HARD TRUTHS

Uncovering the Deep Structure
of Schooling

HARD TRUTHS

Uncovering the Deep Structure of Schooling

BARBARA BENHAM TYE

Foreword by Ron Brandt

Teachers College, Columbia University
New York and London

Published by Teachers College Press, 1234 Amsterdam Avenue, New York, NY 10027

Library of Congress Cataloging-in-Publication Data

Tye, Barbara Benham, 1942–
   Hard truths : uncovering the deep structure of schooling / Barbara Benham Tye ; foreword by Ron Brandt.
      p. cm.
   Includes bibliographical references and index.
   ISBN 0-8077-3934-0 (cloth)—ISBN 0-8077-3933-2 (pbk.)
   1. School improvement programs—United States.   2. School management and organization—United States.   I. Title.

   LB2822.82 T94 2000
   371.2'00973—dc21   99-087493

ISBN 0-8077-3933-2 (paper)
ISBN 0-8077-3934-0 (cloth)

Printed on acid-free paper

Manufactured in the United States of America

07   06   05   04   03   02   01   00   8   7   6   5   4   3   2   1

for Ken

Contents

Foreword

For those who want schools to be different, these are troubling times. The leadership for initiatives to change education now comes mostly from outsiders, primarily politicians. In their quest for accountability, governors, legislators, and state boards of education are reinforcing the very practices that for decades progressive reformers sought to change. Sometimes this retreat to tradition is the unforeseen consequence of naive policies, but frequently it is intentional; a disturbing number of officials seem to think the main problems of schools are lack of standards and educators' pursuit of untested fads. The remedies they embrace—more detailed curriculums, more difficult tests, negative "incentives" to punish low-scoring students and schools—leave unquestioned the institutional framework inherited from earlier generations.

Ironically, the goal of these prescriptions is not just minor improvement but revolutionary reform. Whereas a few decades ago, schools sought to provide for individual differences and accepted varied levels of achievement, today's mantra is "all students can learn." In keeping with that theme, many jurisdictions have decreed that all students will master algebra. Proficiency levels on tests, including those for the National Assessment of Educational Progress, have been set at levels much higher than past performance would justify. All students, even those with identified disabilities, must take state tests and meet challenging standards. Under optimal conditions these new aspirations could represent an exciting professional challenge. When resources and capabilities remain the same, such demands are profoundly frustrating.

A decade ago, political leaders professed to agree with the late Al Shanker, then head of the American Federation of Teachers, that students would not attain higher levels of proficiency without substantial changes in the way schools were organized and run (Brandt, 1990). As Ted Sizer observed, "Those 'reforms' [of the 1980s] were like ordering the Model T to run 60 miles per hour. You can order all you want, but unless you change the vehicle, right down to how the engine's organized, you're not going to get 60 miles per hour. People who made those policies have not understood the necessity of fundamentally reshaping the way schools are run"

(O'Neil, 1995). Backed by an apparent consensus that new circumstances called for new responses, the Bush administration helped found the New American Schools Development Corporation, with its "break the mold" designs. Now, just a few years later, decision-makers seem unaware that schools need "restructuring," and that their policies should encourage, not inhibit, school-by-school revitalization.

Barbara Tye understands the dilemma. Years before the term "restructuring" came and went, she was a teacher and project staff member in schools committed to renewal—with disappointing results. In her moving introduction to this book, she says she learned from personal experience that innovative programs "seldom stick," and began wondering why. (Her experiences were especially interesting to me, because in many ways they parallel my own. She begins her story in 1957, which was the year the Soviets launched *Sputnik*—and the year I started teaching at a junior high school in Racine, Wisconsin.)

To complement her invaluable experience as a practicing educator, Barbara became a researcher in John Goodlad's historic Study of Schooling. That project not only produced extensive documentation about what actually goes on in American classrooms, but provided Barbara an opportunity to refine her ideas about educational change.

Those looking for radical rhetoric will not find it in this book. Those looking for sound suggestions, though, will be rewarded. Barbara Tye has identified elements of American education—what she calls its "deep structure"—that, no matter what we think of them, are so well established that they are unlikely to be changed. She reviews factors, including the financial system, the expectations of parents, and the nature of the teaching profession, that keep this structure in place. She makes a convincing case that isolated efforts to change the deep structure will probably, in the long run, fail. Conceding the possibility that massive alterations in society may in fact be eroding the current structure, she nonetheless advises educators to focus on aspects of schooling that are more malleable.

Wise counsel. Let's try success for a change. We can use it.

Ron Brandt

References

Brandt, R. (1990, April). On restructuring schools: A conversation with Al Shanker. *Educational Leadership, 52*(5), 4–9.

O'Neil, J. (1995, February). On lasting school reform: A conversation with Ted Sizer. *Educational Leadership, 47*(7), 11–17.

Acknowledgments

Many people provided many different kinds of help during the years I was working out my ideas and writing this book, and I welcome the chance to thank them here. First, all those students, teachers, administrators, parents, and board members in the planned communities of Columbia, Maryland; Irvine, California; and Reston, Virginia who agreed to be interviewed about the changes that took place in their school districts between the late 1960s and the mid-1990s. Particularly helpful were Bonnie Daniel, Edward Alexander, and Mary Hovet of Columbia; Stan Corey, Dean Waldfogel, and Greg Copps of Irvine; Diana Schmelzer, Dale Sander, and William Stewart of Reston; and Gordon Peterkin, the pioneer superintendent of the innovative high school in New Jersey which I entered when it opened in 1957. Bob Anderson, who was one of the original consultants to the Howard County Schools ten years before he was my dissertation chair, shared his memories of the early stages of innovation in Columbia with me as well.

The question of why innovative programs so often fade and are replaced with more traditional practices has bemused me for many years, but it seemed to be one of the eternal, almost unresolvable puzzles of our profession best left to recognized thinkers such as Seymour Sarason, Matthew Miles, Michael Fullan, Milbrey McLaughlin and others who staked out the school-change territory in the 1970s. Then in 1980 John Goodlad asked me to write the book on the high school findings of the Study of Schooling, giving me the data base with which I was able to begin constructing the conceptual framework that eventually became the basis of this present work. Maxine Greene has been a steady source of encouragement through the years. My thanks go also to Maria Grazia and Enzo Contavalli of Narni, Italy, who provided a quiet place to write in the spring of 1998.

I am grateful above all to Ken Tye, my professional partner, husband, and best friend. He has been an unwavering source of encouragement, a stimulating co-explorer of ideas, and a perceptive critic of successive drafts of every chapter: without his support, this work could not have been done.

Introduction:
The Origins of an Idea—A Personal Story

In 1957, the Soviet Union sent the very first space satellite into orbit and my high school opened. We knew our school was different—but we couldn't know that it was one of the first in what would be, historically speaking, yet another new wave of efforts to conduct schooling successfully in nontraditional ways. The school day consisted of four 90-minute periods, with a snack break for everyone after first period. Core subjects met three times a week, electives twice. Classrooms had trapezoidal tables and chairs instead of the conventional desks.

The first 2 years passed quickly. Traditions were established. A student newspaper appeared. Student government was treated with respect, and discipline problems were put into the hands of a student-run Judicial Board. Teacher morale was high; turnover was nonexistent. We all thought it would go on forever—why shouldn't it?

But at the end of the third year, the founding superintendent left for an attractive district in Connecticut, and things began to change. Within 5 years, my high school had a traditional 6-period day, a conventional curriculum, and a token student government. Twelve teachers had left. It was still a pretty good school—but the spark was gone.

In 1967, with two degrees, teaching credentials in social studies and speech/English, and a Fulbright year on my resume, I took my first "real" job—in a brand-new Title III project in Dayton, Ohio. Two years earlier, Congress had passed the Elementary and Secondary Education Act (ESEA), and Title III was the legislation supporting innovative educational programs. The Dayton project provided a chance for the city's high school students to participate in an after-school fine arts program that included intensive training in art, drama, music, dance, or creative writing. Another new venture, fueled by the optimism of everyone who became involved. Yet after about 3 years, things began to shift away from the innovative and toward the conventional. The Living Arts Center continued, despite various problems, for another 7 years, finally closing in 1977.

By 1973 I was once more involved with an innovative educational program—this time one of the Experimental Schools Programs funded by the Office of Education during the Nixon administration. When I joined the project team in Greer, South Carolina, the project had already been under way for a year. Momentum was good and morale was high.

My job was to be a general facilitator and ombudsman for the teachers at the middle and high schools (my office-mate worked with the six elementary schools) in the project. All eight schools had agreed to implement the Charles F. Kettering/IDEA model of individually guided education (IGE), which included, at the secondary level, the teacher-advisor concept; heterogeneous grouping of the entire student body (no more ninth-grade English, tenth-grade social studies, or physics open only to seniors); a yearly calendar of four 9-week terms; and a catalog of mini-courses half an inch thick for students to choose from. There also were increased parent involvement, with regular parent/student/teacher conferences (the *student* chairing the meeting), and use of the community as a learning resource. A dissemination strategy was part of the plan. It was expected that, as the project schools mastered each component of the changes, their teachers would help the teachers in the other Greenville County schools to function in the new ways.

It was a lot to take on, but the excitement of being one of just a few such experimental sites in the nation generated enough energy to propel everyone through the first few years. And then—of course—things began to change. The student-run parent conferencing model and the use of the community as a learning resource were the first to go. By the middle of year 3, the unique calendar was in jeopardy and project schools were being told that they could no longer expect to have special exemptions but would have to carry on the project within the same limitations shared by all the other (nonproject) schools in the county. Within a few more years, nothing remained of the IGE legacy except the teacher-advisor system, and even that more closely resembled a traditional homeroom period. My position was eliminated at the end of year 4, and I went back to school.

During the course of my doctoral program, I began to see patterns in my experiences with innovative educational programs. As I reflected upon each case and learned about other, similar cases, a very tentative hypothesis took shape—but it stayed in the back of my mind for a while longer. Meanwhile, 10 years after beginning my first job in Dayton, I completed my dissertation and moved to Los Angeles to join John Goodlad's research team and help with the final 3 years of work on the Study of Schooling. This highly detailed study of 38 elementary, intermediate, and secondary schools across the nation was designed to shed light on the internal dynamics of schools and the communities they serve.

When the Study of Schooling ended in 1980, Goodlad asked me to write a book describing the study's findings at the high school level. While struggling to complete the manuscript, I discovered that the findings provided a data-based answer to my emerging hypothesis about innovative programs and why they so seldom stick: The data pointed to a phenomenon that I started to think of as the "deep structure" of schooling (B. B. Tye, 1985). In choosing this term, taken from the work of some contemporary linguists and poets, I wanted to suggest the underlying (and generally unexamined, even unrecognized) but powerful patterns of schooling that are held in place by society's assumptions about what schooling should be. Others have also chosen to apply literary constructs to the description of educational phenomena; see, for example, Tyack and Tobin's 1994 analysis of the "grammar" of schooling.

The deep structure of schooling, I now believe, is composed of the values and assumptions about education that are widely shared throughout our society. Despite our traditions of local control, Americans do not vary greatly in their views of desirable and appropriate educational experiences for children and young people. They have an idea of what a "real" school should look like (Metz, 1989). These values and assumptions are also shaped by conventional wisdom, by tradition, by vested interests—and by a certain amount of institutional inertia. At this point in time, what we Americans expect of our schools includes the physical similarity of classrooms; the overall control orientation of policy, program, and pedagogy; the general similarity of curriculum and of schedules; patterns of resource allocation; faith in test scores as measures of success; and the practices of age-grading and the labeling and sorting of students.

I further suggest that the phenomenon we might think of as the "deep structure" of schooling is undergirded by a number of interconnected phenomena that exert a conservative pull on efforts to change the way things are done in schools. These inhibiting forces are the following:

1. The social context: conventional wisdom, and the role played by the media.
2. The structural characteristics of the institution itself.
3. Fiscal realities, including the strong influence of the knowledge industry.
4. Parent expectations and community assumptions.
5. The demands of teaching and the nature of the teaching profession.

Any one of these inhibiting forces may be strong enough to defeat change. When combined, their effects are so powerful that unless the proposed change is fundamentally compatible with emerging shifts in the deep structure, institutionalization of the change—*even when adapted to suit local conditions*—may be virtually impossible.

Finally, my hypothesis was complete: Reforms of *any* kind won't "stick" unless they are compatible with the existing deep structure of the society *or with the direction in which the deep structure may be shifting*. If true, this may help to explain much of the failure of both liberal and conservative education reforms in the United States since the end of World War II.

DISCOVERING THE LIMITS OF EDUCATIONAL CHANGE

Following the McCarthy years and as the Cold War intensified—and especially after the Soviet Union developed atomic weapons and successfully launched the first space satellite—the U.S. government, responding to energetic public criticism of our schools, abandoned its traditional hands-off policy. With enactment of the National Defense Education Act in 1958, government entered the public education arena in a big way. No fewer than 214 federal programs supporting educational change were funded between 1957 and 1967 (Fallon, 1967; House, 1974; Kirst, 1974). Bailey and Mosher (1968) put it most dramatically: "In the scant period of 13 years (1954–1967) . . . a sea-change has occurred. The Federal government's interest in stimulating change . . . has unquestionably affected the traditional, decentralized autonomies of American education" (p. 2). The years that followed saw increasing federal-level and private foundation support for a wide array of both structural and curricular changes.

In 1960, with the narrow victory of John F. Kennedy, the political scene shifted. Throughout the decade after *Sputnik*, education was on the front burner. The Justice Department took a proactive role in forcing implementation of school desegregation. The U.S. Office of Education and the Office of Economic Opportunity initiated programs such as the Teacher Corps, VISTA, Head Start, and Follow Through. Congress passed—and funded—a massive education reform package, the Elementary and Secondary Education Act, in 1965. The National Science Foundation supported ambitious curriculum development projects, some of which, like *Man: A Course of Study* and the "new math," also included expensive inservice training workshop components to prepare teachers to use the new materials effectively.

> Beginning in 1961, the Ford Foundation poured millions of dollars into "lighthouse" high schools to demonstrate the value of comprehensive attacks on

> the pedagogical status quo, and in 1968 the Danforth Foundation gave a grant of more than a million dollars to the National Association of Secondary School Principals (NASSP) for a Model Schools Project designed to create the "schools of tomorrow" . . . The experiment took place under favorable auspices, then, just like the Eight-Year Study. The decade of the 1960s was a time of optimism and urgency when innovation was the watchword. (Tyack & Tobin, 1994, pp. 471–472)

In short, millions of dollars were spent on efforts to improve our system of schooling. Then, as the 1960s ended, some researchers began to take a look at what we had gotten for our money. What they found was both surprising and discouraging.

In 1972 an essay by Charters and Pellegrin, "Barriers to the Innovation Process," appeared in the *Educational Administration Quarterly* and the Ford Foundation released a report, *A Foundation Goes to School*, documenting its less-than-successful experiences with funding school change programs from 1960 to 1970 (Nachtigal, 1972). Two years later, Goodlad and Klein (1974) looked "behind the classroom door" to discover why many of the projects of the 1950s and 1960s had never caught on. The RAND studies of educational change, appearing at the same time, identified a number of factors that made successful implementation difficult (Berman & McLaughlin, 1974). At the same time, however, the RAND authors introduced the helpful notion of *mutual adaptation*—that a new program and its environment interact to produce a local variant which stands a better chance of success than if fidelity to the original vision is insisted upon. Evidently, although many innovative programs had either evolved into different forms or disappeared, educators could still learn a great deal from those experiences.

Over the past quarter-century a massive literature on educational change has accumulated. These works tell story after story of specific projects and programs. Most provide templates for successful *adoption*; some address what is needed for successful *implementation*—actually putting the program in place (Fullan & Pomfret, 1977). Comparatively few, however, follow the story further. If they did, we would already know much more than we do about the dynamics of the deep structure: those forces that come into play during the third, fourth, fifth, sixth year and beyond, and that alter the innovation so much that in most cases, 10 years after a school (any school you care to name) adopts a change—whether of structure, pedagogy, or curriculum—you can walk into the school and find *not a trace* of that innovation remaining—except in the memories of the old-timers on the faculty.

KNOWING WHAT WE'RE UP AGAINST

Eight years after the conclusion of the Eight-Year Study, Frederick Redefer (1950)—who had been director of the Progressive Education Association while the study was in progress—pondered the failure of most of the study schools to retain the changes they had made. One conclusion he reached was that insufficient prior attention had been given to the obstacles likely to be encountered:

> Before foundations, committees, or individuals invest sizable sums to im- prove education, before institutions publicize a new experiment . . . it would be well to investigate what are the factors that must be taken into consider- ation if the effort is to have a lasting effect. It would be desirable to face the sources of the opposition, to know what are the obstacles and how they might be overcome. (p. 36)

With Redefer's challenge in mind, the remainder of this book is de- voted to an analysis of each of the inhibiting forces that hold the deep struc- ture in place. In the final chapter, I offer some thoughts about ways in which school change efforts may be able to "work around the deep structure," by focusing on change at the level I call the *unique personality* of each individual school.

Throughout, in addition to referring to appropriate classic and con- temporary works from the literature on educational change, I draw upon data from a study I conducted in the mid-1990s. As a result of doing some reading on more than 30 planned communities built from scratch in the 1960s and early 1970s, it occurred to me that these communities—often designed along the lines of similar "new towns" in Scandinavia—had had a unique opportunity to create new schools unbound by existing traditions and regulations. I also recognized that enough time had passed since those new communities began that it should be possible to explore the ways in which the original visions for those schools had been modified or pulled, by the inhibiting forces mentioned earlier, from the innovative original vision back toward the norm. Information is drawn from archival docu- ments (master plans, planning committee minutes, reports and recommen- dations by consultants, and correspondence) as well as from interviews with key players in each of three planned communities: Columbia, Mary- land; Irvine, California; and Reston, Virginia. I spoke with pioneer board members, superintendents, principals, teachers, and parents. Excerpts from these interviews are included in some of the chapters, as appropriate. In addition, I tracked down and interviewed the pioneer superintendent of my own high school, who went on to serve as superintendent of both the Westport, Connecticut, and the Winnetka, Illinois, school systems; as those of someone with career-long experience of educational innovation, his views are occasionally included as well.

THE THREE COMMUNITIES

In 1963, bulldozers broke ground for what would become the new planned community of Reston, Virginia. Located on 7,000 acres of farmland outside Washington, D.C., purchased in 1961 by Robert E. Simon, Reston would—when complete—consist of five villages and a town center. On October 30 of that same year but 50 miles north in Howard County, Maryland, between Washington and Baltimore, James Rouse publicly announced that he had purchased 14,000 acres of prime farmland and intended to build a new town there. Twice the acreage of Reston, when complete Rouse's Columbia would consist of nine villages and a town center.

On the West Coast, on a quiet ranch south of Los Angeles that had been in the Irvine family since 1870, bulldozers were busy as well. The University of California had persuaded the managers of the Irvine Company to sell part of the ranch for a university campus. President Johnson dedicated the UC-Irvine campus in 1964, and the following year the Irvine Company broke ground for the first of what would become the 10 villages of the new planned community of Irvine, California. By far the largest of the three, Irvine 25 years later would sometimes be compared to Boston in size (though certainly not in ambience).

All three communities included space for business parks in their master plans, hoping eventually to attract major businesses and organizations to situate their corporate offices within their boundaries. Because all three were strategically located in future suburban corridors linked to major metropolitan areas, all ultimately succeeded in doing this.

Although Reston and Columbia each began as the dream of a single person—Robert Simon and James Rouse, respectively—by 1967 all three communities were managed by corporate entities. In varying degrees, homeowners' associations also participated in community decision-making.

Reston celebrated its 25th anniversary in 1990, Columbia's was in 1992, and Irvine's in 1996 (a bit later than the others only because it had not voted for incorporation until several years *after* its pioneer families had settled in).

These three planned communities had much in common, but they had distinct differences too. Though all three new towns attracted primarily well-educated upper-middle-class families, both Reston and Columbia included affordable housing in their master plans. This was done deliberately to ensure some socioeconomic diversity in the pioneer population (both Virginia and Maryland were moving to desegregate their schools during these years). James Rouse, in particular, hoped that this would assure Columbia of racial and cultural diversity as well. No such philosophy was evident in the original plan for Irvine; in fact, the Irvine Company was fairly explicit about not wanting to get involved in social policy.

Columbia built its town center concurrently with its villages, but Reston didn't get around to building its town center until the late 1980s—almost a quarter-century after the town was founded. Reston retained its rural personality longer than the others, and in fact didn't even install its first traffic light until 1973. Irvine, as mentioned, chose not to have a town center as such but focused instead on creating clearly distinct villages that their residents would identify with first and foremost.

When it came to planning new schools for the anticipated influx of pioneer homebuyers, again the three communities had much in common but there were also some important differences. These are summarized for the reader in the capsule profiles that follow. It is hoped that these profiles will assist the reader in making sense of the additional information on specific topics—often in the form of stories or personal reminiscences—that are brought into later chapters of the book as appropriate.

Community Profiles

Reston, Virginia. Virginia's public schools are administered by a county system. Automatically, therefore, the new schools of Reston would be part of the Fairfax County Public Schools. The elected board of education and the professional staff of the County Office of Education would determine when, and where, new schools should be built to serve the newly arriving residents. Because Reston was comparatively small and all five villages didn't go up immediately, Reston students attended schools in nearby Herndon. It would be some 12 years before the first new schools actually opened within the Reston town limits.

Fairfax County was proud of its school system—it was not unusual for graduates to be accepted at respected out-of-state universities—and saw no need for the new schools to be much different from the good ones already available. In fact, a strong tradition of evenhandedness dictated that no school receive special treatment unless for an exceptionally sound reason. Some differences in physical plant were tolerated—Terraset Elementary, for example, was an unusual underground building, with an open-space plan and solar heating/cooling system—and some programmatic differences were approved, but, as a rule, policies and resource allocation formulas were applied equally to all schools. Neither Robert Simon nor, after 1967, the Gulf/Reston management team played a significant role in planning for the new schools.

Columbia, Maryland. Like Reston, Columbia would become part of an existing county district: the Howard County Public School System. Unlike Fairfax County, in 1963 Howard County really *was* a sleepy rural area, with just 9,726 students enrolled in schools that were "accepted as satisfactory by the county population" of farmers and small-town businessmen (Hovet, 1971, p. 35). Those few students who did go on to college tended to choose the local community college or state university.

When James Rouse dropped his bombshell on October 30, 1963, by announcing that he had bought up enough adjacent Howard County farm properties to create a new town, it did not detonate immediately in the Howard County schools office. The explosion came 6 months later, when Rouse presented school officials with an evaluative report by Christopher Jencks, which he had commissioned and which questioned the capacity of the Howard County School System to rise to the challenges presented by the need for new schools in the new town. Though the Jencks recommendations were never formally accepted by the school board, they did serve to goad the staff into a flurry of productive action that led to the reinvigoration of the entire Howard County School System.

Howard County, like Fairfax County, took the position that the new school couldn't have anything that wouldn't also be available to existing schools. Operationally, this took the form of a policy that for each innovative new school built in Columbia, one just like it must be built concurrently in some other part of the county where a new school was needed. As a result, in September of 1968 two model elementary schools opened, and the following year two model middle schools opened in Howard County. As things turned out, when the first high school was built for Columbia (1971), the county did not need a second high school; so an exception was made in that case.

James Rouse took a thoughtful interest in the planning of schools for Columbia, even selling the land for the first elementary school to the Howard County Board of Education for just $1. Although he did not intrude upon the planning process, it seems clear that he had high hopes that the new town and its pathbreaking schools would together form a living laboratory of the best kind of democratic community living.

Irvine, California. Few children lived on the Irvine Ranch when development began on the first village in 1965. For some years, the existing school districts were able to handle the growing school-age population as pioneer families moved to the new town. Before long, however, it seemed desirable to establish a separate school district to serve Irvine alone; this was done in 1973. Residents elected a school board, the new board hired a superintendent, and the Irvine Unified School District was born. It absorbed

the existing elementary school district, acquiring five established elementary schools and one middle school in the process; it also acquired one
existing high school that had been in what was then a neighbor district but
on land owned by the Irvine Corporation.

The new superintendent gathered a team together and began holding
a series of community meetings in the fall of 1973. Early in 1974 the result,
the IUSD Master Plan, was adopted by the school board. It included many
innovative features, among them the decentralization of decision-making,
including fiscal decisions, to the school sites; interdisciplinary curriculum;
high-tech linkages between schools; multi-age grouping; the mainstreaming
of students with special needs (*before* the passage by Congress of PL 94–
142, the original legislation mandating the mainstreaming of students with
disabilities); a strong career education program at the high school level;
district-wide open enrollment; and the option of a year-round calendar for
those schools that chose it.

The Irvine superintendent went on record as being opposed to the idea
of uniformity and encouraged his school sites to be as creative as they could
in responding to the needs of their constituencies. In this important respect,
then, the Irvine leadership differed sharply from that in Fairfax and Howard
counties and, in fact, in most of the more than 30 planned communities that
were springing up around the nation in those years (Burby, 1977).

SUMMARY AND CONCLUSION

Though I opened with a story of my personal experiences and how they
led me to frame an explanation for the disappearance of new programs and
practices, I know that I'm not the first to wonder how it happens; and I
won't be the last. The brief overview of key developments in the past half-
century or so reveals numerous efforts to understand the dynamics of educational change. It also shows that no matter how often we slide back toward what's familiar, practitioners are ever ready to try again. Habitual
optimists, educators always bounce back: There *must* be better ways to do
things—there *must* be ways to solve the big and little problems of schools.

Perhaps, though, we could be more selective, choosing projects with
a chance of real survival. This is where I believe the *idea* of the deep structure of schooling can be useful. If it helps to explain the past failure of reforms to survive as originally envisioned or even to survive at all, it may
also help us to invest our time, energy, and education dollars more successfully in the years ahead. We need more than just a grasp of the idea,
however—we need to understand the way the deep structure works. This
book is dedicated to that exploration.

In Chapter 1, I define the construct of a "deep structure of schooling" in far more detail than I have been able to do in this introduction. Then, in Chapters 2 through 6, I explore, in some depth, each of the inhibiting forces that hold the deep structure in place. The *conventional wisdom* and the *role of the media* are the focus of Chapter 2. Chapter 3 addresses the *structural characteristics* of the educational system, and Chapter 4 examines some of the *fiscal realities* that inhibit changes in the familiar use of time and space, the grouping of students, and the distribution of resources. *Parent and community expectations* are the theme of Chapter 5. Last but certainly not least, I take a look at aspects of the *work lives of teachers* and the professional norms and behaviors that discourage deep structure change just as effectively as do any of the other inhibiting forces explored in this book.

Finally, I want to assure the reader that there is a light at the end of this analytical tunnel, a silver lining to what looks like a cloud. For although it *is* exceedingly difficult to make permanent changes in things that our society really wants our schools to be and do, there is a place where successful action is possible. Chapter 7 shows that, in addition to the deep structure that permeates the entire society, each individual school has its own unique personality. It is at this level that constructive and lasting reforms can be made, and, I believe, it is at this level that educators and community members can become most effectively and happily involved in the life of their schools.

The book closes with some suggestions for projects at the unique personality level, and I can't resist adding a few speculations as to the possible future of some current educational reforms.

1

Defining the Deep Structure of Schooling

Every human society has ways of teaching its young those things that it finds important. Most societies—though not all—accomplish this task through the institution of a formalized system of schooling. Children and young people leave home to attend a place called school for part of each week, and their society expects them to master certain knowledge and skills as a result. Beyond this, the institution of education may also fulfill other tasks for the society it serves, such as sorting and channeling young people into predetermined adult roles and preparing them for the world of work. In virtually all cultures, schools are expected to contribute significantly to the acculturation and socialization of the young, reinforcing the norms of their society and teaching them to behave in acceptable ways.

In agrarian or pastoral societies, much education of the young takes place in contexts other than schools. Children learn how to behave and what to do within the family and village or neighborhood setting. Many may never attend a school as such, and for those who do the experience is focused on extra training, over and above what is needed for full functioning in the adult society. This was also the case in the United States prior to the industrial revolution, and, even as recently as 1930, only 50% of the 14- to 17-year-olds in the United States were attending high school. The other half were learning what they needed to learn by participating in their culture—just as were young people in other cultures around the world.

As a larger and larger percentage of its children and young people attend schools, the institution of schooling loses its mystique—and its status—within the society. From something only a select few could do, over time it becomes something everybody does. Inevitably, everybody in the society "knows" what schools are for and how they are supposed to be, because everyone was a student and experienced it firsthand (Labaree, 1999). A conventional wisdom begins to build: Throughout a culture, certain assumptions about schooling are widely shared and taken for granted. In our own culture, these include our taken-for-granted patterns dictating the use of time (the 6-period day and the 9-month school year, for example) and space (the egg-carton schoolhouse, with classrooms of about the same size regardless of their purpose), age-grading, ability grouping, and the control orientation and custodial function that Americans expect the public schools to fulfill. Local variations and experiments may emerge from time to time, but these do not significantly alter the underlying phenomenon, which is, as a rule, slow to change.

Such assumptions form the deep structure of schooling. It is both a culture-wide *and* a culture-specific phenomenon: All schools in the United States are connected by a deep structure of schooling, and it differs from the deep structure of schooling that connects the schools of Argentina . . . or Korea, Russia, or Zaire. *Every society has its own set of assumptions about what schools are for and how education should properly be conducted—its own "deep structure" of schooling.*

THE EVOLUTION OF WHAT AMERICANS TAKE
FOR GRANTED ABOUT THEIR SCHOOLS

The deep structure can change, and has done so in our country several times since the colonial era. However, *educators* can't change it. Nor, for that matter, can megabucks, or legislative mandates, or pressure from special-interest groups. The deep structure of schooling, being a sociocultural phenomenon, is bound to the prevailing worldview of that culture at any period, past or present. But if a society is changing in large-scale and significant ways, chances are good that its attitudes toward schooling are shifting, too.

1750–1850: The Academy Replaces the Latin Grammar School

> *The history of . . . academies in North America demonstrates the interrelationship among politics, the organization of society, and education.*
> Joel Spring (1986, p. 22)

The earliest schools in the American colonies were established to promote basic literacy for the purpose of religious salvation, and the curriculum of these schools consisted of reading, religion, and in some cases the classics—Latin and Greek. At what we think of today as the elementary level, dame schools and town schools were available in many communities; for the sons of the elite, Latin Grammar Schools provided further education. This pattern continued for 150 years, during which time society changed a great deal—but the Latin Grammar Schools changed very little. By the mid-1700s it was painfully clear that the existing schools were unable to provide the practical kind of education increasingly in demand.

Academies, flourishing in England since the late 1600s largely as a social alternative to Anglican dominance of traditional schooling, began to appear in the American colonies in the 1750s. They were not free, publicly supported schools—they charged tuition—but they did offer a new, utilitarian curriculum that included math, sciences, and practical, career-oriented subjects such as surveying, navigation, and agriculture. In short, these academies were just what was needed by a dynamic, rapidly changing society—and they caught on quickly, spreading from the new cities and towns of the East Coast to the western frontier towns. Within just 100 years, there were 6,185 such schools in the young nation (Sizer, 1964).

As the academy movement spread, the Latin Grammar Schools disappeared. As Gerald Gutek (1991) has pointed out, "The academy tended to replace or absorb the Latin Grammar school, because . . . the academy met the educational needs of a civilization that was both frontier and industrial in character" (pp. 99–100). Daniel and Laurel Tanner (1980), calling the Latin Grammar Schools the educational "dinosaurs" of the 18th century, comment that "Institutions must change in order to meet the changing social, political, and economic needs of society or they die. This is as true of the school as of any other institution. The curriculum of the Latin Grammar School was virtually the same at the beginning and the end of the colonial period. Yet a new social and economic structure had developed in the intervening years that required a vastly different education for youth" (p. 225).

American society had undergone a major change, and the deep structure of schooling had changed along with it. By the early 1800s, the American people shared a set of assumptions about what schools are for different from the one that had prevailed 100 years earlier.

1830–1930: Common Schools: From Many, One

Another significant shift in the deep structure of schooling in America was the change from local control to the state-supported common school, and wide acceptance of the need for unity and stability, for assimilation and preparation for democratic citizenship, in a nation of diverse immigrant groups. According to Kaestle (1973), "The central, transforming institutional development in the history of American education was the creation of a common, uniform school system in the 19th century" (p. vii).

The period of nation building that followed the establishment of constitutional democracy was shaped by three complex and interrelated forces: the industrial revolution, immigration and the westward expansion, and the growth of large cities. Into the mix came hopeful would-be citizens from all over Europe and parts of Asia; and Africans, brought by force from their homelands.

Such diversity posed a challenge to the political and educational leaders of the day. By the 1830s, sentiment was coalescing around the notion of schooling as a way to provide all children with a *common* education, one that would provide all with "American" values and acceptable "American" behaviors. The newcomers themselves, whatever their socal class, generally saw this as a legitimate and desirable goal in the "land of opportunity." Ordinary laborers as well as members of the new middle class, understanding that opportunities existed in the new world that had not been open to them in the old, demanded schooling for their children. They saw the abolition of the classes as part of the meaning of democracy, and education as a way for their descendants to rise into positions of power that had previously been unattainable except to the hereditarily wealthy (Cremin, 1951; McLaren, 1998; Spring, 1986).

Thus, for a variety of reasons, by the middle of the 19th century an ethic of inclusion—though it still did not apply to *all* children and young people—had become an integral part of the new nation's assumptions about the purposes of schooling. It was to shape educational policy well into the 20th century.

Common schools, however, were elementary schools. As the United States moved into the 20th century, most teenagers were still going into the work force right after eighth grade. In 1900 only about 10% of the nation's 14- to 17-year-olds were attending high school. A variety of social and economic pressures would soon combine to change that, however.

The new spirit of inclusion articulated by the avid proponents of the common school was extended to the secondary school as the great debate over the proper nature of the high school was finally resolved in favor of the comprehensive plan. A dual system such as existed in Europe, which sent college-bound and workforce-bound students to separate schools, was eventually rejected in favor of one school offering several curricula. The schools of America would—in theory—reflect the democratic ideal: They would bring people together rather than keep them apart. Learning to live and work together cooperatively in school would prepare the young to live and work together harmoniously—despite differing cultural origins, economic status, and career plans. In retrospect, a national policy of this sort seems almost inevitable, given the historically unprecedented circumstances of a new nation being forged out of an assemblage of diverse immigrant groups.

There is another way to look at that development, however. Although it is true that the institution of the comprehensive high school just prior to World War I brought all students together under one roof, the tradeoff— a differentiated curriculum—provided the mechanism whereby the separation of students into different futures could be legitimated (Labaree,

1987). "In the name of egalitarianism," comments Lasch (1978), "they pre-
served the most insidious form of elitism, which in one guise or another
holds the masses incapable of intellectual exertion" (p. 145).

Nevertheless, the move toward universal school attendance continued. By the early 20th century, an increasing proportion of girls were attending high school, and special public schools were being established for
children and young people with disabilities (Butts & Cremin, 1953). In the
South, the separate schools for black children and youth were maintained
at public expense, a logical outgrowth of the charity-schools movement of
earlier times. This inclusionary impulse has continued in the second half
of the 20th century, making itself felt most clearly through the school desegregation and special education movements.

1930–2000: Schooling as Preparation for the World of Work

The changing nature of the work force played the most important part in
the push to keep young people in school, and thus we see again that the needs
of the culture determine the nature of the deep structure of schooling. The
demographic shift from the farms to the cities changed family life. Adolescents who had helped with farm work could now work in factories, mines,
and mills—or they could stay in school and aspire to something more. From
a macro social viewpoint, having them stay in school kept them out of the
work force and thus made more jobs available to adult workers. This was
particularly true during the Great Depression of the 1930s, when the proportion of 14- to 17-year-olds attending high school jumped to about 50%.
Although compulsory attendance legislation for elementary school was in
place in most states by 1918, similar legislation requiring school attendance
to age 16 was enacted in the 1930s in many states.

It was during this period of time, too, that American society began to
acknowledge what it had been moving toward since the early days of the
academy movement, namely, widespread agreement that the purpose of
formal schooling is to get a good job. Years of schooling were henceforth seen
as a financial investment and a guarantee of upward mobility (Benham,
1979b). Students today can be heard to mutter, when bored with a class, *"Why
do we have to study this? I don't need to know this to be a—."* It hardly matters
what career is mentioned.

From the 1830s, then, to the 1930s, as a diverse society struggled to
weld itself into a unified whole, new educational policies extended schooling horizontally, to children and young people of all backgrounds. It sought
to establish itself as an economic system in a time of change from farming
and cottage industry to industrialization and the factory system; and other
educational policies extended schooling vertically, to increasingly older
groups of students.

1880–1950: The Structures of Schooling Become Fixed

Historians differ on exactly when American society—and the deep structure of schooling—settled into its present form, but most agree that the formative era was over by the early 20th century. Michael Katz (1975) places the date even earlier:

> The basic structure of American education had been fixed by about 1880 and it has not altered fundamentally since that time. . . . It is, and was, universal, tax-supported, free, compulsory, bureaucratic, racist, and class-biased. . . . It is as if the characteristics noted above form the walls of a box within which other sorts of change have taken place. The box is filled with objects that can be moved around and rearranged, but the walls themselves remain solid. (p. xix)

Whatever the date one argues for, it is generally agreed that by the early 20th century, the basic structure of the U.S. public school system was in place: mandatory elementary, junior high, and high school; the school district system; state boards of education; and state certification of teachers. In all but the smallest schools, students were grouped by age and, in the larger schools, they were often grouped by ability as well. The school year and the school day were fixed. School buildings grew in size—especially following the period of consolidation in the mid–20th century—but within those large buildings, individual classrooms remained about the same as they had been in the days of the one-room schoolhouse. Even after World War II, when movable furniture replaced desks that were bolted to the floor, most desks still faced forward, in rows. All of these familiar characteristics are a product and a reflection of the deep structure of schooling in America for most of the 20th century—of the assumptions we have learned to take for granted: the "walls of the box."

Despite this, one might reasonably argue that there have been three shifts in the deep structure of schooling *since* midcentury: consolidation, desegregation, and special education.

The 1950s: Consolidation. Although city schools had been large for some time, in 1930 there were still 130,000 one-room schoolhouses in the rest of the country. By 1980, there were fewer than 1,000. The number of school districts in the nation dropped from 127,531 in 1932 to 16,960 in 1973 (Tyack & Cuban, 1995). Midwesterners of my own generation can still remember local battles to prevent their small-town schools from being closed and their children sent to the larger school in a nearby community. This shift was enhanced by the postwar appearance of a new demographic phenomenon: the suburb. Suburbs, in turn, had been made possible first by the spread of automobiles and then by the related development of the modern highway system. School buses in growing numbers appeared on the roads. Riding the bus became an unquestioned part of a student's experience of schooling, and transportation was added to the budget of most school districts.

The maxim that "bigger is better" quickly became part of the conventional wisdom, especially at the secondary level where it was now seen as important to provide a wide range of courses, each with its own appropriate materials and equipment. This differentiation was accepted as a functional necessity for the complex postwar society. In the name of choice, students were separated into groups and given schooling experiences that would define their futures. The high school grew as large as many a factory and, as in a factory, a sense of community was diminished. That the efficiencies possible in a large high school would be a Faustian bargain did not begin to occur to people until several generations had attended consolidated school systems.

The 1960s and 1970s: Desegregation and Special Education. The two significant changes since the 1960s were the desegregation and special education movements. I would, perhaps, reserve judgment on whether these actually represented shifts in the deep structure of schooling. Although it is undeniable that society has been profoundly changed by both, on reflection it seems that *schools*, at their deepest operational level, function much the same as ever, regardless of what kinds of students are in attendance.

EVENTS AND IDEAS THAT SHAPED THE DEEP STRUCTURE OF THE LATE 20TH CENTURY

The events and ideas of 17th- and 18th-century Europe—the notion of fundamental human equality, the overthrow of monarchies, the rise of a vigorous middle class, and the opening up of a new land, in which anyone might make of himself what he could—combined to undermine the old order of western civilization. People abandoned a world that had always been stable and where life had been predictable, in favor of the chance to make a better life. This idea would have been unthinkable to the common people just a few generations earlier. It seems that the "great ideas" that shape the worldview and assumptions of a society at any given point in time are often heretical when first proposed but follow a predictable path to public acceptance. Thus, the ideas of liberty and equality, radical in the 1600s, were enshrined in the founding documents of the United States 100 years later. The ideas of Darwin, Marx, and Freud, heresies of the 19th century, have shaped the 20th, and so forth (Schumacher, 1973).

That individuals could improve themselves, and that society as a whole, composed of enough individuals intent on self-improvement, would also—inevitably—improve was one of the beliefs of many who supported the common school movement in the mid-1800s and was also a cornerstone of the Progressive movement of the early 1900s. Inextricably entwined among the other inducements that the new nation offered its newcomers were the ideas of upward social mobility and of progress.

As the United States entered the 20th century, there was much that needed improving, and the progressive spirit pervaded many social institutions, including education. Obviously, most people agreed, schooling was a key to improvement, both of individuals and of society. *How* schools were to accomplish this was not, however, a matter of universal agreement. Some progressive thinkers, impressed by the efficiency of factories and swept up by the promise of science to yield answers to the most basic human problems, advocated efficiency measures and standardized techniques. "Both the work-place and the schools, as well as other nineteenth-century institutions," notes Kaestle (1983), "were partaking of the same ethos of efficiency, manipulation, and mastery" (p. 69). Other educators, equally committed to progress, focused on the nature and the needs of children as individual learners.

These two very different orientations led to quite different assumptions about what schools were for and how schooling should be conducted. The "two camps" of the Progressive Education movement were grounded in the larger progressive impulses of the entire society during the period from about 1880 to 1930. Close study of American education in the years since then reveals what appears to be a pendulum-swing from one to the other, with the dominance of either approach partly dependent on the state of the economy and of national security at any given point in time. But one could argue that the child-centered, or "soft progressive," views were the views of educators and others involved with schooling and were not necessarily shared by the population at large. Paul Mort (1957) astutely observed over 40 years ago that educators are sometimes guilty of seeing things normatively—as they wish they were—rather than descriptively—as they actually are:

> Much of the shouting against "progressive education" which is not now, nor ever was, present in public schools to any great degree, is an example of the results that may come of the imprudence of administrators talking about what they'd like as if it were what they have. (p. 185)

That is why periods of child-centered education have never really altered the underlying social/economic/political system of the nation, which has remained reliably skewed in favor of those in power (Martin, 1991) and those who favor efficiency and standardization (Eisner, 1994; Levin, 1991;

Theobald & Mills, 1995). The image of the pendulum-swing must, therefore, be understood as a metaphor that does not truly enlighten. The image
proposed by Katz (1975), of moving the furniture around inside a box
(which doesn't itself change), may be closer to the uncomfortable truth. As
David Purpel (1989) has noted:

> [It is] important to note the persistence and continuity in the stucture and
> content of American public education. Contrary to some folklore, for example,
> the 1960s were not a time of widespread radical changes in public education
> . . . the changes adopted were well within existing frameworks of traditional
> goals and objectives of the in-place system. (p. 14)

What, then, *has* been the worldview of the American people in the
20th century? I believe it to be predominantly behavioristic and mechanistic. The growth of technology and the accompanying faith in science
to improve the quality of life has had a powerful impact on our outlook,
perhaps without our even being fully aware of it. Certainly it has shaped
the deep structure of schooling within which most of us have lived and
worked.

The "cult of efficiency" and the image of school-as-factory have fitted
quite nicely into this behavioristic and mechanistic worldview, particularly
since the end of the consolidation movement left the nation with such large
schools (Callahan, 1962). Americans generally have stood by and nodded
with approval as children were sorted into categories and grouped first
by age and then by ability (as determined by tests that were seen as scientific and, therefore, as reliable and valid). Policies formulated in the spirit
of efficiency were implemented relatively quickly. It's not so far off base
to note that children and young people have been viewed (usually from
outside the educational system but sometimes even from within it) as "raw
material," and that teachers have been regarded—and treated—as "inter-
changeable parts." Occasionally one even finds assembly-line metaphors
applied to the teaching–learning process (though usually *not* by people
involved with the day-to-day challenges of teaching).

The curriculum also has been structured on a behavioral model:
Specify "outcomes" first, then build the content in small chunks, assuming that a study of the parts will lead to an understanding of the whole.
Assume further that all meaningful learning can be seen as measurable
behavior and, therefore, can be tested using norm-referenced instruments;
and that because those instruments have been developed scientifically,
that somehow makes it okay for a certain proportion of the students to fail.

The issue of student failure points to two other elements of the
20th-century worldview that we must consider: the deeply engrained as-

sumptions of social Darwinism and of radical individualism. Coexisting with a belief in the possibility of upward mobility through hard work has been the judgment that those who do *not* manage to better themselves are *less worthy as people*:

> The competitive ethic preached by the social Darwinists was not, of course, new to Americans, for it resembled the old Protestant ethic implanted in the American soil by the Calvinist Puritans. Instead of justifying hard work, discipline and thrift on theological grounds, the social Darwinist did so on the basis of the "latest scientific theory." The Puritan, the capitalist, and the social Darwinist could thus all subscribe to an ethical code that . . . saw poverty as a deserved punishment for the shiftless, inefficient, and wasteful. (Gutek, 1972, p. 265)

Such views continue to shape the deep structure of schooling in America, for if it were otherwise, how can we explain the appalling condition of impoverished inner-city and rural schools, or the vast discrepancies in resources available to school districts even within just a few miles of each other? As a society, we evidently now take it for granted that some children don't deserve our help; we can do that without batting an eye, because the social Darwinist assumption and the mythology of America as the "land of opportunity" tells us that each child can make it, if he or she will only work hard and play by the rules. A clear-eyed, unflinching look at the real world, however, reveals that the playing field is far from level and that children do not have an equal chance now . . . if, indeed, they ever did (Kozol, 1991). Furthermore, if we are being honest, we also must admit that the educational system itself has contributed to the maintenance of this harsh reality. For example, one school restructuring project failed to get off the ground because the teachers "continued to believe that the problems lay with the students, and not with the school, and that the challenge was thus to fix the students" (Raywid, 1994, p. 30).

I have taken considerable time to look at the deep structure sociologically and historically, because it is a construct that is inseparable from context, from the gestalt of any era. Indeed, it is itself a part of the context of our lives; that is its very nature.

RECOGNIZING THE DEEP STRUCTURE— VARIATIONS ON A THEME

As I've said before, what I'm suggesting isn't exactly new. Others have written about this idea, albeit using different language and a wide array of images. What they all have in common, however, is that they address the phenomenon of an underlying set of beliefs and practices that hold familiar and taken-for-granted aspects of schooling in place. Seymour Sarason (1982) taught us to think of the "regularities" of schooling: those structures, behaviors, and habits that are so deeply rooted that we don't even recognize them as problematic. To help us "see" these patterns, Sarason asked us to look with alien eyes: as if we were visitors from outer space. Maxine Greene (1973) posed much the same challenge: to "make the familiar strange," and so to become aware of the boxes in which we as a people have confined ourselves. "One reason the individual can rarely think clearly about the renewal of society or of an institution to which he belongs is that it never occurs to him that he may be part of the problem . . . part of what needs renewing," observed John Gardner in 1963 (p. 160).

Over 20 years ago, John Goodlad (1975) aptly described the process by which regularities become taken for granted:

> When certain expectations for schools become pervasive in the surrounding community and society, schools begin to take on what appear to be relevant tasks, not as goals but as activities and conditions. These, in time, become regularities or givens in the operation of schools and are recognized as such by successive generations. Certain regularities in home and community life tend to grow up around school customs, such as the times for beginning and ending the school day. Innovations in these customs, especially those already regulating home patterns to some degree, are suspect or even taboo. It may be easier . . . for example, to instill a new science program for the upper elementary years than to send children home an hour early on Thursday afternoons so as to provide time for teachers to plan together. (p. 10)

With some caveats, Larry Cuban (1984) has employed the metaphor of a hurricane to convey a mental picture of educational change and the deep structure of schooling: "Images of storm-tossed waves on the ocean surface, turbulent waters a fathom down, and calm on the ocean floor lent themselves well to agitated squabbles over curriculum theories, textbooks, and classroom instruction" (p. 10). Although an impression of change may be created by public excitement about an identified problem and its proposed solution, in fact deep beneath the surface things go on pretty much as they always have.

David Tyack and William Tobin (1994) explore the "grammar" of schooling, and Mary Haywood Metz (1989) speaks of a persistent "common script," noting that it serves symbolic as well as functional purposes (p. 81). Bruce Joyce (1982) wrote about *homeostatic forces*, which pull innovations back to the prevailing norm. Purpel and Shapiro (1995) analyzed public discourse about education and discovered a level of consensus that they found remarkable, given the size and diversity of the nation. Elliot

Eisner (1994) agrees that American schools are driven by "fairly uniform expectations for a shared way of life that is both long-standing and wide-spread" (p. 53). MIT management guru Peter Senge (1990) uses the term "established mental models," noting that they are powerful and deeply entrenched because they are "largely tacit" (pp. 11–12). These tacit expectations or "mental models" are, in effect, the conventional wisdom aspect of the deep structure, which we examine in more depth in Chapter 2.

Peter Airasian (1988) notes that an innovation will achieve social acceptance if it is compatible with the social values of the day. Sarason (1983) makes the same point, even more vividly: "We got to the moon when we did because that abstraction we call 'society' had come to see such a feat as congruent with its interests. . . . Ideas, for good or bad, have transformed the world but only after they have gained a currency that makes them seem consonant with the self-interests of that world" (p. 183). It's ironic that a reform has a good chance of success if it is in tune with the prevailing cultural values—what, then, makes it a "reform"? Nevertheless, this is an important point about the deep structure: It accommodates changes that are compatible and defeats changes that are not. It's wise, therefore, to recognize this before tackling something that is *too* unconventional.

CONCLUSION

At this point, we have established a context for our exploration by reviewing some pertinent historical background and by defining the construct "deep structure." In a nutshell, the deep structure is a composite of widely held beliefs about what schools are for and how they should function, coupled with a number of inhibiting forces that actively seek to prevent change in how schools are put together and work. That changes *do* happen and sometimes even become permanent can be attributed to shifts in what society demands from its schools. It is possible to see that this has happened a number of times in the history of American public schooling, and we can assume that it will happen again—although it's not so easy to recognize a deep-structure shift when it is actually taking place and one is living through it. Supporters of the academy movement in the late 1700s, the common schools movement in the mid-1800s, or the consolidation of small schools and districts into larger units in the mid-1900s, were sure only that they had a better idea. It is unlikely that they were consciously aware of the ways in which those reforms were actually supported and made feasible by other changes that were happening in society at the time.

The phenomenon now commonly known as the "conventional wisdom" is an inextricable part of these other changes, and in every era the conventional wisdom is conveyed within a society both by word-of-mouth and by the media. Broadsheets, newspapers, and the Chatauqua circuit in earlier times; radio, TV, and the internet today—the media of the age spread news and at the same time they promote certain values and create certain images and assumptions in the populace. In the next chapter, we take a closer look at the conventional wisdom, how it works and how it can inhibit some kinds of educational change.

2

The Social Context:
Conventional Wisdom About Schooling

What Americans assume to be true about their public schools may or may not *be* true, but we believe it anyway, even in the face of evidence to the contrary. In 1958, economist John Kenneth Galbraith gave this social-psychological phenomenon a name: He dubbed it the *conventional wisdom.* More recent writers are using the term *popular ideology*, which refers to much the same phenomenon but with the added dimension of belief or value systems. Embedded in both constructs is the notion of *common sense*, which is an integral component of popular ideology. Common sense is a concept that has always been dear to the hearts of the American people. Indeed, as Stuart Hall (1986) has pointed out, the assumption that we can rely on our common sense to see us through most problems is a cherished part of our conventional wisdom: "Common sense is itself a structure of popular ideology . . . reflecting the traces of previous systems of thought that have sedimented into everyday reasoning" (p. 55).

The conventional wisdom is part and parcel of what we absorb in the process of becoming socialized within a particular culture, and it settles into the taken for granted and usually unexamined aggregation of beliefs, values, attitudes, and assumptions that form our worldview. In Sarason's (1983) words,

> It is a characteristic of widely held but unarticulated assumptions that they serve the purpose of defining and bulwarking individual and societal perceptions of what is right, natural, and proper. . . . So, for example, up until relatively recently (by the clock of history) males and females did not have to think about what a woman was, what roles she should play, and where she would play them. These were not issues to be examined, not because people were told not to examine them but because the socialization process put them beyond the realm of questioning. (pp. 25–26)

This is not to suggest that the conventional wisdom is permanent. As we shall see, it does change with the march of events.

WHAT WE TAKE FOR GRANTED ABOUT SCHOOLS

At the close of the 20th century and the threshold of the 21st, what is the conventional wisdom about public schools in the United States? The following may sound familiar:

> Schools are chaotic, dangerous places.
> Teaching is an easy job, with lots of time off.
> Too much money is spent on schools.
> Schools today are not doing a good job of teaching the basics.
> A quiet classroom is one where learning is taking place.
> The most effective teaching is traditional, frontal, and teacher-directed.
> Children should be grouped by age and ability.
> Parents should participate in running the schools.

On a more positive note, we also believe that *any child can succeed if he or she works hard enough* and (against all the evidence) it is part of the conventional wisdom that *we have equal educational opportunity in this country.*

It's also the conventional wisdom that *there is no national consensus about what schools are for,* but is this true? Doesn't the existence of a "deep structure" actually constitute a consensus of sorts? In fact, general agreement about the purposes of schooling in the United States is long-standing. During the period from the end of the Revolutionary War to the beginning of the Civil War:

> People in different classes, with different political perspectives or different educational philosophies, could agree on a list of purposes for common schooling: moral education to produce obedient children, reduce crime, and discourage vice; citizenship training to protect republican government; literacy for effective economic and political participation; and cultural education for assimilation and unity. (Kaestle, 1983, p. 101)

Every September the Gallup Poll provides the nation with a summary of what Americans believe about and want from their schools. Of course, it reveals a range of opinion and some regional differences; but what sticks in most people's minds are those points on which large percentages of citizens agree. This fundamental agreement (despite outlying alternative viewpoints) is part of the deep structure of schooling. In this particular case, it seems that the conventional wisdom maintains a belief that simply doesn't hold up under scrutiny. We all assume that Americans don't agree about schools, when in fact they do. Why, if the conventional wisdom is an integral part of the deep structure, would this seeming discrepancy exist?

The answer may be that the assumption that Americans don't agree on what schools should be or do has some operational advantages, even if it isn't really true; this is probably why we cling to it. Its face validity (and thus its secure niche in our popular ideology) derives from the wide variety of regional or local differences that can be found in individual schools and school districts. If Americans accept the myth that agreement among diverse constituencies is impossible, the illusion of local control is maintained and the inexorable drift toward increased centralization at the state and national levels is masked. Thus, the myth of unresolvable disagreement serves the purposes of those who support the development of a national system as against authentic forms of local control.

Because the conventional wisdom is itself one of the components of the deep structure of schooling—one of the inhibiting forces that pull educational innovations back toward traditional practice—we need to take a closer look at some of its most powerful assumptions, and then we need to think about how these are created and take root in the popular consciousness.

The Appropriate Purposes of Schooling

Both historical and contemporary documents reveal that four basic goals for our schools have emerged over the past 300 years. Furthermore, these appear to be remarkably stable (Goodlad, 1984; Johnson, J., and Immerwahr, J., 1994; Rose & Rapp, 1997). Americans expect their schools to attend to the academic, vocational, civic, and personal development of children and young people. They would be unhappy if schools were to abandon any of these goals.

The Academic Goal of Schooling. This is generally taken to mean mastery of the traditional "basics" (composition and literature, mathematics, natural sciences, history, civics, and—maybe—geography). Physical education, music, and art—and, in the more affluent schools, computer literacy—are also considered important. Beyond this, definitions of what is "basic" tend to diverge according to *which students one is talking about.* The comprehensive high school, with its array of electives, has traditionally taken care of these differences. (I return to this shortly, in a discussion of the conventional wisdom concerning curriculum and instruction.)

The Vocational Goal of American Schooling. To most Americans, this means appropriate preparation for work or for college. Whereas school subjects such as office practices and shop courses come easily to mind, less obvious school expectations such as learning to be on time, tidy, and cooperative are also considered important "vocational" goals.

We often hear, now, that business and industry want our high schools to turn out graduates who have mastered the basics but have not been trained for any specific occupation. "Give us broadly educated, trainable, adaptable young workers," we hear. Some political economists and people whose business it is to study the nature and needs of the work force seem to agree, pointing out that children in school today will fill jobs that don't even exist yet, and so obviously they cannot be trained in specific skills. The rhetoric of "learning how to learn" is heard far and wide.

Taking the broadest possible view, one must admit that in any society at any time one of the purposes of educating the young is to prepare them for their roles as productive adults—whatever that may mean in any particular culture. So our schools can hardly behave as if the vocational goal isn't important. The open questions have to do with whether individuals have some choices and some control over their lives as both learners and workers or whether the marketplace, in the final analysis, determines everything.

The Civic and Personal Goals of Schooling. These are not as easy to pin down. There seems to be general agreement that "citizenship" must be taught in schools, and that it is appropriate for children and young people to develop self-confidence, self-discipline, friendly relationships, and good habits of hygiene as outcomes of their schooling; but within these generalities there is a lot of room for disagreement as to specifics. When it is suggested that schools might abandon these goals, however, there is general protest. In fact, in recent years many *additions* to the required curriculum fall into these goal areas—drug and alcohol abuse units, anti-gang programs, suicide prevention, AIDS and STDs awareness, self-esteem enhancement, community service, and programs for at-risk youth, for example.

Disagreement about specifics, then, is one thing; making any major changes in the widely accepted and deeply rooted goal areas themselves is quite another. They are firmly entrenched in our conventional wisdom about the purposes of schools. Any innovative programs that would change these would face an uphill adoption battle or, if implemented, would be difficult to institutionalize.

The Custodial Function of the American School

One function of the schools that has been important to society for quite a long time but that is seldom publicly acknowledged or discussed (and never included in formal goal statements) is their role as caretakers of children and young people during the workday. In the early 1800s, "Parents who sent very young children to school seem to have done so through a desire to have them out from underfoot as much as from eagerness to get them started on the three R's early" (Kaestle, 1983, p. 15).

This expectation of child custody has effectively prevented any serious rethinking of the traditional 9-month school year in most parts of the country. Where an alternative calendar has been adopted, the change has seldom been accomplished without considerable local argument. This is an example of how one small part of the deep structure—societal assumptions about the proper use of time in schools—can thwart innovation.

The situation can get even more dramatic when changes in the school *week* or *day* are proposed. Numerous districts have faced stiff community or parental resistance, or both, to regularly scheduled shortened-day or student-free-day arrangements that allow teachers to have some planning and decision-making time together. It's odd that in most businesses it is assumed that staff meetings will take place on company time, during the workday; but this opportunity is not extended to K–12 educators at their workplaces. But it isn't odd at all when one bears in mind the strength of the custodial function of schooling in the minds of the American people.

Curriculum and Instruction

The persistence of the subject-centered curriculum is, in itself, evidence of the strength of the deep structure of schooling. In the 20th century it has been most striking that time and again efforts to make the curriculum more interdisciplinary and integrated have held for awhile, then yielded to pressures that reinstitute the old familiar pattern. One can visit schools from coast to coast and border to border and one will find the same subjects being taught, often in the same way and even from the same textbooks. This *is* our national curriculum, whether we admit it or not; and as a society we will not tolerate much change in it. At this level, elementary students have no curricular choices at all, and secondary students have choice only between available electives.

Local variations in curriculum serve to mask these commonalities and contribute to the myth of local control mentioned earlier, but in reality it hardly matters that high school students in the midwest can take agriculture courses while students in coastal communities may have the option of taking oceanography. These remain peripheral to the common curriculum—English, history and civics, math, life and physical science, and physical education—which all must take before choosing electives.

If the common curriculum is one side of the coin, similarity of instructional method is the other. In neither case does society tolerate much innovation, although individual schools may get excited, for a time, about efforts to "reform" in these areas. On the whole, such reforms rarely last beyond the first 3 to 5 years before starting to slide back to the old familiar patterns.

In the case of instructional method, those old familiar patterns include a preponderance of teacher talk/students listen and a hefty dose of worksheets, questions-at-the-end-of-the-chapter, and paper-and-pencil tests. That this is what teachers *do* is discussed more fully in Chapter 6. That this is what parents—and society in general—*want* or, indeed, *insist upon* is of concern as we ponder the role of the conventional wisdom in shaping the deep structure of schooling.

Team teaching is one of those instructional methodologies that has come around a number of times in the past and will, no doubt, be rediscovered again and again. An interesting case study by Gold and Miles (1981) tells the story of the first few years of an innovative elementary school in which team teaching and individualized instruction were among the changes being attempted. The pressure of parent and community expectations, based on conventional wisdom about appropriate teaching methods, was one of several deep-structure forces that combined to defeat these particular changes.

From the RAND change studies we know that planned innovations rarely survive in their original, "pure" form as envisioned by the designers; instead, they normally undergo some kind of "mutual adaptation" that permits them to survive in modified form (McLaughlin, 1978a). In the Gold and Miles (1981) study of Lincoln Acres School, we learn that such adaptation began as soon as *week 3 of the first year*. Single teachers in self-contained classrooms began to replace teacher teams before the end of the first semester. Teams were gone entirely by the end of the first year, and individualization of instruction had been only partly achieved. Gold and Miles point out that "the adjustments made to 'solve' the problems substantially altered the original vision . . ." and, later, that "after a struggle, the school now fit the parents' image of education, not the educators' . . ." (pp. 281, 300, 340).

It seems to me that "adaptations" of an innovation being implemented are always made in the direction of the traditional and familiar, and virtually *never* in the direction of the new and experimental. They are negotiated agreements to modify the original vison in the direction of the tried-and-true, or to abandon the vision altogether and "go back" to business as usual. This may be particularly true in the case of instructional methods, because in this area our collective sense of what is both appropriate and possible (the conventional wisdom) has been shaped by our own experiences as students.

The Myth of Equal Educational Opportunity

The myth that there is truly a level playing field in America when it comes to chances for a good formal education has deep roots in our history. There was the frontier—open for anyone to settle (one had only to sidestep the inconvenient fact that one had to displace the people who already lived on it). There were homestead laws, making it possible for any poor immigrant with a bit of initiative to own land. Completion of the transcontinental railway system hastened the process. In the growing cities and towns, there were niches just ready to be filled by the enterprising. Newcomers flooded the new world, convinced that here, even the most lowly European peasant could become wealthy and powerful. And in fact there *were* chances for upward mobility—up to a point. (No one cared to look carefully at the dark side: the abysmal working conditions that made the boom years of the industrial revolution possible, for example.)

The story we tell ourselves—and others—extended to our system of public schooling. From the Old Deluder Satan Act of 1647 to the common schools movement of the mid-1800s to the establishment of the Office of Equal Educational Opportunity in the 1960s, it has been a cherished part of our national self-image to believe that everyone has an equal chance at the gold ring. We've also liked to think that our system is a meritocracy— ever since Thomas Jefferson proposed his *Bill for the More General Diffusion of Knowledge*, Americans have held fast to the idea that the system allows the best and brightest to rise to the top (and that they can rise from any social class). Herbert Spenser's formulation of "social Darwinism" was just a new way of saying what Americans had believed for quite a long time: that the "fittest" will do well and that, conversely, if one doesn't do well, it must be that one is *less fit*—and less worthy. It's a circular line of reasoning that neatly justified the emerging status quo as the frontier closed and American society settled into the patterns we know today.

Today, there is little room for debate when it comes to equality of educational opportunity. Jonathan Kozol's 1991 book *Savage Inequalities* became an instant classic in large measure because Americans recognized its central truth: that the playing field is far from level, and that complex social forces conspire to prevent meaningful equalization. As others have said, "Should the accident of geography determine the quality of science instruction a child receives, whether he has an opportunity to learn to play the violin, whether her first-grade class will have twenty students or thirty-five?" (Wise & Gendler, 1995, p. 499). And although the answer (provided by state and federal court rulings in school finance cases) has often been *No, it shouldn't*, in fact it *does*—and has done for many, many years. Of course, it isn't geography alone but a complex web of related factors that in effect make the term *geography* a code word for *poverty* and *substandard housing* and *no afforable health care* and *stressed families*—and all the other forces that, combined, prevent equal educational opportunity. As Robert Bullough (1988) has observed, "The race for knowledge and position is far from fair even at the starting line; most of those who get ahead even within a public school setting begin with tremendous advantages" (p. 14).

The American tendency to "blame the victim" instead of recognizing the *systemic* causes of inequity is vividly illustrated by Mary Anne Raywid (1994) in describing a $40-million project designed to "enhance the life chances" of at-risk youth. Changes in both school structure and instruction were agreed upon by all those involved, but 3 years and many dollars later, nothing much had changed, because the staff of the school "continued to believe that the problems lay with the students, and not with the school, and that the challenge was thus to *fix the students* [italics added]" (p. 30).

We also need to acknowledge the role played by racism as an element within the conventional wisdom. At this point in our nation's history, when most white middle- and upper-class Americans think of "poverty," they automatically think in terms of the nonwhite population. We are invariably surprised to learn that higher numbers of whites than nonwhites receive welfare support, for example; or that more teenage mothers are white than otherwise. We exclaim, momentarily, and then settle back comfortably into our comfy old armchairs and assumptions.

The mythology of equal educational opportunity and the realities that it masks seem particularly short-sighted in view of demographic changes presently under way in the United States. With a growing percentage of citizens over 65, a correspondingly smaller proportion are available to do the nation's work, pay taxes, and generally keep the wheels turning. We'll need every one of our young people to take his or her place *in the work force*—not on the streets, and not in prison. Assuming that poor rural or inner-city children are incapable of high educational achievement (and therefore shouldn't have schools as good as those we provide for affluent suburban youngsters) is diametrically opposite to our own best long-term interests. And yet, strangely enough, just this assumption is firmly embedded in our conventional wisdom at this point in time.

Standardized Testing

The 20th-century worldview in the United States has been—as I argued in Chapter 1—predominantly mechanistic and behaviorist. Enamored of the *idea* of efficiency, we applauded the time-and-motion studies and task analyses of the early 1900s. From there it was a small step to mass testing and to the development of behavior modification techniques. Treating human beings like so much raw material in need of processing, and then post-testing to measure the quality of the "product," came to seem normal and natural in a world increasingly dependent on machines of all kinds (Gould, 1981).

A great deal has been written about the factory model and its applications to American schooling; I don't need to review it here. Pertinent to this discussion of the conventional wisdom about schooling as the 21st century dawns, however, is the *intensification* of a shared belief in the power of standardized tests. It seems that, rather than running its course and giving way to a new paradigm, the mechanistic worldview is alive and well and shows little sign of abating any time soon.

Indeed, it has become even more entrenched in the years since 1978, when state-mandated, high-stakes testing appeared and was quickly accepted by the public despite the absence of clear empirical evidence that such tests actually do what their proponents claim they can do: to raise both standards and student achievement. According to Peter Airasian (1988), "the testing programs are powerful symbolically; they strike a responsive chord in the public at large and this response helps explain the widespread and speedy adoption of an innovation that had virtually no track record in American education before about 1979" (p. 311).

In effect, Airasian is saying that the deep structure of the present time supports standardized testing. David Purpel (1989), in discussing the same phenomenon, notes that "The code word for this renewed energy for using the school to sort and weed is 'excellence,' and the basic technique for implementing the policy is testing. . . . 'Excellence' has through a relentless process of reification and reductionism come to mean high scores on normative standardized tests" (pp. 18–19). Here, the conventional wisdom takes on an aura almost of magic or superstition—as if attaching a compelling name (in this case, "excellence") will make something true. And, as with some magic, we believe it despite all evidence to the contrary. Why? Perhaps because, as Purpel implies, the schools are actually doing *precisely* what our society as a whole really wants them to do: acculturate, socialize, sort, and indoctrinate—and, in the process, protect hierarchy and privilege. Standardized testing serves this purpose well.

Kahne (1994) identifies the way standardized tests ensure the success of some students at the expense of others: "Uniform and comparative measures of success can transform efforts to equalize opportunity and achievement into zero-sum arrangements. This occurs when a student's grade in a class or score on a standardized test reflects his or her achievement relative to others. As a consequence, the success of some students comes to depend on the failure of others" (p. 239). Anyone who has ever graded "on a curve" will recognize that no matter how well the entire class does—even if *everyone* did extremely well—there still will be failures: Arraying students around a group average guarantees it.

THE ROLE OF THE MEDIA IN SHAPING
THE CONVENTIONAL WISDOM

Although print media have played a part in both educating the citizenry and in shaping public opinion since colonial times, the 20th century has seen quantum leaps in this area, as electronic media—radio, cinema and ultimately television—entered our lives (and, some say, took over). Social critics such as Vance Packard (1981), Marshall McLuhan and Quentin Fiore (1967), Neil Postman (1985), and others showed us how our values, opinions, and behavior are determined by marketing strategies and by the ways in which national and world events are covered in the print and electronic media. John Goodlad, in 1984 but without irony, asked, "Has television become the common school? If so, what is left for the public school?" (p. 42). As the 20th century ends, educators still have not come to grips with these uncomfortable questions (Maeroff, 1998), and now they are exacerbated by the rapid spread of computer technology as well.

Where Americans Get Their Information

A national research study conducted by Goodlad and his colleagues in the late 1970s included questions about where parents and community members got their information about the schools in their community. "Radio or television" and "the grapevine" were the two most common responses: These adults seemed quite willing to accept as credible what they were told by others, whether on TV or over the back fence (B. B. Tye, 1985). In such a society, we collectively grant our media moguls tremendous power over our minds. Some may argue that the conventional wisdom always has been shaped by those who control and limit the dissemination of ideas, that contemporary media power is just a matter of degree, and that in fact the World Wide Web and the internet are going to take us all in just the *opposite* direction: wide-open access to information. Maybe so. But whatever happens, there will never be a time in which societies are not held together by some common assumptions—whether, as we have seen, they are true or not.

The Attraction of Bad News

A number of respected educators have tried, in recent years, to correct some of the many misconceptions that were being perpetuated in the media and taken for granted by many—perhaps most—Americans. For example, Gerald Bracey's annual *Phi Delta Kappan* articles through the 1990s clearly document the misuse and misinterpretation of data by the media in its coverage of schooling in America. But was he able to find a forum for his position in the popular press? Far from it. Reading Bracey, one might conclude that something about the way in which Americans have been socialized in the second half of the 20th century makes us willing to trust negative news about schools that is *false* and to distrust positive coverage that is *true*. "Why do some 'facts' slip so easily into the popular culture while others that contradict them are rejected outright?" Bracey (1994) wondered (p. 82). Two years later, Bracey (1996) pondered the selectivity of calls for "balance" in reporting the news about schools, noting that coverage of good news often includes rebuttal by dissenters, whereas coverage of bad news is usually left to stand alone.

David Berliner also spoke out to counter the incessant barrage of misinformation and negatives, first in a 1993 article that was turned down by the *Atlantic Monthly* and other mainstream publications, and ultimately published in an education journal (Berliner, 1993). Then, in 1995 he and Bruce Biddle co-authored a book on media misrepresentation of the schools, *The Manufactured Crisis*, which was not aggressively marketed to the general public. For many who were interested, the only way to get a copy was to special-order it.

In June of 1994, Larry Cuban of Stanford University showed how business interests made use of negative media about the schools *when it served their purpose* in drawing attention to the need for a "better educated" work force to improve the national economy. But when the economy did, in fact, improve, the same business leaders never gave any credit to the school reforms that had been put in place in response to their earlier demands. The same point was made in a *Newsweek* column in March of 1998 (Elliott, 1998), but in general this is not a view that gets much media coverage.

Speaking of self-serving attacks on the nation's schools, James P. Comer (1980) some years ago pointed out that school problems "are 'good news' to some, like those politicians, reporters, scholars who advance their own interests and careers on the backs of school problems and people. In too many instances, the more complicated the problem the more simplistic the explanation given and solution proposed" (p. 15).

Social critics such as John Gardner (1963), founder of the citizens' group Common Cause, locate the power of the conventional wisdom in the nature of *vested interests* within the society. Following Gardner's line of reasoning, it is *to somebody's advantage* that schools should be the scapegoat for so many social problems. Daniel Tanner (1998) reminds us that the education establishment itself must share some of the blame for placing bad news in the public eye. When flawed research produces evidence of serious problems in the system, the media are all too ready to trumpet the findings as "news." He uses a 1993 study of adult illiteracy to make his point, showing how despite the study's weaknesses in definition, sampling, and item validity, the popular press seized upon the report with glee.

I mention Tanner's analysis because it serves no useful purpose for us to assume that all the negativity is caused by "others," and because it is a good illustration of Gardner's point about vested interests. Readers will readily recognize that many other people, groups, organizations, and institutions in our society contributed to the negative attitudes about public education popular at the end of the 20th century.

The image of public schools as dangerous places that one finds depicted in recent feature movies and in television programming is rarely what one would encounter on a visit to most schools, though a series of real-life schoolyard shootings by armed children and young people in the late 1990s added to that impression. The image of pervasive chaos and danger does reflect what many Americans have come to believe, and it contributes to the perpetuation of these beliefs, however warped, and to the consequent difficulty faced by educators when they attempt to correct such misconceptions. "Most reporters realize that public opinion often seems to have a life of its own. . . . Conventional wisdom quite frequently rules, in spite of evidence to the contrary" (Watson, 1998, p. 734).

The power of the conventional wisdom to shape popular opinions and attitudes is seen most clearly in the discrepancy between what people say about schools in general and what they say about the schools that their own children attend. Year after year, the Gallup Poll on education shows that parents in a controlled national sample give their children's schools a grade of average *or above*. They should know, after all. But this is never "news." The power of one vivid negative story to overshadow the thousand daily accomplishments of students and teachers is, literally, awesome.

Some educators, taking a longer sociohistorical view, trace the current antipathy toward public schooling to the willingness of educators, in the years since the end of World War II, to take on greater responsibilities. It is ironic, and considerably depressing, to understand that to some extent school people have themselves contributed to the problem of negative conventional wisdom by raising society's expectations of what the schools would be able to accomplish. On the other hand, what has changed in the past will change again. Cremin (1961) brings us full circle, noting that "The conventional wisdom accommodates itself not to the world that it is meant to interpret, but to the audience's view of that world. And since audiences tend to prefer the comfortable and the familiar, while the world moves on, the conventional wisdom is ever in danger of obsolescence" (pp. 350–351).

Ultimately, even the media cannot resist the pull of a changing world, whatever the vested interests that tug against that pull.

PERIODS OF TRANSITION IN THE CONVENTIONAL WISDOM

I proposed in Chapter 1 that the deep structure of schooling changes only when the nation comes to want something different from its schools. Now it needs to be said, in addition, that such shifts are invariably accompanied by changes in the conventional wisdom. The power of the conventional wisdom (or popular ideology) holds institutions in place. Once in a great while, it helps to overturn or alter them; then it coalesces and solidifies around the new beliefs and practices, legitimizing'them as it once did earlier formations.

So integral to the deep structure is the conventional wisdom that, in fact, I find it virtually impossible to envision one without the other. But are they then, perhaps, merely the same phenomenon called by two different names? No: The *deep structure* is the complex of accepted educational policies and practices existing at any given historical moment in a culture; the *conventional wisdom* is part of a sort of ideological glue that holds those policies and practices in place. The popular ideology must change before the deep structure of schooling will change—it cannot be the other way around, because the deep structure of schooling is, by its very nature, reactive. It sits ponderously in place, like a very old bear, until prodded or jostled into shifting to a different position. Even a very old bear can move, though; and the conventional wisdom can shift, pulling the deep structure along with it.

Is the bear on the move again? Are we now, at the end of the 20th century, in a period of significant social transition? Michael Apple (1993), among many others, suggests that the nation lost its moorings in the 1960s and 1970s, and has not yet formed a new anchoring self-image. Sarason (1983) implies that the incessant barrage of negative criticism of the schools may indeed be an indicator of profound social change-in-progress: "Precisely because society expects so much and so many different results from schooling, criticism of schools tends to be sustained and varied. Ordinarily the criticism is muted and unorganized, but *when there are sea-swell changes in the society, criticisms become stronger and more focused* [italics added]" (p. 36).

Robert Bullough (1988) has suggested that Americans may have simply given up on the idea that almost everyone is capable of understanding public issues and making informed decisions. Public education is still supported, but primarily because it is a ritual we are accustomed to, and because it keeps young people off the streets. "Education," he concludes, "is not the primary aim of schooling. Rather, it is the socialization and control of other peoples' children. For our own children we parents want something better and many of us would gladly abandon the public school to achieve it if necessary" (p. 16). This provocative statement assumes even greater significance in light of recent turn-of-century reforms such as charter schools and various attempts to privatize the institution of public education.

There have been many other indicators that suggest that profound changes are under way in the United States. It is tempting to conclude that western society in general is, indeed, in a period of transition. And yet . . . we are all so culture-bound that we might mistake transitory ripples for sea-change.

SUMMARY AND CONCLUSION

In summary, the conventional wisdom undergirds the deep structure of schooling by providing the "taken-for-granted" ideas that are used to justify the way things are done. Such ideas include the following: that Americans cannot agree on the purposes of schools (even though we really do); that schools should play a custodial as well as an educative role; that there is certain appropriate subject matter that should be taught; that teaching methods shouldn't deviate far from the banking model (deposit information into their heads); that all children have an equal chance to achieve success in school; and that standardized testing yields educational excellence.

Some of these are openly acknowledged and vigorously defended, whereas others can almost be viewed as *subconscious* assumptions shared among the population as a whole. Whatever the degree of public recognition, however, as aspects of the current conventional wisdom, they are part of the deep structure: Their very existence goes far to inhibit changes that might be attempted in these areas of educational endeavor. As I have tried to show, they shape every aspect of the schooling enterprise; and they themselves are shaped by the workings of the print and electronic media of our time.

Strange but true: The messages we receive from the media are more powerful than what we know from personal experience. As I noted earlier, national polls repeatedly show that parents of school-age children are reasonably pleased with their own child's school but are at the same time convinced that American schools in general are going to hell in a handbasket. One would think that a generally satisfied parent might be just a little bit skeptical of so much negative media coverage, and willing to say: That's not *my* experience. That they are neither may, sadly, suggest one of the real failures of our system of public schooling: promoting the rhetoric of democracy while at the same time discouraging generations of Americans from raising their voices in constructive critique of the status quo. All that is left to us is the mindless mouthing of the conventional wisdom, articulated for us by others.

3

Myths and Realities of Schooling as a Bureaucratic System

Most people take it as a given that the institution of education in America is a bureaucracy, and in most ways it is. But it's become clear that a bureaucratic hierarchy can't contain all the complexities of an essentially nonroutine endeavor such as the teaching–learning process. Bureaucratic structures by themselves fail to account for much of what goes on in schools. The structural characteristics of contemporary schooling form the focal point of this chapter; the goal is to understand the ways in which these structures inhibit many efforts to improve what is done in schools and classrooms.

HISTORICAL PERSPECTIVE: THE BIRTH OF BUREAUCRACY

Bureaucracy . . . was first developed in a few limited and specialized industries after the Civil War; it was not generalized to a widely applicable model until the 1920's; it became fully "worked out" in its details only during the 1950's.

Heckscher and Donellon (1994, p. 4)

In Chapter 1, the ethos of the 20th-century United States was characterized as essentially behavioristic and mechanistic. That worldview found its expression in education through the adoption of the corporate models of organization that emerged during the 19th century as part of the industrial revolution. This change was, in itself, a deep structure change from the localite and entrepreneurial systems that had been the norm before the Civil War.

The concept of age-grading is a case in point. Heterogeneous, multitask classrooms had been the norm in the small communities of the young nation. But as the cities grew and city schools became enormous, some kind of organizing principle became necessary. Grouping children by age seemed to have a certain face validity that grouping by some other criterion—student interests, for example—lacked. As Tyack and Tobin (1994) point out, the age-graded school "mirrored . . . the hierarchical, differentiated organizations in which urban dwellers increasingly conducted their business" (p. 459).

It is likewise no accident that the public high school appeared on the scene when it did and, in many respects, reflected the national mood even better than did the elementary school of the time. By the 1920s, the high school went beyond age-grading: In offering a newly differentiated curriculum, it sorted adolescents in not just one but three ways—by age, by future plans, and by ability. It served the emerging corporate culture well to have the future work force pass through schools structured to prepare them for life in a hierarchical work environment (Gutek, 1991; McLaren, 1998).

Oddly enough, it was a series of hearings at the Interstate Commerce Commission in the fall of 1910 that first brought the idea of "scientific management" to public attention. It's a measure of how fertile the ground already was for an ideology of efficiency that educators began applying the principles of scientific management to schooling *just 3 months later* (Callahan, 1962). A popular practice during World War I involved marching groups of children from room to room for departmentalized instruction. This "platoon" system, also known as the Gary Plan, was considered an efficiency measure because it was thought to make better use of the physical resources of the school building, keeping all rooms in use at all times during the school day.

During the 1920s a public reaction to such mechanical treatment of children set in, and a compromise was reached: The humanity of the self-contained classroom *and* the efficiency of age-grading would coexist henceforth in American elementary school classrooms. As expressions of the deep structure of schooling, both subsequently have been extremely resistant to change.

At the secondary level, World War I had even more direct consequences: The impulse to sort students not only by age but also by planned careers and academic ability got a big boost from the IQ-testing and task-analysis movements.

The early 20th century also saw a massive wave of immigration, and the influx of non-English-speaking families from southern and eastern Europe played right into the hands of American educators and policy-makers, who recognized the tools of "scientific management" as a way to contain and control the newcomers. It was necessary to inculcate the immigrants with American values, and uniform treatment seemed a good way to do it. Systematic training of teachers in the normal schools and state teachers' colleges provided communities with cohorts of schoolteachers prepared to teach more or less the same things in more or less similar ways. McGuffey readers and other popular textbooks added another kind of consistency to the schooling experience. Finally, where the teachers and a headmaster had once been sufficient for schoolkeeping, now the addition of new administrative roles led to the development of a more multi-layered and complex institution—one that bore a good deal of resemblance to the complex corporate entities that were, increasingly, conducting the business of the nation.

But . . . was it a bureaucracy? Is it still? If so, how does it work? If not, what is it, and how does *that* work? We need to take a look at questions such as these, because one thing is clear: Structural factors do get in the way of constructive change and pull it back to the tried-and-true, familiar way of doing things.

THE INSTITUTION OF SCHOOLING VIEWED
AS A BUREAUCRATIC SYSTEM

To most of us, the first thing that comes to mind when we think of a "bureaucracy" is *hierarchy*: distinct levels of authority, status, and responsibility. Inextricably interwoven with the concept of a hierarchical system is the notion of *role differentiation*: People at each level have certain functions and tasks to do within the organization.

Training, recruitment, and promotion are based on an individual's *competence* in performing the technical requirements of his or her role, in playing by the rules, and in achieving the goals specified for that position. Whether the individual is related to the boss or has been in the business since it was a mom-and-pop operation isn't supposed to have anything to do with it; appropriate role performance is what counts. It follows from this that the environment of a bureaucratic organization is intentionally kept as *impersonal* and neutral as possible.

All of this is held in place by a management system based on the maintenance of *documentation*: policies, rules, and paperwork. In addition to these, one can also think of other ways that an organization can demonstrate that its workers possess technical competence: supervision using standardized evaluation instruments, institutional accreditation, and so on (Nohria & Berkley, 1994; Pinchot & Pinchot, 1994).

Finally, whatever its structure, every kind of human organization has a characteristic *culture*. When people come together to perform a certain kind of work, they find that in addition to the formal, explicit rules and procedures, there is an informal, implicit, and symbolic side to the job. There may be a specialized language to be mastered as well. The norms of bureaucratic life include the following: be stable, self-disciplined, and reliable; obey the boss. *Don't* be impulsive, unpredictable, or self-indulgent; don't play favorites or do things your own way. "The bureaucrat has a will, but it is an officially limited will: it cannot transcend his or her role. It is a will whose origins lie not in personal conscience but in machinery set in motion by a superior, the work rules, or the understanding of one's jurisdiction" (Hummel, 1977, p. 6). The bureaucratic mindset promotes specialization and diverts people from considering context—or ethics—in the performance of their work. "Just go by the book" is the operative guideline (Heckscher, 1994; Purpel & Shapiro, 1995).

To what extent does American public education have these bureaucratic characteristics? Does the educational system have *levels of authority*, a chain of command? Yes, at the upper levels, but not "on the shop floor." On the contrary: When one reaches the school site, the organizational structure flattens out abruptly. Even in schools that have a number of distinct teacher roles—resource specialists, for example—these are nearly always staff, rather than line, positions. In fact, as we see in Chapter 6, within the culture of teaching there are strong egalitarian norms that tend to discourage making status distinctions between members of a faculty.

Are school districts and school sites places where *roles are clearly defined*? In this case, the answer is definitely yes. In fact, boundaries are traditionally quite firm and there is usually little or no overlap. Test this proposition, if you like, by imagining what would happen in your school if any one of the following people were to begin doing the tasks assigned to any one of the others: custodian, librarian, nurse, principal, third-grade teacher, superintendent, personnel director, school bus driver, school board member, and so on.

Is *technical competence* in performing one's assigned tasks the sole criterion for hiring and promotion in our public schools? Yes: Would-be educators must pass through state-certified training programs and earn a certificate of such competence in order even to be considered for a teaching or administrative position. Once hired, there are established procedures for the supervision and annual evaluation of competence, at least for teachers. Things get a bit obscure when it comes to the formal evaluation of administrators—ordinarily, if an administrator is running the show within the budget and not rocking the boat too much, it seems the person is viewed as technically competent.

There is another way in which technical competence as a characteristic of a bureaucratic system may not apply to schooling in every case: room exists for subjectivity, even favoritism, in hiring and promotion decisions. It's not unheard of, for instance, for a school district to do a national search for a new superintendent but then fill the position from inside—even though an outside candidate may clearly have been superior—simply because everyone in the system is more comfortable with the person they already know.

Are school systems *impersonal and neutral environments*? This is one characteristic of a bureaucracy that doesn't seem to fit the institution of education well at all. A heated board meeting is hardly a neutral environment; nor is a strong demonstration of support for the principal, or for a teacher. Try as they might, teachers seldom treat students impersonally—at least not by choice. On the other hand, the system does have certain norms and practices that preserve a certain measure of neutrality.

Finally, is the educational enterprise held together by *systems of documentation*? Most school people would, I suspect, say that not only is this the case but that the pressure for documentation has grown far beyond what is really necessary. Paperwork? Tell us about it. Submit your annual objectives. Hand in your daily lesson plans. Document daily attendance and follow up on absences as needed. Develop a grant proposal and send in six copies to the funding agency. Are you a principal? Carefully record every teacher observation and evaluation conference. Do the budget in quadruplicate. Prepare the school's self-study and submit ten copies to the state. Examples go on and on—and these are only at the site level. The same is true at the district office, the county office, the state department of education and the U.S. Department of Education.

This quick review of the primary characteristics of a bureaucratic system suggests that the institution of schooling may be considered a bureaucratic system in some respects but not in all. As it turns out, bureaucratic structures seem to work pretty well at the mid- and upper-management levels. Much of what administrators have to do to keep the schools functioning lends itself to a certain amount of routinization and standardization, but the closer one gets to where the really important things happen—the classroom—the less that holds true. Yet, because bureaucracy does work at the upper levels, people at those levels tend to assume that it must work at the other organizational levels as well. Every single top-down reform mandate reflects this assumption, whether it comes from the district, the state, or Washington.

Structurally, then, we seem to have a two-part system: largely bureaucratic at the administrative end, and something else at the instructional end. What is that "something else"? I'm not the first to suggest that it is a *loosely coupled system* (Meyer & Rowan, 1983; Scott, 1995; Weick, 1976). Such a system can be envisioned as an organism (or organization) with component parts that are not tightly bound together. Where they interface, they meet as needed, smoothly interact, then move on to play their separate parts in the functioning whole. The way this plays out in the educational system is dealt with in more detail later in this chapter.

I do not want to imply that the institution of formal education consists organizationally of two neat boxes balanced on either end of a systemic continuum. It would be much too simplistic to say that classrooms are loosely coupled systems and the superordinate system functions bureaucratically. Certainly, fingers of the bureaucracy reach down into the classroom, and there are ways in which the various components of upper-level education administration, although bureaucratic in themselves, are loosely coupled to each other and to the classroom.

All the same, loose-coupling theory is very helpful in thinking about how and why some of the structural features of schooling defy efforts to do things differently. I suggest we shall find that the characteristics of a loosely coupled system work to defeat change just as surely as do the characteristics of a bureaucratic system, though in different ways.

HOW A BUREAUCRATIC SYSTEM HELPS THE DEEP STRUCTURE RESIST EFFORTS TO DO THINGS DIFFERENTLY

Hierarchy: Top-down Decision-making

Because it is the essence of a hierarchy that those at the top have more power than those at other levels, it sometimes happens that such power is used to stifle a new program or process. This can be done actively, as when a school board votes to discontinue block scheduling. It can also be done passively, as when a superintendent or a principal simply fails to give the project his or her support.

The power of position can also be used by policymakers to promote reforms that are actually *inappropriate*. Jean Anyon (1995) has observed that some proposed reforms are accepted by inner-city school district administrators because it may be politically wise to do so, but that since the proposed changes "have little if anything to do with [the] district's students and the cultural and economic realities of their lives, and in part because of this sociocultural inappropriateness, the reforms actually impede the students' academic progress and thereby *preclude reform success* [italics added]" (p. 77).

These policymakers—the "policy elite"—whether they are in Washington, the state capital, or even sitting on the local school board, have generally been well-served personally by the public schools. They were "successful": They quickly learned how the game is played, they got good grades, graduated from high school, and earned one or more college degrees. They are also, for the most part, happy with the way their own children are being served by the schools. They have difficulty understanding how very different school life is for children of working class or unemployed parents, for non-English-speaking children, or for children with disabilities. It is understandable—though not excusable—that they should devise reforms that are inappropriate for many students.

Legislators and others in a position to make educational policy can also do so for purely political reasons and, as such, these too are likely to be poorly conceived and inappropriate. For example, as part of the reaction to *Sputnik*, the state of California passed a law in 1962 *requiring* foreign language instruction by 1965 for *all* students in grades 6 through 8. *But no money was appropriated for this huge new addition to the middle grades curriculum.* By 1965 the dust had settled, the nation was focused more on the War on Poverty than on the space race, and very few California districts were teaching foreign languages to all their early adolescents. Most districts, in fact, had applied to the state for an exemption to the law. By 1968, the law was rewritten to make foreign languages optional, not mandatory (K. A. Tye & Novotney, 1975).

When educational reforms are mandated by politicians in the form of new state or federal laws, they may also fail because of the "magic feather" fallacy. It seems that the further a person is from the classroom, the more likely he or she is to believe in the magic feather: Wave it, and change will happen. Name a thing, and you make it real. Pass a law, and the problem will be solved. "Build it, and they will come." There is a great temptation to go for a quick fix (Darling-Hammond, 1997; Fullan & Pomfret, 1977; Hall & Loucks, 1977; Tye, K. A., 1992). This is "symbolic politics"—the formulation of policy that doesn't actually change anything (Bentzen, 1974; Crain & Street, 1969; Fullan & Miles, 1992). Purpel and Shapiro (1995) suggest that such public discourse, which separates schools and society, is a way to protect the status quo: Policymakers talk about change in general terms; school people talk specifics—everyone talks past each other and nothing happens.

This tendency to confuse normative and descriptive—to assume that the gap between *what should be* and *what is* can be closed by the simple act of passing a bill or issuing a directive—"waving the magic feather"—is exacerbated by the status assumption inherent in the top-down structure of a bureaucratic system: that those in higher positions know more, and make better decisions, than those in "lesser" positions within the organization.

Although this may hold true in some institutions, it doesn't work for schooling. The literature contains plenty of examples of top-down mandates that failed to take possible unanticipated consequences into account and thereby contained the seeds of their own ultimate failure (Tyack & Cuban, 1995; Wise, 1979). "Legislated learning suggested by those who do not work in schools," comments Wasley (1991), "has unintended consequences that cancel the good intentions of the hopeful reformers" (p. 16). And, as Susan Ohanian (1996) suggests in her inimitable way, policymakers *just don't get it*: "Point out to a bureaucrat calling for curriculum reform that his state is eliminating librarians and art teachers even as it passes standards to increase the emphasis on student research and artistic performance, and he will merely shrug his shoulders" (p. 281). Ignoring the suggestions of teachers—seen by the hierarchy as line subordinates and therefore less knowledgable—has until fairly recently been quite common, and perhaps even today may be more the rule than the exception, despite the rhetoric of participatory decision-making.

Finally, when politics drives education reform and politicians, rather than educators and communities, frame what is to be done, the timetable for change can become problematic in two ways. First, our system of government virtually guarantees a short institutional memory. Freshman legislators have no sense of the reasons for education reform laws passed before their time, and if they do not take the trouble to educate themselves, they are more than likely to gut the earlier programs or else to reinvent the wheel. The story of political changes in California's math curriculum shows that this phenomenon is a perennial one: The math curriculum of 1938 came under attack in the early 1940s and, in 1946, was "again revised, essentially returning it to its previous design" (Rowan, 1982, pp. 270–271). The California math curriculum underwent precisely the same reform/reversal cycle 50 years later, in the 1990s. Reverting to familiar patterns and reinventing the wheel are, clearly, likely to continue when politicians decide what should be happening in schools.

Second, the political need to show quick results produces pressure for the premature evaluation of new programs. Both legislative turnover and the limited tenure of governors make long-range planning and ongoing commitment to the support of school improvement projects unlikely. "The nature of state-level educational politics offers little hope that many states will be able to sustain the ten years or more of consistent effort required to achieve lasting school reform," noted Richard McAdams (1997, p. 142) in his critique of the highly touted school reform legislation enacted by the state of Kentucky in 1991, but faltering by 1996 (Holland, 1997; O'Neil, 1994).

One final point must be made about top-down mandates for change: At whatever level they originate, they *always* assume that what practitioners are currently doing isn't good enough; and those who design them *never see themselves* as part of the problem. "It almost has the status of a law to

say that those who advocate educational reform seek not to reform themselves but to change someone or something else," Sarason (1993) has said
(p. 19). "Recommending reform to others is easy," Ohanian (1996) adds,
"blue-ribbon panels do it all the time" (p. 284).

Role Differentiation

The second characteristic of bureaucratic systems is the allocation of roles
and the attachment to each role of a very precise set of rules, norms, and
performance expectations. Some anthropologists and sociologists suggest
that role specialization is more than just a characteristic of bureaucratic
organizations; it is a characteristic of all human societies when they reach
a certain level of developmental complexity. Some also propose that human
beings, as social animals, always organize themselves into groups that
contain various status positions—in effect, into hierarchies—and, further,
that as they assign higher status to some roles, they create natural oligar-
chies. If hierarchical systems are an expression of human nature and
not merely a way of organizing human activity, then changing behavior
grounded in assigned roles may be all but impossible (Krackhardt, 1994;
Michels, 1949).

Be that as it may, role differentiation is done in an attempt to eliminate ambiguity (Zacker, 1973) and enforce accountability: "With centralization and specialization of functions, in theory, would come accountability—one could pin down the responsibility for success or failure. The
organization chart showed who was in charge of what," note Tyack and
Cuban (1995, p. 76). In practice, however, as they go on to point out,
clearly separated roles also give workers in a bureaucratic system a natural excuse for *not* making a decision or providing an answer: "It's not my
department."

The organization chart has in fact proven to be quite a useful device
for making *symbolic* changes within the system: As many students of the
change process have observed, it's much easier to tinker with the structure than to actually get people to behave in new ways. Educators involved
in "strategic planning" in recent years have become accustomed to seeing
a new organization chart trotted out, with great fanfare; perhaps new tasks
have been assigned to some roles, but, in reality, nothing much changes in
the way the school district does its business.

Although easier to make than behavioral changes, sometimes structural changes, too, fail to stick. The story of differentiated staffing is a good
example of this—from NASSP's Model Schools Project in the 1970s to recent experiments with new roles for teachers, differentiated staffing has
been one of the most difficult innovations to retain (Trump & Georgiades,

1977; Warren, 1978). Bonnie Daniel, one of the original teachers at the first high school built in the planned community of Columbia, Maryland (and, some years later, its principal), admits that differentiated staffing was "probably the thing that we have managed *least* well over the years." The original plan, which was in place when the school opened in 1971, followed the Trump-Georgiades/NASSP model (Jenkins, 1977). It included an instructional aide and a clerical aide for every department. The clerical aide role worked out well, Daniel recalls, and in 1993 there were still five in the school, but

> the teacher/instructional aide relationship never really developed as the model intended that it should. In the early days, many of our instructional aides were credentialed teachers who just, for one reason or another, didn't want to teach full-time. They were perfectly well qualified to monitor kids, to assist with questions that kids might have when they were working on independent assignments, and yet—it didn't work. I have to say that, as a group, the teachers—and I was one of them—were unable to let go of the reins, to accept that somebody besides us could talk to that kid about the composition, help him revise it. We just didn't do it well; and eventually we lost all of that staffing.

When Irvine High School opened in 1975, its first principal tried redefining the assistant principal and counselor roles: People holding these positions would also teach part-time. This blurring of the traditional role categories was one of the first things to "snap back," he recalls. The pull of administrative responsibilities was too strong and when something had to give, it was the teaching that was seen as most logically expendable.

> Employees are not paid to think broadly: their job is to stay within the "boxes" defined by their job descriptions. (Pinchot & Pinchot, 1994, p. 29)

At this point in our consideration of how the educational bureaucracy works as part of the deep structure of schooling, we need to move inside the "boxes," to take a look at the various roles found in the school system, and to see how each can do its part to inhibit change.

The Board Member. Historically, school board members have been appointed or elected from among the civic elite of a community. Business leaders have been disproportionately represented, and over time this has tended to give a business management orientation to the decisions made for schools (Callahan, 1962; Counts, 1927; Kimbrough, 1969).

The board's designated role is to set policy and to hire the superintendent, who will manage the district in accordance with that policy. "Boardsmanship" training is available through workshops offered by the American School Boards Association or its state affiliates, or both, but because such training is not necessarily required of new members, participation varies greatly from district to district. The result is that in some communities, board members have a good deal of background knowledge and considerable skills in areas such as deliberation, goal setting, decision-making, and conflict resolution. In other communities, where this is not the case, board members rely on conventional wisdom, common sense, and whatever knowledge and skills individual members may possess. Stan Corey, the pioneer superintendent of the Irvine Unified School District, saw board members generally as "good people who want to do good things, but in a great many instances they have no sense of the complexity of the organization they are to govern."

Skilled or not, one thing is for sure: School board members, as elected officials, have little institutional memory. Like state and federal legislators, they are unlikely to have a clear understanding of the context of policies that are in place when they arrive on the scene. Dismantling the work of predecessors and reinventing the wheel are inevitable consequences, and, of course, this often means the death or drastic modification of new programs or efforts to improve the schools.

Some boards do a good job of providing leadership within the framework of their designated role. Others micromanage, assuming role responsibilities that are not technically theirs. An example of the former was the way the Howard County board handled community/school differences of opinion in the years when the Columbia community was new. Mary Hovet, an activist educator in those years, recalls, "We had many issues—we still do—where the Board would have the parents come in and the school people come in and we really would argue it out; and either one could win because the parents haven't always been right and the school staff hasn't always been right, either. But it really gets a hearing all the way."

Micromanagement is something else again. This impulse to cross the lines of authority and responsibility in the hierarchy can create tremendous friction; it runs counter to everything a bureaucratic organization is constructed to be. Micromanagement by board members, whether individually or as a group, can run the gamut from naive but well-meaning interventions to truly unpleasant adversarial incidents. One of the former superintendents I interviewed told me this story:

> A school board member came in one day to tell me that I needed to spend more time out in the schools. The reason, she pointed out,

was that in the kindergarten at one elementary school there were only three geraniums in the window and she felt that this showed that I simply wasn't spending enough time at that school. I tried to explain to her that if I told the teacher how many geraniums she should have, I would be in deep trouble. But this did not affect the school board member *at all*. This was her opinion and by gosh I had better do something about it.

Another time, something more serious happened—a very shrewd and aggressive woman on the school board simply issued a newsletter to the community without discussing it with me. The first I knew about it was when a copy showed up on my desk. When she came in, she said she'd done it because it was clear that I was too busy with other things. Which was quite correct; but it still was not her place to do something like that unilaterally. That's not what board members are supposed to be doing.

When the lines get crossed and board members usurp the authority of those who are hired to run the schools of their district, no one wins. Consider this small but telling story from a Fairfax County principal:

The board made one decision that the principals didn't agree with and it was within our rights to make a different decision, so the board had to go back and change theirs. And when they did, one of the school board members' comment was, "You guys got away with it. You did it. But you better fall in line or you are going to pay for it."

Micromanagement by board members can be problematic for the life of a new program or reform effort—whatever the motivation of the board members, the fact is that they are taking action that is not theirs to take.

Finally, if a board *really* wants to prevent change in the district, a sure-fire way to do so is to fire the superintendent. As early as 1982, Bruce Joyce observed that

A number of mechanisms are now in place that have the effect of stabilizing the school in its present form. One of these is the relatively regular practice on the part of so many school boards of firing the superintendent. New superintendents . . . know that they will be judged by conservative criteria and that the price of innovation will surely lead to failure. (pp. 57–58)

The Superintendent. The career path of a superintendent typically starts with some years of teaching followed by a move into administration, first at the school-site level and then at the district or county office. Moving on through the directorship of a department (finance, personnel, curriculum) and an assistant superintendency, the ambitious education administrator arrives at last in the large corner office with the windows, carpeting, and state-of-the-art computer. In the process, as John Gardner noted in 1963, most career school administrators not only learn to "play the game" but end up thoroughly indoctrinated by the bureaucratic culture.

It's hardly surprising, then, that so many superintendents seem to be what Rosenholz (1989) characterized as "stuck" as opposed to "moving." Job security at this level is tenuous at best. As we've already noted, an experimentally oriented superintendent can be fired, and this has a damp-ening effect on the extent to which that person will encourage his or her subordinates to try anything unusual. "The new superintendent comes in knowing that the average tenure for a superintendent these days is 29 months or whatever, and tries to be responsive to what the Board is ask-ing for," one retired superintendent said during a discussion of turnover in district office leadership.

The superintendents already in place in the Howard and Fairfax county systems when Columbia and Reston were built in the early 1960s had come up through the traditional career path and were products of a rural conser-vative time and place. Typical of the vast majority of such school officials nationwide, they were neither comfortable with nor well suited to the chal-lenges presented by the new towns and the strange new school plans being proposed for them. In Rosenholz's terminology, they were "stuck" superin-tendents; Carlson (1972) would describe them as place-bound, rather than career-bound.

Superintendents hired to create new school systems where none ex-isted before—the "pioneers"—are more likely to be "moving." That is, they give their subordinates ample opportunity to exert professional autonomy and to experiment, within a supportive framework of orderly processes. Their mandate, after all, is to build something special. Stan Corey, the pio-neer superintendent of Irvine, provided such "moving" leadership, as the following quote reveals:

> None of us is wise enough and strong enough and bright enough to be all things to all people, to know all things at all times. Therefore, it's only rational to bring around you people that you feel are brighter than you are, to give them major responsibility, give them colossal credit when they do it—make it plain to everyone *who* did it—and you build yourself a mighty fortress. Your power is almost limitless because no matter what comes up, somewhere in the pack you have a trusted colleague with the skills and the answers.

It's fairly rare to find this type of management philosophy actually working in practice. Most superintendents, however—whatever their management style—do try to find a workable balance between keeping their districts on an even keel and being at least partly on the cutting edge of what is considered to be best educational practice. Unfortunately, this can lead districts to devote a good deal of time and energy to projects that, worthwhile as they might be, run out of steam in a few years' time. Robert H. Anderson, who was retained in 1961 as the outside consultant for the new elementary schools being planned for Howard County, Maryland, describes the 1958 annual conference of the American Superintendents Association in terms not too different from what one might find today:

> There was such a willy-nilly, pell-mell, hurry-hurry adoption. When team teaching hit the streets, it hit them running 100 miles an hour. . . . I remember at the superintendents' convention in 1958, every superintendent that you ran into would say, "Gotta get into team teaching, can you come and work with us?" The word was around that if you're anybody in this business, you've got to start with team teaching. And that was sort of a death knell for the movement, because it became a bandwagon that got out of control.

Pauly (1978) agrees with Anderson's implication that district administrators keep an eye on their own career needs when they decide what new programs or practices to support. "If it will further the careers of school district officials to innovate, they will do so; if it will not, they will support the status quo. The underlying principle here is that innovations are a product of school organization rather than of 'educational' concerns" (p. 284). This may sound cynical, but it echoes what we already know about the power of a hierarchical system: Operatives at each level look to their superordinates for clues as to what will lead to professional advancement. The lesson here for educators interested in doing something new in their schools is that support from the district office (or from the administration in their own building, for that matter), may be contingent upon factors other than the merit of the change itself.

The role of school superintendent, then, is framed by the hierarchical structure of the organization, and its prerogatives are limited by the realities of the district itself. As one would expect, this is true nationwide; it is part of our deep structure of schooling. The role is further defined by the kind of administrator training programs provided in most universities, endorsed by all regional accreditation agencies, and reinforced by professional administrators' associations.

Finally, there is another, more subtle way in which the superintendency has played a part in maintaining the homogeneity of our educational system: The professional superintendent—shaped as we have seen by the career path he or she has followed—moves from district to district, bringing personal values along, thus spreading them around (Eliot, 1969).

Being a superintendent of schools is not easy. As Gross found in his classic 1958 study of superintendents in Massachusetts, negative pressures dominate the job: Both school personnel and members of the community are much more likely to *complain* about something than to urge *support* of something. That little has changed in the intervening years is suggested by the parting words of a Milwaukee superintendent, who said that "his reforms were doomed to die a death of a thousand cuts" (Pipho, 1995, p. 102). Corey spoke of the sheer exhaustion that came from continual battle with a board that was always split, 3 to 2, with one swing vote that might—or might not—support him.

One gets the impression that the relationship between school boards and superintendents in many communities is far more adversarial now than it used to be. One possible cause is the growing tendency of boards to micromanage, which has already been discussed. Another may be the resurgence of right-wing ideology in the 1990s and the orchestrated effort of political and religious conservatives to assume control of local school boards—and *then* to micromanage. Whatever the cause, today it seems that school superintendents must fight battles on many fronts and learn to be very savvy and always on the alert.

On the other hand, superintendents have always found ways to control their "territory"—the designated areas of responsibility attached to their official role and codified in their job description. One strategy, for example, is learning how to control the agenda at board meetings: "The things they *know* they talk about, like sidewalks, sites, and so forth. I let them go on sometimes because I don't want them to talk about curriculum" (Kerr, 1964, p. 159).

The management style of each individual superintendent is revealed in the way in which he or she treats subordinates, and this is important because it sets the tone for the entire school district. School people have intuitively known this forever; the Rosenholz (1989) study found that "both stuck and moving superintendents were near-perfect mirrors for how principals treated teachers, and teachers treated students" (p. 211). Unfortunately, the institution of schooling as it exists today usually attracts those who are comfortable in the traditional top-down, hierarchical bureaucracy.

The District Office Staff. There are many supporting roles at the district or county office, and their job—whether directly or indirectly—is to help the teachers do theirs. That is not always clear, however. Bureaucracies have a way of becoming self-perpetuating entities, and people higher in hierarchical organizations get used to thinking that *their* work is more important than that of their subordinates. In the institution of schooling, just the reverse is true: The *most* important work goes on at the "bottom" of the organization chart, and all other positions exist in order to make that work possible and successful. (I have long hoped to meet an educational leader whose "org. chart" shows the classroom at the top and all the support positions—including the superintendent and district office staff—at the bottom; I'm still waiting.)

The other point that needs to be made about the various roles at the district office is that many of them serve gatekeeping functions, limiting access of people to each other and controlling the flow of information within the organization (House, 1974). It's important to keep this in mind if one is trying to build support for a new program or a new way of doing things.

The Principal. The role of principal is a pivotal one in the bureaucratic hierarchy of schooling, positioned as it is between the tightly coupled *administrative* level at one end and the loosely coupled *instructional* level at the other (Crandall et al., 1982; Meyer, 1983). Though the reward system of a top-down structure keeps the principal attentive to the expectations of those above him or her in the district (and relatively powerless with respect to these), the principal does have considerable power to create (or stifle) a productive and cheerful work environment at the school site. Like Janus, a principal must continually look both ways.

This position permits the principal to act as a buffer between the superordinate system and the site staff, a function that has become essential in recent years as so many new demands are being made of our schools. A few principals do this well, protecting their people from pressures that distract from the tasks of teaching and at the same time stimulating them to think creatively about their work. Others either do not see the need for it or just can't seem to do it well. In either case, they fail to distinguish between what really needs attention and what doesn't.

Ken Tye's study of the leadership styles of 17 elementary and secondary school principals over a 4-year period from 1985–1989 bears this out. He found that principals handled goals and demands in one of three ways. Without claiming that these include all possible categories, he suggests that when it comes to goal orientation, some principals have a *coping* style; basically, they limit themselves to managing the school and respond only to directives or demands from the district office or from parents. A second group are what Tye calls *diffuse*: They are aware of new trends and tend to set all kinds of goals for their school in an indiscriminate, sometimes conflicting way. Finally, some principals are *goal-focused*. They and their teachers carefully select a few reasonable goals and concentrate on them, excluding others on which they place a lower priority. It was principals of this latter type (incidentally, the least common of the three) that were able to serve as good buffers for their teachers (B. B. Tye & K. A. Tye, 1992).

The principal who is goal-focused is also likely to be the one who has what Hall (1987) would call a "strategic sense." This intuitive feel for what is important (and what is not), combined with the willingness to risk the displeasure of higher-ups by declining to carry out some of their demands at the school, is what makes the buffer principal successful.

A study of school administration programs offered in the southern states during the mid-1990s revealed widespread lack of attention to the development of leadership skills, particularly in school districts that were financially stressed (Crews & Weakley, 1995). There is no special reason to assume that the situation is much different elsewhere: As with superintendents, the system produces site administrators because that is what best serves the needs of this role within a hierarchical bureaucracy. The solid but conventional top-down school administrator produced by most current training programs is not, however, the kind of person who can build an innovative climate in his or her school. Willis Hawley (1978) noted that "conventional models of assertive, take-charge leadership are not appropriate to adaptive schools" (p. 235), adding his observation that although directive principals may be very likely to *adopt* a change, they are equally *unlikely to actually implement it*—in other words, such a principal will talk a good game but won't join with the teachers, roll up his (or her) sleeves, and help to make the change really work.

Many principals—perhaps even a majority—are more laissez-faire than controlling. They get caught up in the day-to-day maintenance agenda and find there's no time left for anything else. As one of the pioneer principals in the Irvine school system put it, this can happen even to the lucky ones who have a chance to open a new school—unless they stay focused on their original purposes:

> In a new organization you have an opportunity to dream your vision and think through your philosophy because there is energy to devote to that, but the longer an organization exists, the more likely you are to have to devote energy to maintenance types of issues, so you have less time to spend on innovations. And if, as a leader, you fail to focus on your improvement agenda, then your maintenance agenda will fully consume you; but if you focus on the improvement agenda, some of the maintenance issues will take care of themselves.

It's not easy to be a good principal these days. The role requires that the person who fills it be a buffer, a leader, an administrator, a PR person, a mediator of differences, and a team player with the superordinate system. Furthermore, the *way* in which all this is done is what sets the tone of the entire school. And if it's so difficult to be even a *good* principal, as defined by these well-established expectations of the role, it's all but impossible to be that rare creature, a genuinely innovative educational leader. Even a *savvy* principal—one with both a clear vision and that special strategic sense mentioned earlier—can succumb, over time, to the expectation of various constituencies that he or she will act in familiar ways (Heckscher, Eisenstadt, & Rice, 1994).

Pioneer Principals. With one or two remarkable exceptions, the first principals in the new schools of Reston and Columbia were local educators who had come up through the ranks in the quiet, rural Fairfax County and Howard County systems of the 1950s, and were rewarded by being given the new schools. For example, the first principal of South Lakes High School, Reston's first high school, was within 2 years of retirement when South Lakes opened in the fall of 1978.

These, then, were people who had played by the rules all their lives. Their management style was conservative and by-the-book, and in retrospect it can be seen that in most cases they were poorly suited to guide the new, innovative schools through their early years. As one Howard County board member recalls, "They made some terrible mistakes in bringing old county principals into the new schools of Columbia; they just couldn't do what needed to be done."

The process used to hire the first principal for Wilde Lake High School, in Columbia, was completely different. By that time the county office—and the pioneer parents of Columbia—had had several years of experience with starting new schools. The board and the superintendent were ready to support an outside hire, and went along with an unusual screening process proposed by the high school planning committee. As a result, a genuinely innovative leader was found, and his vision for the new school was compatible with that of the planning committee. In fact, he took the school beyond the early planning, by networking it with other innovative projects of the 1970s—it even became one of the NASSP's Model Schools. Flexible scheduling, a "no-fail" mastery grading system, advisory groups, differentiated staffing, team planning—under Jack Jenkins, Wilde Lake became a showcase of mid-1970s reforms.

When such a pioneer principal leaves and the superintendent and school board must agree on a successor, it often happens that the new principal who is chosen is less experimental, less of a risk-taker, and more of a classic school administrator than was his or her predecessor. According to one observer, the 9 years after Jenkins's departure in 1978 saw a dramatic slide toward the mean.

Administrator turnover almost inevitably causes some modifications in the reform agenda of the departing principal. Interestingly, many school districts have a built-in mechanism for *encouraging this to happen*: an institutionalized policy of moving site administrators around to different schools every 5 years or so. This prevents them from becoming too attached to any one school, its staff, and its community, and suits the need of a bureaucracy to maintain the allegiance of each level in the system to the level above it.

Finally, the pioneer principal can be wooed away. "The training and visibility which accrued from participating in the programs sent the leaders on to bigger and better positions within the existing system," commented Angela Fraley (1981) in her study of efforts to create democratic schools (p. 162). In a careful analysis of the Chicago reforms of the early 1990s, Bryk, Easton, Kerbow, Rollow, and Sebring (1994) noted that "many of the initial principal leaders have already moved on to other jobs, typically outside of the system" (p. 78).

Whether a school is new or not, if it is trying to do something innovative, when the principal leaves that process becomes vulnerable. This is true whether the person is transferred within the district, retires, or is wooed away. What happens next may not *always* be a turn for the worse, but it very often is. School people and their parent and community supporters who are trying to implement a new program or change some aspect of their school's structures, policies, or procedures need to keep this in mind and develop strategies to ensure continuity for the effort.

The Teacher. Before the institution of education became bureaucratized, there was much more variation in the teacher's role because it was shaped to a considerable extent by local conditions (Sedlak, 1989). With consolidation of the enterprise and the appearance of regulating factors such as state teacher certification and the accreditation of teacher training institutions, the role itself became both more specifically defined and more standardized across all types of communities—large and small, urban and rural. The early 20th-century press for the application of scientific management techniques within a bureaucratic organizational framework led policymakers outside the educational system to support schemes for differential salaries and merit pay. These were defeated, however, by teachers and other education professionals. Tyack and Cuban (1995) describe how the National Education Association fought for a single salary schedule during the 1920s: From the 1930s on, in most states no longer would men be routinely paid more than women, high school teachers more than elementary teachers. The hard-won contracts stipulated simply that level of education and years of service in the school district would be the basis of annual salary increases. This is still the case, despite the occasional renewal of outside calls for merit-pay plans.

The job description of a teacher includes other duties in addition to the direct instruction of students. The contract is likely to specify a number of inservice days per year in which participation is required, expectations of interaction with parents, hall monitoring duties, and attendance at faculty meetings. In some communities, it has been necessary for teachers to insist—through collective bargaining—upon contract language limiting the amount and type of extra duties that can be required.

A teacher achieves tenure by earning good evaluations from the principal for the first several years on the job. Frequently seen by the public as a way to protect poor teachers, this contractual provision actually evolved as a way to protect the majority of good teachers from the capricious favoritism or punitiveness of administrators, and still serves this purpose. Tenured or not, every teacher is evaluated every year, and, in cases where it is needed, the administrators do have procedures they can follow to request the dismissal of a truly poor teacher.

It must be understood that teaching is much more intense than it used to be. Teaching has never been a 9-to-5 career, and in the past 15 or 20 years the work load has, to be blunt, exploded. Resources for teaching are more scarce, requiring extraordinary creativity or promoting overreliance on that old standby—the textbook. The latest wave of immigration has placed new demands on teachers straining to work with youngsters who themselves are struggling to master a new language and culture. Since the mid-1970s, the practice of mainstreaming has stretched teachers in another new direction, as they learn to work with students who have a wide variety of physical and learning disabilities. A renewal of public demands for more parent and community involvement, mandated additions to the curriculum, and the increased use of standardized testing all add in one way or another to the work load of a teacher. Listen to these teachers as they describe their school day *after* classes are over:

> I'm sorry to run in and out like this. There's a parent waiting in my room, I've got an assignment to complete, and I'm already late for another meeting!

> I'm coaching the academic decathlon team, mentoring a first-year teacher, advising the yearbook and the National Honor Society,

coaching tennis, and getting a Masters degree. I'm the union rep for
this school, and I do my share of departmental curriculum work.
That's about all I can handle this year. (Tye & Tye, 1998, pp. 111, 124)

In such a context, the profession responds with some defense mechanisms that can have the unintended side-effect of dampening teachers'
enthusiasm and support for new projects. First, exhausted teachers may
meet proposals for change with the argument that the principal would
never agree to it, so why try? This kind of tactic works perfectly in a hierarchical organization, because each level can claim that the one above it
would withhold approval. Principals use it, too, by assuring their staffs that
the district or county office, or the board of education, would never approve. Ironically, sometimes the higher-ups *would* approve the new plan
but never get the chance because it's cut off at the level below.

A second tactic that teachers can use to hold competing demands at
bay and define the parameters of what is (or is not) possible is the use of
disparaging comments about a new idea, put-downs suggesting that for
one reason or another it cannot work and shouldn't even be tried. This
behavior can be used by site administrators as well as by teachers, and in
fact is most often used by those at the school who are viewed by their colleagues either as having power or as being the opinion leaders, or both
(Hargreaves, 1984; Joyce, 1982).

The third way in which the perfectly understandable defense mechanisms of classroom teachers today can inhibit the permanent incorporation of an innovation into the life of a school is the "wait it out" approach.
The protection of tenure has already been mentioned: If a teacher is performing adequately, job security is assured. Teachers, therefore, generally
stay in a district—often in the same school—for many years. They come to
think of themselves as long-term participants in the life of the school, as
opposed to administrators, whom they view as temporary (Metz, 1986).
Teachers who have been around awhile will have seen numerous good (and
some not so good) projects and programs come and go (old-timers may
have seen the *same* idea rediscovered several times in the course of their
careers). Under the pressure of competing demands, it might not be unreasonable for a teacher to hold back from participating, knowing from
experience that if she can just hold on awhile, this too shall pass.

The Nonteaching Professionals. Counselors, librarians, and nurses provide professional services that are available in most schools but that are
among the most vulnerable in the system: In recent years, these positions
have often been the first to go when budget cuts are necessary. In the culture of a school, teachers generally view these colleagues as equals—work

comfortably with them on committees, and so on. The comparative insecurity of these jobs, however, suggests that the superordinate system in fact regards them as lower in the pecking order, thus more easily expendable.

In a district that is not financially stressed, these auxiliary professionals participate in the life of the school more or less in the same way that teachers do. They work directly with students, but owing to the nature of the services they provide, they interact with far greater numbers of youngsters than teachers do. A counselor, for example, may be responsible for meeting the psychological, career, and academic guidance needs of *hundreds* of students. A librarian may serve the *entire student body*, and a nurse might be assigned to *more than one school*. Indeed, the very fact that these positions often require one person to do the work of two (or three) may be another indicator of the low regard in which they are held by the administrative bureaucracy.

How might the nonteaching professional role inhibit efforts to try new things in a school? Guarding of territory may play a part. For example, it isn't unusual to find counselors up in arms when a school begins to consider implementing a teacher-advisor system. Rather than welcome a reconfiguring of their own admittedly overwhelming responsibilities, counselors may see this innovation as a threat. If teachers are doing the counseling, what will remain for *them* to do?

It is an intriguing irony, however, that schools that do adopt a teacher-advisor system often find it is one of the best changes they ever made. It frees the counselors to do much-needed group sessions and the more serious psychological work with individual students that they imagined doing when they entered the profession.

Parents.   Obviously, parents play an important role in the educational system. They can act to inhibit or to promote change, and their influence and potential for support or opposition should never be overlooked or underestimated. Within the established bureaucratic organization of public schooling, however, parents (like the informal community structures discussed below) are an *unofficial* group. Individually and collectively they can be a powerful force in the life of the school, but they do not tend to play a daily role. More often, they respond situationally, when circumstances arise to prompt their concern.

Parent and community expectations are much more thoroughly examined in Chapter 5.

The Informal Structure.   Some scholars see the real power of a school system as residing *outside* the formal bureaucratic structure, with its designated roles and responsibilities. It is certainly true that in many communities it is possible to identify a "civic elite," the members of which are the true decision-makers not only in matters pertaining to the local schools but in other community issues as well (Lindblom, 1994; Martin, 1962).

The informal structure tends to be a homogeneous in-group of people (historically, almost exclusively male) who share similar values and have often known each other for years. They belong to the same service clubs— indeed, it is often at meetings of such clubs that the real decisions of the community are made (Kimbrough, 1969)—and live in the same neighbor- hoods. When gathering to anoint their preferred candidates for school board, they select people much like themselves and thereby ensure that the same values will be reflected in school district policies, in decisions about whom to hire as superintendent and, in turn, what kind of people are chosen to be the site administrators. "When members of the civic elite choose school board members . . . they have in mind an operational image when they say they want a 'good man' for the job. It is hardly a surprise that they get the kind of man they want most of the time" (Crain & Street, 1969, p. 361).

The workings of an informal decision-making structure, where it exists, take place *outside* the formal bureaucratic hierarchy with its designated roles. But it is a powerful force for maintaining the status quo, and must be care- fully considered by educators who hope to make changes in their schools.

A Final Thought About Roles. The allocation of roles and assigned re- sponsibilities is greatly reinforced when people develop a vested interest in keeping their own role the way it is. Not only is there a certain comfort level connected to doing what one has always done, but there may also be material advantages to preserving the boundaries of one's job. "Vested interests may be found," John Gardner commented in 1963, "wherever a man acquires a shirt for his back or rights and privileges he would be re- luctant to lose. In any organization many of the established ways of doing things are held in place not by logic or even by habit but by the force of one powerful consideration: changing them would jeopardize the rights, privileges, or advantages of specific individuals—perhaps the president, perhaps the maintenance men" (p. 65).

Impersonal Environment

We have dealt with hierarchical structure and with role differentiation; we turn now to the third characteristic of bureaucratic systems in general: the maintenance of an impersonal work environment. Is this characteristic found in the institution of schooling? If so, does it play a part in pulling innovations back to the tried-and-true?

An elementary or secondary school can be a fairly cozy and personal place to work, especially if it isn't too large (teachers in large secondary schools can confirm that they do not even know all of their colleagues by sight, let alone by name). A school district office, on the other hand, is often much less personal and much more "bureaucratic." The various work stations may be separated by flimsy partitions that provide neither quiet nor privacy; this design also permits easier monitoring by superiors. A pecking order may be more evident—it is unlikely that the clerical staff and the professional staff will go out to lunch together or know much about each other's personal lives.

At the school site, the design of the building also helps to keep teachers separated from each other for much of the day. In addition, the norms of the profession dictate that teachers honor each others' privacy when they are working in their classrooms (Little, 1990). Teachers come together before and after school and during planning periods, however, and some school faculties socialize together at other times. In teachers' lounges and faculty work rooms one may hear personal conversations and the sharing of both private as well as professional concerns. Some school staffs refer to themselves as a "family."

All in all, although the *general* pattern prevails (an impersonal environment at the administrative/bureaucratic end, and a more personal climate at the instructional end), there are exceptions. In particular, the very fact that a bureaucratic system separates the various roles in the organization provides teachers with their own niche in which to do what they're assigned to do, and that's just fine with them.

I have suggested that bureaucratic impersonality is, indeed, a characteristic found at the administrative organizational levels outside the school site. The "district ethos" is a complex phenomenon composed of six closely interconnected elements: the *management style* of the superintendent, the extent to which the district insists on *standardized practices* throughout the system, the district's level of *service orientation*, the nature and directionality of *communication* and *information flow*, the *way in which workers are treated*, and the *locus of decision-making* (B. B. Tye & K. A. Tye, 1992, pp. 116–122). This ethos, or climate, reinforces organizational impersonality in a number of ways; three in particular are apt to inhibit change. These are (a) the "don't rock the boat" norm found in most school districts, (b) the policy of treating all schools precisely alike, and (c) the policy of moving principals around.

Don't Rock the Boat. Superintendents set the tone for the district, but even those who regard themselves as flexible and innovative can go only so far in the direction of encouraging divergent views and unusual projects. As we have seen, the way the system works tends to produce superintendents who are system-maintainers. Such people aren't likely to come in and rattle the cage too much. They may tolerate a certain amount of boat-rocking from their subordinates; but this will be mostly for show and will be kept within manageable limits.

And the subordinates know it. As Warren Bennis (1993) notes, "Evidence and research demonstrate conclusively that subordinates tend to withdraw and/or suppress views that are at variance with those of the boss" (p. 232). The newly appointed principal, eager to appear well chosen for the job, may be especially quick to make changes that he or she sees as being desired by the superordinate system, and in doing so may sacrifice some of the innovative features of the school (Metz, 1986). Having worked hard to get there, and played by the rules along the way, the school-site administrator isn't going to jeopardize his or her career by alienating the superordinate system.

> For school administrators trying to do a difficult job in a hostile environment, the strategy of tending to their careers by concentrating on headquarters affairs is the best possible adaptation to the uncertainty, complexity, and peer-recognition reward system that characterizes American public education. (Pauly, 1978, p. 263)

Bruckerhoff (1994) tells an interesting story about an NSF-funded math project for inner-city middle schools in Cleveland. The project, which emphasized process-oriented problem-solving approaches, was in direct conflict with the district's established policies supporting traditional math teaching reinforced by annual standardized testing. Knowing full well which side *his* bread was buttered on, the district's mathematics curriculum coordinator "chose not to collaborate," and teachers who served on the committee behaved in ways that revealed their belief that the project was doomed from the start—as, of course, it was.

Treat All Schools Alike.

> There is a tremendous confusion in American society about standardization, about *same* being *good* . . . standardization never raises everyone to excellence; it merely assures a similar level of mediocrity, and no excellence anywhere. (S. Corey, interview by author, June 18, 1993)

The bureaucratic organization's characteristic impersonality is also expressed in policies requiring absolutely identical treatment of all schools in a district. No exceptions, no special considerations. No school receives a budget line that other schools don't also receive. If one school gets a grant to implement a new program, it must do so within the district calendar: no extra staff development days. If another school obtains permission to try something new, it must do so within the same budget parameters as its sister schools. (Indeed, one of the conditions upon which the permission was based may well have been that the school be required to show that doing something different won't cost any more than what has been done in the past.) Many a pilot project, approved by the school board partly because it is seen as small and nonthreatening, has disappeared in time as the result of pressures to prove itself within the same set of constraints required everywhere else (Metz, 1986).

The policy of equal treatment took an added twist in the Howard County system when the Rouse Company began to build Columbia on the farmland it had bought. The county board of education decided that anything done in the new town, insofar as schools were concerned, had to be replicated elsewhere in the county. Would an air-conditioned elementary school be built in Columbia? Another just like it would be built outside Columbia. A long-time Howard County administrator explained it this way:

> They all have to live by the same rules, they all have to live by the same staffing formulas. It was true then and it's true now. For example, ever since I've been Director of elementary schools for Howard County—which is since 1977—I've been pushing for differentiated staffing based on the needs of each school, rather than strictly by formula, but they are still going strictly by formula.

Around the country, this policy may be in the process of accommodating somewhat to recent political pressures on school districts to provide several types of schools for parental choice. Nevertheless, norms of equal treatment continue to be powerful. In discussing the problems of small alternative or charter schools within school districts, Deborah Meier (1998) notes that in many cases individual schools "flicker brightly," but that still, policymakers want reforms that can be implemented across the board. In making that a requirement, they deprive the unique schools of the very conditions that would permit their success to be replicated. She goes on to say that

> Without deep-seated changes in the system that surrounds these small schools of choice, history suggests that . . . most will water down their innovations or give up altogether. The existing system is simply not designed to support such oddball entities. It believes in its mission of control and orderliness. . . . If it's not good for everyone, it's not good for anyone. To make exceptions

smacks of favoritism and inefficiency. Each exception must thus be defended over and over again. (p. 360)

Meier here eloquently describes the way the deep structure works (in this case through policies of equalization and supposed "fairness") to prevent small alternative schools from surviving with their original vision and purposes intact. The same dynamic is at work to pull any new effort—whether program or process—back to what everyone recognizes as a "real school."

Move the Principals Around. A third way in which some districts attempt to maintain an impersonal work environment for the adults in the system is by transferring principals and vice principals around from school to school. This practice suits the need of a bureaucracy to maintain the allegiance of each level in the system to the level above it; and it also may serve the purpose of squelching the innovative experiments of an outgoing administrator, who is faced with starting all over again at a new site *and* watching from a distance as a new person with a different agenda dismantles what had been accomplished at his or her old site.

Transferring the principal really can contribute to the atmosphere of impersonal bureaucracy at a school, at least for awhile. Teachers wait and wonder if their new leader will be better or worse than the one who is leaving. "Will he support us in what we are doing?" "Will she give us a chance to try something new?" "Will he be friendly and accessible, or distant and officious?" "If we invite her to our Friday afternoon gatherings, will she come?" Though it may get harder as the years go by, the teacher culture sets about each time to undermine the system's efforts to keep distance between the various roles in the organization. The extent to which it succeeds is contextual. It depends entirely on the individual administrator's personality and management style as well as the levels of teacher warmth and cohesiveness in the building.

Technical Competence and Personnel Evaluation

Training, recruitment, and promotion are based on an individual's *competence* in performing the technical requirements of his or her role, in playing by the rules, and in achieving the goals specified for that position. How does this aspect of a bureaucratic organization help to stifle new ideas and pull changes back to the mean?

Earlier, the point was made that technical competence is used to make decisions about hiring and promotion in the institution of education—*up to a point.* In a bureaucratic hierarchy, the levels above *always* supervise—

and judge—the work of those at the lower levels. "The principal expects some supervision and advice from his superiors," comments Warren (1978, p. 156), "but none from peers or inferiors." This is what Bruce Joyce (1982) calls a *homeostatic force*: "In most schools there is a tacit understanding between administrators and teachers that their respective domains are not to be encroached upon" (p. 48). Requests from teachers that they be permitted to evaluate the principal, therefore, generally meet with firm resistance. A suggestion that principals be allowed to evaluate the superintendent won't even be taken seriously; it is seen as the board's prerogative to judge the superintendent's behavior, and the views of those who work with and for him or her are not considered pertinent.

Earlier in this chapter, the point was made that the organizational structure requires school administrators to attend to the wishes of the superordinate system if they want to move up in the hierarchy. There may or may not be room for moral and ethical behavior in this picture. As Pinchot and Pinchot (1994) point out,

> Success in the bureaucratic organization is defined as a lifetime career of advancing to higher levels in the chain of command. . . . Promotion is achieved through technical competence in one's speciality and efficiency in carrying out orders. . . . The employee's primary responsibility is not to do what is right or what needs to be done but only to follow exactly the orders of his or her immediate boss. (pp. 26–27)

In the context of our present concern—technical competence as a characteristic of bureaucratic systems, and the way in which this characteristic may inhibit educational change—several points come to mind. First, we have already seen that "playing by the rules" as a way of conducting one's professional life is unlikely to lead to the maverick behavior needed for experimentation and innovation.

Second, someone who is seen by the system as technically competent may not be the best person for the job when it comes to building a consensus for change or creating a work environment that will nurture and protect a new program. Those are not usually the skills that are taught in master's degree programs or district inservice workshops. Nevertheless it may be the "technically competent" person, rather than the best person, who is put in charge of the project.

Finally, a focus on technical competence emphasizes form over substance. While this is characteristically bureaucratic behavior, it can deflect attention from what is really worthwhile in a proposed change. Over time, the project may be modified beyond recognition, completely gutted of its original purposes: Only the rhetoric remains.

Documentation, Rules, and Paperwork

Last but not least, documentation holds the bureaucratic edifice together. Rules and regulations, codes and policies, paper trails for various purposes, job descriptions, publications such as curriculum standards, frameworks, and guidelines, and the entire realm of program evaluation including accreditation self-studies, school improvement plans, standardized testing, and annual teacher competence assessments—this list represents just the tip of the iceberg. Documentation is required by the site, district, state, regional, and federal levels of the system. For many conscientious educators, bureaucracy *means* paperwork. The irony of this is dramatic. "That the demand for paperwork intended to improve school accountability actually undermines productivity by taking time away from the core functions of the school is a paradox most policymakers and administrators have not fully appreciated," comments Linda Darling-Hammond (1997, pp. 42–43). Not only can the time needed to do mandated record-keeping and form-filling eat into time needed for working with students, but some documentation policies also demean teachers, thereby reinforcing their lesser status within the organization: Requiring that they sign in and out of the school building is one example that comes to mind.

Premature Exposure and Evaluation. One example of how the bureaucratic need for documentation can help to kill a change before it really takes hold is what happens when a new program or practice is both exposed to the public and evaluated too early. Premature exposure and evaluation are powerful ways in which the bureaucratic system manages to maintain the status quo, and to do so while *seeming* to support new efforts to make improvements in schooling.

Premature *exposure* can have the unintended effect of halting the evolution of a new program and freezing it into place at an incomplete point in its implementation. The excitement and buoyancy of the first year or two of a new project can lead its supporters to welcome media coverage and visitors from outside, eager to see the promising new program for themselves. Teachers living in such a fishbowl willingly demonstrate the new practices they have already mastered but, understandably, hesitate to attempt new ones while being observed. It is possible that under these circumstances they may never go much beyond what is already comfortable.

Premature *evaluation* can, however unintentionally, create the impression that because no significant gains appear, the new program isn't working. For one thing, in the evaluation process no one asks about the problems being encountered during implementation, the kind of question that *could* be helpful—unfortunately, all the questions are directed toward outcomes; and it is too early to expect any concrete outcomes (Pincus, 1974).

In her 1978 review of the literature on the implementation of Title I programs, Milbrey McLaughlin (1978b) suggested that "Title I programs, as they have been evaluated, have never existed . . . Title I has not yet been evaluated as intended by reformers" (p. 164). Title I programs (authorized under the Elementary and Secondary Education Act of 1965 and reauthorized in 1994 under the Improving America's Schools Act) included a range of compensatory programs designed to help "disadvantaged" children. With hindsight, we can recognize the magic feather principle at work again—it was assumed that because legislation existed, funds were allocated, and conscientious educators were at work on implementation, the problems were well on the way to being solved. Poverty has proven to be intractable, but it is also fair to say, along with McLaughlin, that many programs intended to alleviate it were abandoned before they were able to produce genuine results. (Furthermore, the conventional wisdom of the 1990s has been that "those programs of the 60s" were tried, but failed. This has the effect of discouraging new efforts to try again.)

"The demise of a reform initiative is often due not to its ineffectiveness, but rather to its inability to deliver immediate results, however inappropriate or impossible that expectation might be," comment Rallis and Zajano (1997, p. 707). They go on to make a helpful suggestion: Educators with new projects in mind should identify for their constituents—in advance—the expected final outcomes *and* the intermediate benchmarks to anticipate in the course of implementation. In this way it should be clear to the public when evaluation of outcomes should take place. Above all, it should not be too soon. The press for quick results is self-defeating; very little substantive change can move from idea to accepted practice in fewer than 10 years (Goldberg, 1995; Sarason, 1991). Intermediate benchmarks can be helpful, however, especially in times when the public feels that many programs are not being adequately evaluated.

Myths and Ceremonies. Finally, we mustn't lose sight of the ritual significance of policies and regulations and how this, too, can prevent needed change from taking place or inhibit appropriate practices. Perhaps too many of us take institutional policies and documents at face value and fail to recognize the ceremonial nature of some pronouncements. These nearly always have to do with the need of an organization to rally public support and, in the process, to legitimize its own existence and activities.

The easiest of these ritual behaviors to identify is the political rhetoric designed to give the impression that something is being done: for example, the claim to be—or desire to be—an "education president," or to issue a list of outrageous "education goals" and a promise that they will be achieved by a certain date. Promising more than can reasonably be delivered, and thereby ensuring failure, is a good way to undermine our system of public education: This strategy reinforces the pervasive contemporary belief that our schools are beyond hope. It is frustrating to watch national leaders fall for this line and participate, knowingly or not as the case may be, in this weakening of one of the nation's strongest and most successful institutions.

If American education is concerned with legitimization in the eyes of the public, it will cater to prevalent anxieties and currently fashionable myths in its attempt to gain (or keep) public support. A state-mandated curriculum that is developed in response to political pressures may not be appropriate for certain students; but that is what they will be taught nonetheless. For instance, the termination of bilingual programs by a school board and the substitution of English immersion may be more a response to current anxieties and political myths than a solidly researched program designed to meet an educational need. Similarly in the case of early reading instruction, the retreat from whole language approaches and the rapid return to phonics and decoding can be recognized as ritual policymaking, undertaken in response to public concerns.

Classroom teachers respond to all this ceremonial activity by simply closing the door and doing it their own way. The organizational coping mechanism is *decoupling*. This permits everyone to behave as if the organization is functioning as it should: At the official level, policy statements and curriculum mandates show that public concerns are being heard and attended to; at the instructional level, life goes on and teachers do their best for the students they see every day—no matter what the policies say (McCloskey, Provenzo, Cohen, & Kottkamp, 1987; Meyer & Rowan, 1977; Wise, 1979).

At this point we turn our attention from the bureaucratic organization to the loosely coupled organization. In its way it, too, has characteristics that can support the deep structure and inhibit changes that would challenge it.

HOW A LOOSELY COUPLED SYSTEM HELPS
THE DEEP STRUCTURE RESIST CHANGE

I have suggested that the characteristics of a bureaucratic organization are not found from top to bottom of the educational system, but that they are limited primarily to the administrative and staff positions that are charged with supporting the educative mission of schooling. At the instructional level, the idea of a "loosely coupled" system is much more useful. The characteristics of such a system are not, however, simply the inverse of those found at the bureaucratic end. Furthermore, the various characteristics of a loosely coupled system overlap and double back on each other in distinctly nonlinear ways, as we shall see.

Characteristics of a Loosely Coupled System

An organization that is loosely coupled contains components that have their own *identity* and a certain amount of *autonomy*, yet they are also *connected* to and *responsive* to each other. "Thus," says Weick in his classic 1976 essay on this topic, "in the case of an educational organization, it may be . . . that the counselor's office is loosely coupled to the principal's office. The image is that the principal and the counselor are somehow attached, but that each retains some identity and separateness and that their attachment may be circumscribed, infrequent, weak in its mutual effects, unimportant, and/ or slow to respond" (p. 3).

A loosely coupled system can *provide niches* in which possibly outdated aspects of the organization can continue to function long beyond their usefulness. Most people would see this as a negative. On the other hand, it can also *provide for local adaptations* without making system-wide adjustments either necessary or inevitable. Thus, such an organization will allow for change in a small subunit while at the same time rendering broader implementation extremely problematic. This could be seen as a positive attribute by proponents of site-based reforms but as a real drawback by those who would like to mandate sweeping, across-the-board educational change.

Another way to look at this is that a loosely coupled system is more *resilient* than a bureaucratic system, because by its very nature it can absorb changes without disturbing the organization as a whole. Resilience may be seen as either a positive or a negative, of course, depending upon one's viewpoint and one's purposes. If society is calling for educational change and the schools continue on much as always, *I* may say that they are wisely resisting political pressure; but *you* may say that they are refusing to meet the needs of a changing world.

The cultural norms of a loosely coupled system, although different, aren't simply the opposite of bureaucratic norms. It is still expected, for example, that people working in different roles will pretty much confine themselves to doing their own work. The big difference lies in the amount of regulation and oversight that is considered acceptable. Norms found at the loosely coupled end of the educational organization include the fol-

lowing: Allow others their own space; assume your colleagues are working in good faith for the best interests of the enterprise; don't watch your
neighbor too closely; and *don't* report the unorthodox behavior of your
peers. In schooling, "Just close the classroom door and teach" is the operative guideline (Goodlad, 1975, 1984; Goodlad & Klein, 1974).

The Absence of Hierarchy Weakens Top-down Authority. First, the loosely
coupled system is flat, or nearly so. Horizontal connections and egalitarian norms are more prevalent than the vertical connections and status-based
relationships found in the bureaucratic side of the institution. The teacher
culture usually discourages status distinctions within its ranks. Substitute
teachers may sometimes feel like second-class citizens, it's true. But full-
time credentialed faculty members, among themselves and in the name of
collegiality, can go to great lengths *not* to seem self-promoting or as if some
are "better" than others.

The flat *structure* and the egalitarian *culture* together form a powerful
bulwark against top-down mandates and lend credence to the suggestion
that the search for excellence in schools must happen one classroom at a
time. The existence of many successful classrooms in a school may give the
impression that the school itself is "excellent," but it is doubtful that any
single, specific school-wide policy or practice can take the credit for this.
"Successful classrooms may have created the *appearance* of effective school
policies that never existed. . . . When prescriptive policies run up against
the power of teachers and students to control events in their classrooms,
the prescriptions are trounced. This suggests why prescriptive policies
sometimes work for a short time, but never consistently" (Pauly, 1991,
pp. 102, 112).

It is also possible that life at the school and classroom level is not just
loosely coupled but is actually dependent upon the voluntary compliance
decisions of individual participants. This is the ultimate expression of loose
coupling, it seems to me: "Students," observes Cusick (1992), "decide how
and to what degree they will participate in class. Teachers decide how and
to what degree they will comply with administrators. Each reserves the
right to alter the definition of the situation and to make judgments from
his or her own perspective" (p. 97). There is a body of literature on the
negotiated reality of classrooms and schools, dating from at least the 1970s,
that supports this thesis—no wonder administrators devote so much energy to *control*.

In a decentralized educational system such as that in the United States,
even the bureaucracy at one end can't force loosely coupled practitioners
at school sites to actually do something differently, and to keep doing it
that way indefinitely. The administration can make a one-sided decision

to adopt a new program or practice, for example. Teachers may even be included in the decision-making process. But *no mechanism exists to guarantee compliance*: Each individual must still make a decision to buy in.

Loosely coupled systems, then, can make institutionalization of change difficult because the various participants have a great deal of latitude to decide whether or not to comply. This is frustrating for administrators, of course. But it can be frustrating for teachers, too, if they have made a commitment to the new program or practice and hope to see it succeed. Because the organization is loosely coupled and because of the norm of professional autonomy, they cannot necessarily assume that even their own colleagues will join wholeheartedly in the effort.

Role Relationships Are Not Based on Status. Second, roles are not kept rigidly separated at the instructional level but may overlap to some extent as circumstances warrant. Granted, everyone at this level is a teacher; but within the role there may be some fuzziness. Two examples come to mind. First, not every teacher is teaching in his or her credential area, and yet no one bothers too much about that as long as the job is getting done (the people who are bothered by it are more likely to be the bureaucrats at the state level). Also, in grade-level teams or subject-area departments, the job of chair (if it exists) may be passed around within the group from one year to the next; no one is seen *by reason of status* to be more entitled to be chair than any other. If one person serves as chair more often than some, that is more likely to be because he or she possesses certain skills that the group values in a chair, or because no one else wants to do it.

Although they may not be rigidly defined or kept distinctly separated, functions at the instructional level *are* connected and responsive to each other. Weick's (1976) example—previously mentioned—is of a princpal and a counselor. We might as easily imagine a teacher and a librarian, a teacher and a resource specialist, or any other of several combinations. Each person goes about his or her business in the school; as needed, they come together to deal with specific situations and then move apart again. Although different areas of expertise are acknowledged in this process, the relationships are still collegial and task-determined rather than status-based.

This may have implications for the ways in which new knowledge flows into the system, and thus for the exposure of a school staff, as a group, to new ideas. For example, the special education teachers in a school might attend a conference together and there they might learn of a new practice they feel should be used in their own school. When they return, some may begin using the new practice successfully, others less so. They may or may not share it with the rest of the faculty: The change might lodge in one small corner of that school. As Ken Tye (1981) observed following analysis of the

Study of Schooling findings, "The change literature assumes that the school is an 'open' system. The reality may be that it is hardly open. Our findings indicate that knowledge flows unevenly, without focus or plan" (p. 15). This characteristic of a loosely coupled system may also do its share to prevent change, or to pull attempts to change back toward more conventional and familiar practice: If knowledge is unevenly distributed, concerted group action in continuing, *long-lasting* support of a change is unlikely.

The Adult Work Environment Sends Mixed Signals. Third, the deliberately neutral and impersonal work environment valued in a bureaucratic organization is alien to the culture of teaching. Teachers empathize with each other and with students; they *care*. What is more, this is important to young people, whose overall satisfaction with any specific class has been found to correlate highly with their perception that the teacher is concerned about them (B. B. Tye, 1985, p. 277).

The extent to which a warm interpersonal work environment is important to the job satisfaction of the *adults* in a school is less clear and deserves more study. Given the norms of autonomy and professionalism—what Miles (1965) called "low interdependence"—one might hypothesize that the majority of teachers would say that the relationships they have with their students are far more important to them than those they have with their colleagues. Perhaps this is inevitable. However, the nature of the adult interactions in a school can have a direct bearing on the life—and death—of a faculty effort to do something new or different. An adult work environment characterized by friendliness and mutual respect may well allow such a faculty project to thrive instead of to wither. There are, nonetheless, at least three kinds of "subtle conflict" that, when found within a faculty, can prevent success. These are (a) *covert* conflict, when a group suppresses its inclination to dissent; (b) *latent* conflict, when issues are dismissed as being no more than "personal troubles"; and (c) *inaction through self-censorship*, when individual members decline to participate (Gronn, 1986).

Oddly enough, the motivation for any of these conflicts may be well-intentioned. For example, group members may suppress their inclination to disagree out of a desire to preserve harmony. Paradoxically, in so doing they may create covert conflict that could erupt at a later time and do far more damage. Latent conflict can develop when an individual or subgroup on the faculty feels as if an issue of importance is being dismissed by the majority as merely a personal matter, not relevant to the task at hand. And, of course, when enough members of the faculty simply sit back and do nothing, real friction can emerge as the rest feel they are being left to carry the project without the full support of their colleagues.

The "Logic of Confidence" Makes Close Supervision Unnecessary. Fourth, while teachers as well as nonteaching educators are *hired* on the basis of technical competence as reflected in credentialing requirements, once hired another dynamic takes over. Annual evaluation visits can be largely pro forma once a teacher has achieved tenure. Instead of tight supervision, the "logic of confidence" supports the teacher's job security. The logic of confidence is the assumption "that everyone is acting in good faith. The assumption that things are as they seem, that employees and managers are performing their roles properly, allows an organization to perform its daily routines with a decoupled structure" (Meyer & Rowan, 1977, p. 358).

Not only do teachers work more willingly when they are not too closely monitored but the logic of confidence serves another purpose as well: If what goes on isn't too closely inspected, evidence of inconsistency is masked. In other words, it isn't readily obvious that the mandates and pronouncements made at the upper (and more public) levels of the system aren't always followed to the letter in the classroom. According to Meyer and Rowan (1983), this is to everyone's advantage and is a functional necessity if life in classrooms is to go on.

The logic of confidence, then, seems to be a necessary element of the loosely coupled system found at the teaching end of the educational enterprise. Connected to the logic of confidence is the assumption of professionalism. If teachers are professionals, after all, then we can relax and assume that they know what they are doing. Close supervision, such as that required within a bureaucratic system, would thus be unnecessary. Any teacher can verify that he or she relies on professional judgment in doing what needs to be done—and also that what needs to be done is not always what the superordinate system has decreed.

Documentation Is Not Always Taken Seriously. Finally, the documentation, policies, and regulations so important to the maintenance of a bureaucratic system are largely irrelevent to the real work of the classroom teacher. Few teachers welcome the additional paperwork that does not directly serve their own instructional purposes and the needs of their students; most would welcome a drastic reduction in what the system does manage to require from them. More often than not, official documents may be found gathering dust in the classroom cupboards or the storage room.

A Flexible Structure Can Absorb Systemic Disturbances

As we have seen, then, the loosely coupled system that exists at the instructional end of American schooling is resilient—more resilient by far than a bureaucratic system, because by its very nature it can absorb changes in one part without disturbing the organization as a whole.

This is not to say that it *always* does so, of course. During the 3 years that I was studying schools in the three planned communities of Columbia, Reston, and Irvine, I watched as a problem between a principal and one teacher had an impact on the entire faculty. In another school, a demand by a parent affected only one department, while other departments remained unaware of it. A new effort to promote team teaching at a middle school in one of the districts had no impact at all on the other schools; but a request by another school to try a teacher-advisor plan sent a ripple of response through the entire system. The point is that at the classroom and team or department level, American schooling can be understood as being nonbureaucratic. There may be other images that would serve as well, but for me the notion of a loosely connected set of entities (classrooms, teams, etc.) rings true as a way to envision how things work in that part of the total organization known as the public schools. Weick's (1976) term captures the essentially nonlinear, flexible, and resilient character of life at the instructional level.

Also, as Weick (1976) himself noted, if a loosely coupled system survives over time, one may hypothesize that it serves a purpose or confers some advantage on its constituents. The purpose served by a loosely coupled structure in the case of schooling is the protection of the classroom from inappropriate interventions. A bureaucratic hierarchy just cannot contain all the complexities of an essentially nonroutine endeavor such as the teaching–learning process; but a loosely coupled structure can.

SUMMARY AND CONCLUSION

In this chapter, I have suggested that what we think of as a monolithic edifice is actually two very different—though connected—structures: at one end, a tightly coupled bureaucratic hierarchy with roles, rules, and standardized procedures; at the other, a loose assemblage of connected but independently functioning components including people, processes, and less tangible elements like norms, beliefs, and assumptions. There are historical as well as functional reasons why each end of the system is the way it is, and it would be as futile to imagine the instructional side's becoming bureaucratized as to picture loose coupling on the administrative side. Each kind of structure seems to work for what it has to accomplish. My task has been to suggest how each works and how each, in its way, contributes to the deep structure of schooling and supports its resistance to change.

Having explored the social context within which schools are embedded (Chapter 2) and the organizational structure of the institution of schooling (Chapter 3), we turn now to an examination of how fiscal realities can effectively derail or stifle reform. I suppose many readers will assume that financial constraints are the worst of my "inhibiting forces," especially in recent times when public schools in many parts of the country have been so impoverished. It's not enough to say that the problem is lack of funding, however. As we shall see, sometimes it's not so much that money is (or is not) made available for reforms, but *how* it is made available: with strings attached.

4

Hard Truths About Innovation and Money

In this chapter, we look closely at the financing structures and fiscal support of schooling, resource allocation, and the use of short-term external funding ("soft money"). Money is also at issue in the role played by the knowledge industry in efforts to adopt and implement change, so we look briefly at some examples of how that works as well.

Before we begin, it may be useful to review what the deep structure of schooling in the United States *is* at the present time. In the introduction to this book, I suggested that it consists of the physical similarity of classrooms; the overall control orientation of policy, program, and pedagogy; the general similarity of curriculum and of schedules; faith in test scores as measures of success; and the practices of age-grading and the labeling and sorting of students. With the economic angle in mind, I now suggest that *inequality in the allocation of educational resources and opportunities* and *superordinate control of the purse strings* must be added to this list.

A NUTSHELL HISTORY OF SCHOOL FINANCE

Most Americans don't realize that the tradition of shared fiscal responsibility for schooling is older than our nation itself. In 1647, over 130 years before the Constitution was ratified, the Massachusetts Bay Colony set the pattern by passing a bill that required all villages of 50 or more families to assess their members for the support of a school for the community's children. A 1785 ordinance of the Continental Congress, which predated ratification of the U.S. Constitution, expanded on the same principle by mandating that every new community would reserve a designated section of public land for a schoolhouse. Public funding of elementary and secondary schools was an idea grounded in the essentially new democratic notion that the entire community has a stake in the education of the young. This idea was reinforced in the 19th century, when Horace Mann and other public school advocates campaigned for tax support from all Americans—whether or not they had children in the public schools. They were effective in arguing that an educated citizenry gives both economic and social benefits for a community, and this premise endured throughout the 20th century (Schultz, 1968; Spring, 1998).

In practice, however, school finance has never been a simple matter. Together, adoption of the district model of organization and of property taxes as the primary mechanism for funding schools locked the nation into a pattern virtually guaranteed to produce and sustain inequality. In 1973, the U.S. Supreme Court upheld the principle that all matters pertaining to public schools are the responsibility of the individual states (San Antonio School District v. Rodriguez, 1973). Since then, only a few states have tried to find ways to equalize funding and level the playing field. New Hampshire was caught off guard in late 1997, when the State Supreme Court ruled that its "system of paying for public education with property taxes was unconstitutional because it creates widely unequal tax burdens" (Associated Press, 1997). It remains to be seen if this was a wake-up call inviting New Hampshire and the other states to do some creative problem solving in the arena of school finance.

Consolidation in the 20th Century: Schooling Becomes Big Business

In the early 1900s, policymakers and educational administrators alike were attracted to the idea of standardization as applied to school-keeping. At midcentury, they accepted Harvard president James B. Conant's argument for the consolidation of small schools and districts into larger units. Such a change would produce economies of scale, it was thought, and the money thus saved could be used to provide a wider array of learning opportunities than small schools and districts could afford.

The consolidation movement was one of the deep structure shifts of mid-20th-century schooling in the United States. In retrospect, given the significant social, economic, and technological changes taking place in society, the move to consolidate and enlarge the schools seemed virtually inevitable. So many other elements of American life were intertwined with this change that it soon was taken for granted by most Americans that this had been the right thing to do, particularly at the secondary level.

The larger the districts became, the more they needed the help of professional business and personnel managers, so new job niches appeared at district and county offices. School boards and superintendents, too, found that more and more of their time was being spent on fiscal matters (Gross, 1958; Martin, 1962). As related services were added, school districts employed growing numbers of nonteaching personnel—cooks, custodians, school bus drivers, nurses. Other needs were met by contracting for specific purposes, such as the building of a new school. One way or another, by the 1950s many people in a community were working in many different ways as employees of their local school system: Education had become big business.

Federal Funding Enters the Picture

Postwar Needs. The U.S. Office of Education, established in 1867, had traditionally restricted itself to service activities such as the collection of statistical data. Though the Constitution left control of schooling to the individual states, by the mid-1950s policymakers in Washington began to see the quality of elementary and secondary schools as a matter of national interest. There didn't seem to be any reason why the federal government couldn't provide the states with additional money for certain purposes. It was badly needed. Before the war there had been 10 years of depression, during which capital outlay for schools dropped. Investment in schools had been further deferred during the war, and postwar inflation limited the ability of school systems to meet long-overdue needs for new buildings, equipment, staff, and services. Communities and states began to look to Washington for help with their schools.

Washington Responds. So it was that, between 1954 and 1967, over 200 federally assisted programs supported various educational change projects around the country (Fallon, 1967; House, 1974; Kirst, 1974). "In the scant period of thirteen years (1954–67) . . . a sea-change has occurred," said Bailey and Mosher in 1968. "The federal government's interest in stimulating change and improving quality in public education at the pre-collegiate level has been increasingly visible . . . [and has] unquestionably affected the traditional, decentralized autonomies of American education" (p. 2).

The most massive federal funding during this period came as a result of the National Defense Education Act (NDEA) of 1958 and the Elementary and Secondary Education Act (ESEA) of 1965. The NDEA legislation was passed by Congress as one response to the Soviet Union's successful deployment of the first orbiting space satellite the year before. Its policy intention was to beef up the math and science curriculum so as to attract more American young people into science research and development. In this way the United States might recapture the lead in the emerging competition for supremacy in military and space technology.

Shifting Purposes. The ESEA legislation 7 years later came from an entirely different motive—the War on Poverty—but, like the NDEA, its fundamental purpose was the improvement of education for the nation's young people. Its five original sections targeted different needs. Title I included compensatory programs, such as Project Head Start and school breakfast programs. Buttressed by subsequent supporting legislation in 1994, Title I is still with us in schools serving poor communities.

Title III, on the other hand, was specifically intended to stimulate creative educational problem solving and innovative programs, and most of those projects have long since disappeared. A good part of the reason for that was the failure of the funding to work its magic in the way that the distant planners in Washington had envisioned. Not only were there dozens of conflicting local forces combining to alter the projects every step of the way, but the use of temporary funding or seed money as the instrument of government policy proved to be a flawed approach to educational improvement (McLaughlin, 1990). For a complex web of reasons, school districts and other local funding sources declined to pick up the tab to continue the projects once the federal money dried up.

Readers who have had similar experiences will recognize that underneath the surface *impression* of support suggested by a government grant lurks this trap: Even exciting and worthwhile projects may die sudden or lingering deaths because they were started with seed money. "Soft" money, it's sometimes called—and so it is, and too often unreliable as a way to make permanent change. We return to this topic shortly.

Flaws Appear. Other government agencies were involved with school improvement as well in those years, with varying degrees of success. The U.S. Office of Education and the Office of Economic Opportunity initiated programs such as the Teacher Corps and VISTA. The National Science Foundation supported ambitious curriculum development projects in math and the natural and social sciences. By the early 1970s, however, it was becoming increasingly clear that managing local change from the federal level was extremely difficult—perhaps impossible. One of the primary reasons for the failure of such projects was that local people had not been sufficiently involved (Doyle, 1978).

> From the perspective of those at the planning level, it was eminently rational. There were national priorities (goals) to be achieved. The infusion of large sums . . . distributed through curriculum project centers, regional laboratories, and R&D centers in universities would assure the creation of attractive answers to perceived needs. Unfortunately, much of what was developed and diffused turned out to be answers in search of problems. Practitioners perceived their problems differently and, frequently, did not see these answers, however elegantly packaged, as relevant. (Goodlad, 1975, p. 16)

In an effort to apply what it had learned about the importance of local ownership, during the first Nixon administration the federal government made another stab at supporting significant educational change by allocating funds for the Experimental Schools Project (ESP). Supervised by the National Institute for Education (NIE), the ESP focused its attention on just 16 school districts and made a concerted effort to decentralize much of the decision-making to the local level. It didn't work; in a few years these projects, too, had fallen by the wayside. Again, this was due to many complicated factors—the tension between outside funding and local implementation was just one of them. Seymour Sarason (1982), who was involved in evaluating the ESP, called it a "disaster," and noted that the federal level and the local level are two incompatible cultures and that "the people in each of these cultures did not comprehend each other" (p. 87).

During the 1960s and 1970s, money also poured into school systems across the country from private foundations interested in helping with the improvement of schooling. Ford, Carnegie, Mott, Danforth, Kettering, and other foundations supported projects such as the construction of open-space school buildings, differentiated staffing and community involvement efforts, inservice teacher training, and demonstration schools of various kinds. Like the government-funded projects, the foundation-funded ones also were based on the seed-money principle and, like them, few were continued with local money once the foundation funding was gone.

From Boom Times to Belt Tightening . . . and Beyond

Two of the planned communities being used as case studies in this book were built during the 1960s, when all of this federal and foundation funding was available. The Howard County, Maryland, school system began in the mid-1960s to plan for changes stimulated by the building of the planned community of Columbia, then in progress; the first two new elementary schools opened in 1968–69. The district had received both Title III and Ford Foundation grants to help in the planning for those first schools—money that it might never have received "had not the *idea* of Columbia and its possibilities interested foundation people" (Hovet, 1971, p. 90).

When the Grant Money Ends. For a few years, the federal and foundation grants bought the Howard County planning team the flexibility to make some significant changes. Local people seemed to feel that some experimentation was okay, as long as outside funding was paying for it. Of course, it was precisely that attitude that eventually pulled some of the Columbia innovations back to conventional practice and limited others to partial implementation, because when the federal and foundation money ran out—as it inevitably did—the county didn't pick up the bill for full continuation of all the new programs and practices.

This happened before the first high school in Columbia was completely finished—it opened in 1971—but luckily other sources of help were still available. The newly hired high school principal managed to get the school into the NASSP Model Schools Program, which brought in some additional funding for the school's differentiated staffing structure. Eventually, however, the board of education chose to cut almost all of the instructional aide positions. Because it had been those positions that had allowed the faculty to do some truly innovative teaching, the end of funding eroded the changes, pushing the overworked and weary teachers back toward more traditional pedagogy simply because it was too exhausting to do more with no help.

The new planned community of Irvine established a school district in 1973. Like Columbia, Irvine was built on farmland within commuting distance of a large city and, like both Columbia and Reston, it attracted primarily well-educated and fairly affluent professionals as its pioneer home buyers. The early years were exciting years for the school district. Real estate values were high, so the tax base was solid. Pioneer parents were interested in schools that would have the best of everything, and the new district was wealthy enough to oblige. One of the many innovative programs developed in Irvine in the late 1970s was an interactive television production capability, run by and for students in grades 4 through 6. Stan Corey, the first Irvine superintendent, describes that program and what happened to it:

> We found out from a friend at UCLA that for something like $3,600 a school, using surveillance cameras and other Japanese equipment, we could inter-connect our schools. That we didn't need any master control room or battery of technicians, the kids could do it all.
> You'd have a cart that was half the size of my desk; on top you'd have two TVs and on the shelf below was some magical switching equipment.
> The channel would only work one way, so the control mechanism was social. My kids would switch on our transmission button and start talking to yours. And when your kids wanted to reply, they'd simply flip their transmission switch and it'd make a blip on our screen, and your kids would take over. The whole point is that it was student-driven, socially controlled, inexpensive, and it became an open forum. Any classroom or group of kids in the district could talk with other kids in other schools, about projects—it was just great.
> We had children in 4-5-6 grade who developed some powerful skills. They could get on camera with students in, say, four other

schools, conduct a half-hour interview show—with no script—call the students in each of the other four schools by name, time the questions, do the switching, and close out that show in 30 minutes sharp. I remember during the oil crisis one day they went down to the gas station and interviewed people who were sitting in line for gasoline, and put it in the show for the benefit of other students, parents, or whoever. They were very, very good.

Then in 1979 we hit Prop 13, and unfortunately that program coordinator position was one of the first things to go. Use fell off after that. (S. Corey, interview by author, June 18, 1993)

Withdrawal of Public Support. Corey was referring to the California tax revolt of 1978–79, which led to the passage of Proposition 13 by the voters. This citizen legislation ended property tax funding of public education in California and shifted school finance, along with a good deal of the decision-making authority, to the state level. Communities were also prevented from raising other taxes for schooling. The tax revolt—which spread to other states—coincided with a period of national recession and inflation during the Reagan years. Foundations, too, were no longer making large grants for education projects. School districts nationwide went into a rather prolonged budget downturn. From the boom years of the 1960s and 1970s, American schooling entered a period of scarcity from which it has not, at this writing, yet recovered (K. A. Tye, 1978).

Students were the ultimate losers, as programs were dropped and class sizes rose. There were, as well, hidden costs of which the general public was unaware but that made the work of educators increasingly difficult. Deferred maintenance rendered school buildings uncomfortable, scruffy-looking, and, in some cases, actually unsafe. Buildings meant for 1,000 students were stretching to accommodate up to twice as many, which meant that classes had to meet in spaces originally intended for other learning activities, such as media centers, gymnasiums, and on the stage in the auditorium. Library work, indoor sports, music, art, and drama disappeared from the school experience of many American children. Portable classrooms bloomed on the playgrounds, eating up the outdoor activity areas. Because of the numbers, it was that much harder to keep the buildings clean. Finally, there were fewer supplies to use in engaging students with their learning. For example, in 1980–81 the relatively affluent Irvine Unified School District spent $120 per pupil on materials and supplies—from paper and chalk to test tubes and textbooks—by 1994–95, that figure had dropped by 30%, to $82.50.

I'm speaking here of wealthy suburban districts, as well as the chronically underfunded urban and rural ones. It is important that we recognize the ways in which reduced investment in public education has altered the landscape of innovation and educational change.

> When cuts come, the new and experimental are sacrificed to preserve the traditional. The reason is simple: innovations rarely have widespread public or professional support, and they may be highly controversial. Majority decisions dictate the priorities to be preserved; hence when money is scarce schools tend to revert to generally accepted programs and instructional procedures. (Stiles & Robinson, 1973, p. 266)

THE SHIFTING LOCUS OF CONTROL

The 1980s and 1990s saw power and control over schools shift upward throughout the system. Fiscal decisions that had been site-based were reclaimed by school boards; some that had traditionally been the responsibility of local school boards moved to the state capitals; and during the Reagan, Bush, and Clinton administrations, the U.S. Department of Education sought to exercise more influence over states by issuing national goals and standards and moving to link these to national testing programs. This trend to centralization may be another deep structure change in progress. Whether or not that is the case, in the final years of the 20th century it certainly had a devastating impact on efforts to *decentralize* decision-making that were under way in some states and communities. One of two things seemed to happen to site-based management efforts: Either the decisions that had been allocated to the school sites were pulled back into the district offices, or those decisions had been so insignificant in the first place that they had never truly moved the power away from where it had always been.

An example of the former can be found in the way Chicago's ambitious effort to move power down to local site councils in the early 1990s shifted back to a more traditional top-down model in just a few years. People involved with evaluating the project after its first 4 years found uneven implementation and success, and predicted that even *more* resources would be needed for the next phase (Bryk et al., 1994). However, the power elite behind the project was already in the process of deciding to return most of the important fiscal decisions to the superordinate system. "Local site councils still exist and make decisions for their schools, but they are no longer major players in reforming Chicago's schools" (Cuban & Shipps, 1997, p. M2).

Much the same thing was happening elsewhere. In Fairfax County, Virginia, for example, two principals in the adjacent towns of Reston and Herndon both noted in 1992 that the budget crunch had meant the loss of recent efforts to decentralize some hiring decisions to the school site level. As one put it in 1992,

> We had some really good school-based management in the last few years, but we've lost it. As the budget has gotten tighter and they've had to cut programs, they've taken away our school-based management and told us what we will do. I assume they just don't feel they can trust the principals with this money. If you're a school person, as I am, you shudder—you *shudder*. But *they* don't. . . .

Locating and wielding fiscal power at the administrative, bureaucratic end of the organization rather than at the instructional end is nothing new. Indeed, it's been the rule rather than the exception: When it comes to money matters, superordinate control of the purse strings is part of the deep structure. In the early 20th century, states made financial aid for school districts contingent upon the districts' meeting stringent standardized requirements set forth by the state authorities "according to the model of a modern school proposed by the policy elite" (Tyack & Cuban, 1995, pp. 19–20). K. A. Tye and Novotney found in 1975 that local boards most often defer to the state and federal levels in financial matters.

Attempts to decentralize significant areas of decision-making—like fiscal management—represent challenges to the established deep structure of schooling. As such, they are probably doomed either to fail outright or to undergo such radical modification that they may be unrecognizable within 10 years of initial implementation. Educators who are involved with or considering a project that includes decentralization of power over financial matters would be wise to take a clear-eyed look at the situation before devoting too much energy to an initiative that may sound just great but have little real potential for success.

THE HIDDEN WITHDRAWAL OF BUSINESS

Another reason the locus of control of public education in the 20th century shifted was the pullout of business and industry from the local tax bases that had traditionally provided most of the financial support for schools. In effect, corporate America withdrew its support of public education: By 1987, the overall corporate share of property taxes had declined to 16% from 45% in 1957 (Weisman, 1991). New developments in the global marketplace, including deregulation and the increasing ease of moving production units to Third World locations, gave businesses the leverage they needed to win tax exemptions from local community and state governments (Martin, 1991; Rosenblatt, 1993; Spring, 1998).

Big business masked its withdrawal from support of the public sector with small concessions and token gestures. School people were glad to form "partnerships" with local business and industry, happy to get some guest speakers, field trips, and donated equipment, and unaware that these represented just a small fraction of the contribution those same organizations had made to support public education not so many years before (Boutwell, 1997b; Shor, 1986).

It's ironic that business no longer supports the public schools financially, because the private sector is one of the primary beneficiaries of the services of those same schools. By sorting and sifting students, the elementary and secondary schools assure the nation of the differentiated work force it needs. When factories needed assembly-line workers in blue shirts, or large bureaucratic corporations needed faceless men in gray suits, schools began to separate students and to give them different lives. Batch processing through the use of a differentiated curriculum has been the means by which this sorting and sifting has been accomplished. It has been reinforced by standardized testing, which serves as the gatekeeper to higher education and thus to upward mobility.

This role of the schools has become part of the deep structure of schooling, and any number of rationalizations and myths have been developed to justify it. The myth of "student choice," for example, continues to help Americans believe that all options are open. In fact, some choices are *not* available to some students. And although a 15-year-old who "chooses" between, say, an art course and a foreign language as a 10th-grade elective may feel good about being allowed to make that decision, what she doesn't realize is the extent to which that choice will define the paths her life can—or cannot—take.

As the industrial age gave way to the corporate society and then to the postindustrial era, fewer unskilled, blue-collar workers were needed—so the schools held more students in school longer. Preventing dropouts became a goal, so money was put into programs for young people judged to be "at risk" of leaving school too early and possibly becoming a burden to society. As we stand on the brink of the 21st century, robots assemble automobiles and poor women in China and Mexico make fancy running shoes for the American market. Young people stay in school, as they are supposed to, then go on to college and university in unprecedented numbers. The common assumption that higher education would open the doors to a better job and a more comfortable life, however, slowly but surely turned into a myth. This myth sustains the forward momentum of higher education and, indeed, the encouragement at all levels to "do well in school." But it no longer masks the fact that a college degree is not the guarantee of job security that it once was. The corporate downsizing of the 1980s and 1990s has created an economy that doesn't have enough jobs for educated people (Boutwell, 1997a; Kuttner, 1993; Lasch, 1978; Martin, 1991; Molnar, 1997; Reich, 1991). It remains to be seen how (or if) the institution of public education will adapt to these new realities.

THE IMPACT OF AN AGING POPULATION

Another development that few people have been talking about in relation to the vitality of American public schools is that our population is aging. Since midcentury, a steadily growing percentage of Americans are over 65. Furthermore, thanks to the success of the Social Security system and to the thriving economy of the 1960s and 1970s, when our present seniors were in mid-career, now most of them are living much more comfortably in retirement than their own parents did. Projections into the first third of the 21st century show this demographic shift continuing. Will these seniors feel a responsibility to support the schools, both through their taxes and in other ways?

It has been recognized for some time that older citizens tend to vote against school bond issues (Agger, 1969). This isn't surprising; after all, retirees live on fixed incomes. If their home is paid for, the pension check or Social Security may cover living costs and increasing medical expenses, but wouldn't necessarily be able to accommodate annual tax increases. If they still have mortgage payments or are renters, their financial situation is likely to be more precarious. In either case, it is understandable that they would not welcome higher and higher tax bills.

Traditionally, the most active support for schools has come from young parents when their own children are in school. The ethos of the late 20th century has been, as I have said before in this book, fairly self-centered. It is fueled by the "zero-sum" assumption that there isn't enough money to pay for everything, so that if you get what *you* want, I can't possibly have what *I* need. Some fresh thinking will be needed early in the 21st century if the United States is to escape the trap of assuming that it can't support both its children's education *and* the needs of its senior citizens. If serious consideration were given to ending the use of property taxes to finance the educational system, and workable alternatives can be found, we might be able to regenerate our public schools without pitting grandparents and grandchildren against each other at the ballot box.

THE UNEVEN DISTRIBUTION OF RESOURCES

I suggested at the beginning of this chapter that *inequality in the allocation of educational resources and opportunities* must be considered just as much a part of the deep structure of schooling as the uses of time and space, control ideology, and tracking. Subsequently, we saw that *superordinate power over the way money is spent* should also be added to the list. At this point, more needs to be said about the uneven distribution of resources, because this inequity wouldn't be a part of the deep structure of schooling if it didn't in some way do something that our society seems to need.

Historical Perspective

This used to be a primarily agrarian nation, with thriving agricultural communities wherever the soil would sustain farming. As the cities grew they, too, had a vitality of their own. Higher paying work in the cities, the dust bowl failures, the depression, and, more recently, agribusiness buying up the small farms—all played a part in people's decisions to leave the land. In the cities, too, forces were at work to lure people elsewhere: After World War II there were suburbs and automobiles; for the first time ever, those who could afford it chose *not* to live in the community where they worked. On the farm, and in the "inner" city, many of those who stayed were those who could not afford to go anywhere else. A cycle of rural and urban poverty was allowed to develop, held in place by other economic forces such as segregated housing and limited transportation. Today, pockets of poverty continue to entrap a significant portion of our citizenry, and the schools play a part in this.

First of all, as noted earlier, the traditional manner of financing schools—the local property tax—established dramatic inequities: Wealthy communities could afford better schools, poor ones could not. Children of affluent parents, having gone to those good schools, were equipped to get into college—and their parents could afford the tuition. Children of poor parents pretty much had to take what they could get; usually, it was much less. This pattern was not seriously challenged until the civil rights movement of the post–World War II years. By then, however, it was too late: Even the Great Society programs of the mid-1960s and the court cases of the 1970s mandating the equalization of funding failed to make much of a dent in what had become part of the taken-for-granted reality of American education.

> The six public schools we studied, although chosen to be ordinary and not including any really elite schools, provide eloquent testimony to the differences in public education that economic and racial segregation create in this

country. . . . Different levels of funding available from local tax bases were visible in the schools' architecture, the nonteaching duties expected of their faculties, their extracurricular activities, and their supplies. Not only parents and students but school staff entertained very different visions of students' futures; these visions shaped the relationships of staff and students and the curricula-in-use. (Metz, 1989, p. 86)

Traps of External Funding

When the faculty of an impoverished elementary, middle, or high school in a poor community wants to try to make some improvements in the quality of education it is offering to its students, where can it turn for support? The local school district budget doesn't contain adequate funds to meet all the basic needs of the district as it is, let alone have anything to spare for new initiatives. More often than not, such schools are forced to find outside sources of funding for any new projects they hope to undertake. Some of the traps of external funding—government and foundation grants specifically—have already been mentioned. These include (a) the fact that the culture of the school is so different from the culture of the distant funding agency that the inevitable misunderstandings put insurmountable barriers in the way of project success, and (b) the temporary nature of "soft" grant money coupled with the predictable refusal—or inability—of the local school district to continue providing the necessary money means an abrupt end to funded projects once the grant period has ended.

Related to the first of these is the possibility that the donor will provide money for a project out of a motivation that Freire called "malefic generosity" (Benham, 1978b; Freire, 1970; Greene, 1976). Believing that it understands the situation and with the best of intentions, the funding agency imposes its values upon the requesting school or district by attaching conditions and expectations to the grant allocation that may well not be appropriate. This weakens the chances of success significantly, as the practitioners may not see the project goals as relevant to their real needs.

Funders may also fail to take into account aspects of the larger context, offering an overly simplistic solution to a very complex set of problems. Another possibility is that outside funding may have unanticipated consequences that are as problematic as the situations the funding was intended to alleviate. For example, some categorical funding actually seems to have made the fragmentation of children's experiences *worse* (Darling-Hammond, 1997; SooHoo, 1990).

The second of these "traps of external funding"—the difficulty of finding ongoing financial support once the outside grant has ended—has already been touched upon. Suffice to say at this point that after the pattern repeats itself enough times (of top-down funding and poorly matched projects plus failure to find permanent fiscal support), even the most determined teachers are bound to become discouraged and cynical about the possibilities of improvement. It does seem as if the deck is stacked against success.

Another of the cards in this deck, which has also been briefly mentioned before, is the zero-sum game we play—it's one of the myths of our economy that there isn't enough money to go around, and this myth has at least two disastrous consequences. One of these is unnecessary competitiveness ("I need to *prevent you from getting what you need*, because if you get it, there won't be enough left for me"). The other is even worse: the legitimization of comparative advantage ("I've got more than he does, because I deserve it and he doesn't, because if he did, he'd have it, too").

Public Opinion

Yet a third card in the deck is what happens to public opinion when, time after time, reforms seem to fail. As we know, bad news sells. Every time a reform fails to solve a problem and this failure is trumpeted on TV and in the print media, more people become convinced that the schools are beyond hope. And because real, lasting improvement seems more difficult for schools in poor communities than for schools in middle-class communities, more people will come to believe that money spent in efforts to help poor children with their education is going to be money wasted. It's a short-sighted view, and one that both oversimplifies the situation and conveniently overlooks the fact that our society and its schools are *organized to ensure the failure* of school reform. That is, it contains mechanisms by which the deep structure protects itself from change.

The strangest thing is that we do it to ourselves. First, we convey the impression that a reform is needed because *what is in place isn't working*. (That may not, in fact, be true; but after all, if it wasn't broken, why would we want to fix it? So people assume that it must be broken.) Second, when designing school improvement projects and writing our grant proposals, we often promise more than we can realistically deliver. Such grand hopes get grants; funders seldom suggest that we be more modest in our goals. But by promising too much, we may be guaranteeing our own failure. First, we admit to failing in the past; then, we ask for money in such a way as to guarantee failure in the future. It's rather bizarre, actually. And it's self-defeating, too, because for many Americans it's just a short jump to the conclusion that America's system of free and open public education has outlived its usefulness and that something else must be tried.

A possible explanation—or part of one, at any rate—may lie in Paul Hill's (1978) suggestion that a "reform industry" has developed within the institution of education in the United States. In 1978, Hill observed that "In the ten-year period since the large-scale establishment of federal aid to education, the staffing of the American educational system has changed in a way that reinforces the pressure for innovation. Federal, state, and local education agencies are now dominated by people with advanced training in curriculum design and program evaluation" (p. 254). If that was true in 1978, how much more so now, many years later? After all, people with such training need work; and we need by our work to justify our expertise. Perhaps those of us who work within these categories should ponder the extent to which we depend upon continuing educational change for our livelihoods and sense of efficacy.

Of course, Hill's analysis doesn't cover all the possibilities, nor is the situation entirely bleak. Although in this book my focus is on the forces that defeat reform and change, it is also true that there have been some projects that have not only survived but have been disseminated with some success and are now, years later, established practice. Adequate funding has a good deal to do with this, and so does the use of appropriate expertise. I would argue that when this happens, it is because either (a) the societal conditions were already inclined to support the change, or (b) the change was not aimed at altering a deep structure element.

State-by-State Differences

> *The American commitment to equality is violated at its very roots by the fact that local and state governments continue to pay more for one child's education than for another's. . . . The failure to educate millions of children is turning the potential for social profit into grave deficit, the cost of which American taxpayers will bear both financially and socially.*
>
> McLaren (1998, pp. 15–16)

We've looked at the institutionalization of fiscal inequity in schooling historically and seen that both structural and attitudinal factors play a part in holding these disparities in place. Most of this discussion has focused on the evident differences between affluent, middle-class, and poor communities or school districts, but it is worth noting that dramatic differences also exist between *states.* Local exceptions notwithstanding, it is beyond question that some states provide a much richer educational experience for their young people than do others. As we consider the many facets of institutionalized inequity, perhaps we should confront the possibility that it is past time for a *national* plan to equalize the education funding process.

Distribution of resources for schooling is uneven; because of this, the school one attends matters a great deal. A really bright African American or Hispanic girl of 14 with the potential to earn a Nobel Prize in medicine or physics one day may never even have the chance to *learn* chemistry or physics, because her rural Louisiana high school does not offer those courses or cannot afford well-equipped science labs. Not having had the right courses, she may not get into college. An average White girl with the potential only to get through with barely passing grades will nonetheless be accepted to several good colleges, simply because she attended a high school in suburban Connecticut and was steered into all the right courses by a competent guidance counselor. Other factors are at work, of course; but it's not entirely untrue to say that because there is such disparity in American education, it really is an accident of birth that determines one's opportunities (Tyack & Cuban, 1995; Yeo, 1998).

The way our system operates, therefore, ensures that a tremendous amount of talent is never tapped. For many students, some doors never open. *Why* do we, as a nation, tolerate this incredible waste of human talent?

Structural Inequities Serve a Purpose

The unequal allocation of resources that limits the chances of the poor and minorities is, I now believe, no mistake. It exists for a functional reason, one that has nothing to do with the development of learners to their highest potential or even to prepare each of us to achieve upward socioeconomic mobility. American schools serve the interests of the state, and the interests of the state require a class-based society (see, among many others: McLaren, 1998; Meyer & Rowan, 1983; Molnar, 1997; Oakes, 1995; Spring, 1998; Yeo, 1997).

There is ample evidence in recent educational literature showing how this happens. Linda Darling-Hammond (1997), for example, describes how a self-fulfilling cycle of failure is created when tighter, more prescriptive curricular mandates are decreed for low SES and minority urban and rural areas. The resulting instruction is relatively uninteresting and therefore less likely to engage youngsters actively with their learning. The students are evaluated using inappropriate tests that yield meaningless scores that are then used to hold them back—despite substantial research showing that such grade retention *leads to higher dropout rates*, an outcome none of us desires. First we make it so difficult for poor children to succeed in school, and then we punish them for not being successful.

One of the hard truths seems to be that the economic system of our nation cannot provide good work for everyone. There have always been mindless tasks to be done, and until the development of robotics, these all had to be done by people. Many still are. In a pragmatic society, a high-powered intellectual education doesn't seem necessary if one is likely to make one's living selling shoes, coring pineapples in a canning factory, tightening bolts on an assembly line, or cleaning other people's houses. In the best of all possible worlds, these jobs should probably be well paid: People who don't want to do them should be willing to generously compensate those who will. But capitalism, of course, doesn't work that way. So the system has a vested interest in producing a work force that will be glad to do whatever work it can get, and that will not be so well-educated as to be aware of how it is being manipulated.

> Of course, given the democratic commitments of American life, none of this sorting and selecting can be too easily admitted. The idea that schools are not fundamentally about enhancing the personal and social opportunities of young lives but are, instead, about regulating and channeling kids into the existing social order—perpetuating and reproducing systems of inequality—contradicts our most cherished myths concerning opportunity and freedom. (Purpel & Shapiro, 1995, p. 100)

As Purpel and Shapiro suggest, we have myths and rituals to protect us from knowing these things too clearly. One of the myths is that *anyone can get ahead if he or she will just buckle down and work hard.* Even the poor have bought into this myth—Chomsky (1987) has shown how people can be led to believe that the system is fair when it isn't; he calls this process the "manufacture of consent." This is how those with power arrange the public world in such a way as to ensure that they *keep* that power (Grant & Sleeter, 1996).

One of the rituals may be our earnest support of the never-ending cycle of innovation. As we have already seen, American schooling as an institution goes from one reform movement to the next, always hopeful . . . and too often disappointed. Our common need to feel that our efforts *can* make a difference, and that each new innovation might be the one that works, is one possible explanation of why we invest our energies in this ritual.

But should we continue with this pretense of myths and rituals that masks the discriminatory nature of our work? Once we understand how the system works (and how it protects and perpetuates itself), should we not admit this knowledge; and would that not be a liberating act that might lead us to more constructive solutions?

> *If we don't intend to educate all children well, it's cruel to keep pretending.*
> Deborah Meier (1996, p. 34)

GAMES WE PLAY WITH SOFT MONEY

America as a nation seems to have withdrawn its fiscal (and emotional) support from its schools within the past 25 years. Consequently, school budgets are tight. Even the basics are in short supply in many districts. Many programs have been cut, sharply limiting the range of learning experiences available to children and young people. Conditions continue to be even worse at schools serving poor children than elsewhere. School people feel defensive and undervalued—as well they might. We continue to hope that each new answer might be the one to set the enterprise back onto an upward spiral, so with characteristic optimism we continue to invest our precious time and energy in new projects. A few succeed.[1] Some of them fail, for reasons that may lie in macro forces of which we are only dimly aware. A number of those have been described thus far in this book.

Finally, some succeed for awhile and then falter, yielding to one or another—or several—of the micropolitical events that the deep structure uses to protect and perpetuate itself. It could be a defeated bond issue, a parent protest, a teacher rebellion, or simply the slow attrition of the original participants and the arrival of newcomers who don't feel the same commitment to the project. It could be turnover on the board of education, the departure of energetic leadership, a shift in community support, or the growing exhaustion of teachers unable to continue carrying a work load twice what teachers are asked to carry in other nations of the industrial world. It could be—and often is—the inevitable end of short-term external funding.

Possible Pitfalls

We have looked from different angles at the issues involved in obtaining limited government and foundation grants to make curricular, pedagogical, or even structural changes in our schools. There are a number of additional cautions to be made at this point.

First, outside funding may come with strings attached that are contrary in intent to that of the project itself and thus may pull the project away from its true goals. Examples of this can be found in the tension between the *control orientation of schooling* (an element of the deep structure) and the *nurturing impulse* intrinsic to the teaching–learning process. These two sociopsychological dimensions coexist in the American system of formalized education. Some reforms target one or the other; but as Pauly (1991) has observed, occasionally policymakers will respond to *both*, by providing money for nurturance programs but attaching control stipulations to the funding. When applying for outside funding, we should be quite sure we can live with any conditions attached by the donor, and that those conditions won't pull us away from what we really want to accomplish.

Grants are made by agencies that are seen as superordinate, as having more status and power than those on the receiving end. A government agency, a private corporation, or a foundation with money to hand out and the conviction that it knows what should be done with that money is unlikely to just make grants with no strings attached. Unfortunately, too, private funders prefer start-up projects rather than existing ones in need of, say, 4th-year funding.

Second, a real drawback of external funding is its limited time frame. "Well," you say, "at least we can do some good things for kids while we have it, and that's better than nothing." Perhaps—but if that's our position, why not just be open about it? Shouldn't it be possible to say, "This is a project that will last 3 years, and then we will go back to doing things the way they were before, because to do it properly requires an annual budget and we won't have that after 3 years"? We don't *want* to leave it at that. We want to believe it will be permanent. But when we admit that it might not be, we then must face the more difficult question: Is it still worth taking the grant, knowing it will end and the district won't pick up the tab to continue it? Do those of us who will have to do the actual work have the time and energy to give to something that is unlikely to last?

Yet we continue to perform these rituals, poring over RFPs and slaving over grant applications. Administrators and teachers alike go to annual professional meetings and learn about the newest trends, picking up on the excitement that attaches to a popular new idea and bringing it back to try (or require others to try) on home ground. No one wants to seem old-fashioned and, besides, careers can be built on successfully riding the waves of educational change. On the other hand, perhaps it's time we began politely but firmly to decline to participate in change just for the sake of seeming *au courant*.

Take the Money and Run

When it comes to soft money, district administrators may be even more inclined than principals and teachers to do whatever it takes to obtain such funding. Charters and Pellegrin reported in 1972 on their study of four schools that were implementing differentiated staffing plans. Vague and abstract funding proposals masking a "just get the money" attitude, plus general agreements to "just work out the details as we go along" were two of the characteristics that caused problems with implementation in the very first year. They also found that plans had originated at the district office and had not included significant participation of the teachers who were expected to do the actual work.

House (1974) made the following observation after studying the federal school reform programs of the 1960s and early 1970s:

> Local school administrators traditionally "divert" federal funds to items in their own budget, treating federal programs as windfall money that may soon evaporate. Hence, there is a great reluctance to institute federal programs on a permanent basis since the district may be caught "holding the bag" and absorbing costs for programs in which it is not really interested. (p. 205)

Pincus (1974) also noted this tendency of administrators to devote more energy to getting grant money and much less to making sure that subsequent implementation is successful and permanent in their districts.

The seminal 1974 RAND study of educational innovations found that adoption that is opportunistic is less likely to stick; it simply will not earn the support of those charged with implementation (Berman & McLaughlin, 1974; Doyle, 1978; Fullan & Pomfret, 1977). In reflecting back on that study, Milbrey McLaughlin (1990)—one of the original RAND study authors—said that "resources alone did not secure successful implementation or project acceptance" and that "even successful implementation did not predict long-run continuation of projects initiated with federal funds" (p. 12). According to McLaughlin, projects can be *successful* during the funding period—and *still* disappear when the money goes.

Opportunity Knocked: The Story of Open Space. The impulse to take soft money without giving much thought to the consequences leaves a residue of problems to be dealt with, whether the context is a single, specific school or hundreds and hundreds of schools and districts across the nation. The story of open-space school buildings is a complicated tale of opportunism in obtaining external funding combined with the power of a popular new idea about how change can be achieved, plus all the counterproductive dynamics of top-down decision-making. It left its mark in thousands of communities. Each open-space school that was built had to deal with the consequences in ways that were compatible with its particular, unique personality. What all had in common, though, was the original willingness of school boards and district administrators to go along with the wave of enthusiasm and to take advantage of additional funding that was being made available for designing such buildings.

In the late 1960s, on the basis of the assumption that the way to change teachers' behavior was to change their work environment, the Ford Foundation was actively supporting the building of open-space schools. Flexible spaces would, it was felt, provide more options for teaching and stimulate more creative pedagogy.

This movement was at its peak during the years when the new planned community of Columbia was taking shape on former farmland in Howard County, Maryland. The county school system was planning the new schools it would build to accommodate the children of the pioneer residents of Columbia. Several nationally known consultants were hired to make recommendations, and because hopes were so high for flexible space as an innovation just then, these consultants recommended that Columbia's new schools should be designed that way. Their reasoning was that such innovative buildings would encourage more innovative teaching and, conversely, that innovative teachers would be attracted to Columbia partly by the exciting new schools that were being built there. A number of key decision-makers of that time—including Robert H. Anderson, one of the consultants—recall that what really sold the school board on open space, however, was that it was *less expensive* than the traditional egg-carton style of school building:

> When the school board discovered that those schools not only didn't cost more but actually cost *less*, they were anxious to do it. Fewer load-bearing walls; the understructure could be much more free-flowing . . . but teachers' voices weren't heard. It was mostly a top-down kind of affair; and, in addition, they failed to provide suitable training—even for their principals. (R. H. Anderson, interview by author, April 25, 1993)

A Howard County board member of that time concurs with Anderson:

> That (open space) was a decision the board made, and if you want to know the truth I think it was because it was cheaper. The open space has certainly been modified now; but once the county made that commitment, and began to build all the schools that way, they had a pretty heavy investment. . . . What *didn't* go along with open space schools was the sort of training it would take to make it work.

Howard County received a Ford Foundation grant to support the design of an innovative plan for an elementary school. According to Mary Hovet (1971), a member of the county leadership team at the time, "It is notable that the building design was evolved in advance of the curriculum, responsive to the philosophy of the foundation that curriculum often becomes a limiting factor in school building design" (p. 91).

Still, when the new schools opened, despite the dramatically different physical surroundings, *instruction* hadn't changed much. Teachers coped—as they always do. Some liked the new buildings, some didn't. Some teachers closed the folding walls, and they generally stayed closed. If they didn't have folding walls, some teachers improvised to create visual barriers and carried on with what they had to do. Because excellent teachers had been hired, excellent teaching took place whether in open or modified spaces.

Howard County still has some open-plan schools, but it hasn't built any as dramatically different as those first few for a long time now. Many school districts in the United States can tell much the same kind of story. Apart from the pitfalls of short-term external funding, which has been our focus here, it also should be noted that *how a culture makes use of space* in its formal school buildings is a deep structure element and, as such, is impervious to change. Thus, in *our* culture, egg-carton schools have proven extraordinarily resistant to change. Any American community's story of what happened to its school plant design policies over the past quarter-century will most likely be a story of slippage back to those old, familiar, self-contained classrooms.

Pilot Projects

A strategy used by some districts to obtain external funding is the pilot project. The selling point with a pilot project design is usually that the proposed changes will be made in a subset of the organization—one school in a district, say—and that when all the bugs have been worked out and it is running smoothly, the rest of the organization will also adopt the changes. So many constituencies must be consulted about a proposed reform—and persuaded to support it—that sometimes the best a district can do is to obtain everyone's agreement to try the change on a pilot basis, as this vivid description by a Fairfax County administrator shows:

> The okay to do something different would take approval and support from the area office; from curriculum specialists if it has curriculum implications; if it involves funding, the finance people will have their say, and if it involves facilities, those people will have their say—all the heads of the various departments and the Assistant Superintendents sit on a leadership team; it would have to come before the leadership team. The Superintendent would have to be supportive of it. The school board members of that area would have to be supportive of it, because they're going to hear from parents. The *other* board members would have to be comfortable enough that it's happening in one place but not in others. And "should I support this if it's going to send resources to somebody else's area?" Everybody wants their part of the pie. It's a huge system, and to do anything different means lots of people will want to have a say . . . careful pilots often do get approval. But we proceed fairly cautiously.

Three Possible Outcomes. In the course of implementing a pilot project, one of three possible scenarios may emerge. First, the plan can work as originally proposed, with the entire organization ultimately adopting—

successfully and permanently—the new structure, program, or whatever changes had been set as the goal. This outcome seems rare. Second, and more likely, is the possibility of a successful pilot that does not, however, spread to the rest of the organization: "Those projects that do implement dramatic reform are often run as small 'demonstration projects' within a larger school that remains largely untouched by the innovative programs" (Lee, Smith, & Croninger, 1995, p. 2). In her study of recurrent efforts to create democratic schools and classrooms, Angela Fraley (1981) described this process as it played out in the schools of one Massachusetts school district: "Schools not receiving funding were negatively affected and took no notice of the innovations. The ideas were *not generally picked up by non-funded schools* [italics added]" (pp. 205–206).

The third and most common scenario is that the pilot project succeeds while the external funding is available and begins to disappear after the funding has ended. A few years later, little evidence of the changes can be found either in the piloting unit or in the school, or district, as a whole. This is another example of the soft-money fallacy in action, but there is another factor besides money that pulls innovations back and prevents permanent success: the powerful influence of legitimization by groups outside the educational system. As Rowan (1982) explains, "Educational innovations tend to gain legitimacy and acceptance on the basis of social evaluations, such as the endorsement of legislatures or professional agencies" (p. 260). Having such a public "stamp of approval" can help win authorization of a new project, program, procedural or structural reform. (Having the support of an organization as prestigious as the Ford Foundation certainly must have helped convince the Howard County school board to move toward open-space school designs, for example.)

But as Rowan (1982) also makes clear, such legitimacy can just as easily be *withdrawn*, and when it is, school systems become timid about what they have undertaken to accomplish. Internal support may become lukewarm and wither, while other ideas gain currency:

> Local school systems respond as actively to the decline of institutional endorsement as they do to its growth. . . . During one period, expanding organizations might rush to adopt science programs, because this is the type of innovation currently endorsed by legislatures and professional agencies, whereas at another time they may add electronic data processing units. . . . When negative evaluations emerge, even from only a portion of the institutional environment, local school systems hesitate to adopt or retain the innovations in question. The innovation is no longer diffused widely, and local schools that have adopted it soon drop it. (pp. 260–261)

Educators need to keep these dynamics in mind when deciding how to allocate their time and energy to new initiatives that they may feel are worthwhile.

Finally, why do so many project proposals fail to spell out what will be needed if the new program is to be continued beyond the grant period? Why don't funding guidelines *require* school districts to build a line for the new project into the permanent budget, so it's there when the grant money runs out? How can this tendency to "forget" to provide for maintenance be explained? Is it just another game we play with soft money? Could we behave differently, try to maximize the chances of ensuring our new project a long and successful life?

Calling these tactics "games" may make them seem too personalized, as if I am criticizing people who are involved in making such decisions. In one sense, these mechanisms are *institutional* responses to efforts to make changes in some aspect of the deep structure. That is the theme of this book. On the other hand, of course, *somebody* makes these decisions; there *are* individual actors in this drama. A group of teachers develops a grant proposal, knowing full well that the project may be impossible to sustain when the money runs out; the principal encourages them; the superintendent endorses the proposal without even *suggesting* to the board that the project should be considered for permanent inclusion in the budget; board members don't consider that possibility either, and in fact may simply regard the possible grant as a welcome, but temporary, windfall. Thus the stage is set for the drama to play out predictably.

That "take the money and run" games are still played when extra money is made available is suggested by the experiences of teachers who was involved in the statewide school reform effort made by Kentucky in the early 1990s. Although state legislators increased the number of days and amount of money allocated for teacher inservice (so the teachers could learn about the changes they were being asked to make), most districts still used the money for traditional one-shot workshops. These are known to be ineffectual ways to conduct staff development. Additionally, some districts dropped the extra training days within the first 5 years and used the money to cover added *instructional* days (Holland, 1997).

"Let's just take it and do what we can." No wonder massive amounts of money have been spent since the 1960s, with not much to show for it 10 years after the funding ended. What would happen if educators began refusing to accept soft money and short-term external grants? What if teachers refused to begin implementing a new initiative until a permanent line for it was added to the district's annual budget? What if we started to say, "We'll just continue to do the best we can with what we've got—let's not allow RFPs and passing fads to drain the energy we need to give to our work."

It's a thought.

> It is necessary to remember that American educators . . . have undertaken the most ambitious educational task in history—to educate all the children in a mass industrial society to the best of their ability . . . to do this in a nation which wanted as much education as it could get for its children but was *unwilling to pay for it*. In retrospect, America might have been better off in the long run if American educators had taken a realistic look at what was expected of them, and the means that were being provided, and had closed the schools. (Callahan, 1962, p. 259)

THE KNOWLEDGE INDUSTRY:
A VESTED INTEREST IN THE STATUS QUO

Next to personnel and physical plant expenditures, district purchases of text materials constitute a large budget item for any school system. The nature of the districts' relationship with the textbook industry is, therefore, part of the story of financial realities and it is useful, I think, to be aware of the companies' perspective on this relationship.

Textbook publishers wield enormous power in shaping the knowledge system of the entire society (Apple, 1985, 1993). They also have a tremendous financial stake in schools as a reliable market for their product and will mobilize to protect their interests when proposed changes threaten their profits. Two organizational features of public education are compatible with those interests, and publishers value both. One is the large scale of purchasing units; the other is the bureaucratic structure of education at the administrative/decision-making (as opposed to the instructional) end of the enterprise.

Consider the size of the market: It is *huge*. This is what makes it attractive, and that very size provides the rationale for a standardized—rather than a customized—product. Publishers would much rather produce a single text and sell it nationwide than tailor it to regional, state, or district-by-district specifications.

Textbooks: Our National Curriculum?

As a result, the mass production of textbooks is a major homogenizing influence within our culture (Bailey & Mosher, 1968). Students from coast to coast learn from the same books, produced by just a few big publishing houses (Benham, 1978a). Classic text analysis studies such as Frances

Fitzgerald's (1979) *America Revised* show how textbooks reflect the cultural biases of their time, thus indoctrinating the next generation with what is considered culturally acceptable knowledge (even though it may be inaccurate or incomplete). Michael Apple, who has written extensively on how textbooks are produced and marketed, also documents this process.[2]

Consider, also, the role of the education bureaucracy in textbook purchasing. Although one might think that textbook selection would be a natural function of the *instructional* end of the organization, because after all the books are used in the teaching–learning process, such is not the case. In most states, individual school faculties are not allowed to make their own purchases from among the whole universe of textbooks available (any more than they are allowed to make hiring decisions). Instead, decisions about how the money is spent are kept carefully centralized at the district or even state level. This is just fine with the major publishing companies. Corporate bureaucracies themselves, they are far more comfortable dealing with district or state department of education purchasing agents, or both, than with individual school faculties. They can offer a uniform product at a competitive price with some confidence of making a big sale, whereas if they had to deal with separate schools, they might be asked to provide a different edition or risk losing the sale to another publisher.

Textbooks *provide the curriculum* by defining what knowledge is of most worth and publishing it, and what textbook publishers want to avoid most of all is any possibility that teachers might take charge of curriculum decisions. How might teachers do that? Actually, numerous innovations involving alternatives to textbooks have been attempted over the years. Consider 9-week minicourses, popular in the 1970s: not cost-effective for publishers; they want to provide a book that will be used a whole year. What about the movement in the 1980s to teach using primary sources instead of prepackaged anthologies? Publishers didn't necessarily own the rights to primary sources and, anyway, collections of primary documents on scientific, historical, or literary topics would be too specialized to sell broadly. Integrated curriculum? "A passing fad, not worth investing in product development." Teachers who want to develop materials for integrated thematic units, a core curriculum, or a problems-based or activity-based curriculum are left to do it themselves.

Publishers can relax: This is not a major threat. Teachers might start out on such a project with high energy and enthusiasm (and even a small grant), but after awhile it just gets exhausting to be doing the research, going to the meetings, developing the plan, preparing materials for students to use, and designing ways to evaluate student mastery for the unit, over and over again, for an entire year's curriculum. Too many competing demands pull teachers away from this activity; then, when all the energy is gone, the textbook for their subject and grade level is right there, ready to use.

Textbook publishers also have an ally in *parents*, who may get anxious when their children don't bring home a textbook to use in homework assignments. Teachers can explain the use of alternative learning materials until they are blue in the face, but for many parents it still doesn't seem like "real school" if there isn't a textbook.

The knowledge industry has a firm hold on how and what is taught in our schools, and many inhibiting forces—some obvious, some obscure but nonetheless powerful—act to keep this element of the deep structure of schooling in place. Teachers have found ways to quietly circumvent the textbook, most often by using it primarily as a supplement rather than as the focal point of the curriculum. It is ironic that even when textbooks sit gathering dust on a shelf, the content of instruction rarely wanders too far from what they cover. The conventional understanding of what ought to be included in, for example, a basic biology course is so deeply entrenched that most Americans could quickly identify the major study units they would expect their children to encounter in the course. The same holds true for every discipline. As products of the same system, teachers—even if given carte blanche to design a new biology curriculum—are unlikely to come up with anything radically different. This is another source of support for the knowledge industry, for, after all, if textbooks and other mass-marketed teaching materials cover what we all "know" is the appropriate content for a course, why not use them? Here is the deep structure again, speaking through the conventional wisdom about what's worth knowing.

Teachers who do have different ideas—that a basic biology course should include strong units on the history of scientific ideas and on current bioethical issues, for instance—and who have access to opportunities to put their ideas into practice, simply need to keep these deep structure forces in mind. As they take steps to modify the biology curriculum and win system approval for the changes, they should not naively assume that the district will happily provide money for supplementary materials; nor should they be blindsided by pressures to use a standard textbook or by the objections of parents—or even of students, who may also have conventional ideas about what they should be studying. If the teachers obtain a grant to develop or purchase extra materials, what happens to the new units when those materials wear out or become outdated, and the district declines to pay for replacements? By being aware of these pitfalls and pressures in advance, educators may be able to develop plans to protect their projects from the pulling-back forces of the deep structure.

SUMMARY AND CONCLUSION

Money *does* matter. Allocation of funding, when it is ongoing, can produce change—much has been done in the area of special education, for example, because federal support has continued. On the other hand, when funding is short-term, it can inhibit change, encouraging it for awhile but ultimately pulling it back to past practice.

Money determines what learning opportunities are (or are not) available to children and young people. The playing field is *not* level when it comes to school finance, and those who have both money and power in our society would never dream of sending their children to schools such as some of those described in *Savage Inequalities* (Kozol, 1991). Why are we so willing, without a twinge of conscience, to provide inferior schooling for poor children? The answer has to do with the deepest prejudices and motivations of our culture as well as with the underlying assumption that the purpose of our schools is to provide the appropriate kind of work force for our changing economy. A variety of myths and rituals help us to avoid seeing these uncomfortable matters too clearly.

There is a certain amount of game playing associated with school finance and, in particular, with the funding of innovative programs and new ways of doing things. Such behavior may be seen as a mechanism for protecting the status quo.

Finally, money plays a part in deciding what knowledge will be included in (and what will be excluded from) our children's learning.

We educators need to keep these factors in mind as we plan new initiatives, in order that we not waste our time and energy fighting battles that cannot be won. Knowing something about how the deep structure is held in place by money, or lack of it, may help us to implement successful *and permanent* improvements in our schools. Policymakers outside the schools can only go so far. They can't actually *make* the changes; but they can create the conditions that will allow practitioners to do so. They are also in a position to equalize school finance across states and districts (Tyack & Cuban, 1995). Whether they will ever rise to that challenge remains an open question.

NOTES

1. Following his analysis in 1983 of data from a major study of dissemination efforts supporting school improvement, Matthew Miles suggested that three groups of organizational conditions are needed if an innovation is to become

permanent: (a) supporting conditions, such as *"operates on a daily basis"* and *"competing practices eliminated"*; (b) *"passage completion,"*—and here Miles specifically mentions *"goes from soft to hard money"* and *"routines established for supply and maintenance"*; and (c) "cycle survival," for example *"survives annual budget cycles"* and *"survives departure or introduction of personnel"* (p. 16). All three of these are pertinent in considering the inhibiting forces that hold the deep structure in place, but the second and third have special relevance for our present discussion of the problems involving acceptance of limited funding from external sources.

2. Readers interested in deeper analysis of the production and influence of textbooks should refer to Apple's *Teachers and texts* (1988) as well as his chapter in the *1985 ASCD Yearbook*, pp. 73–90. Other sources include Eisner (1987), "Why the textbook influences curriculum," in *Curriculum Review, 26*, 11–13; Woodward, Elliott, & Nagel (1988), *Textbooks in school and society*; Elliott & Woodward (1990), *Textbooks and schooling in the United States*; and Spring (1998), "The Knowledge Industry," pp. 161–178, in *Conflict of interests* (3rd ed.).

5

Parent and Community Expectations

Our concern in this chapter is to address two questions. First, how do the expectations of parents pull innovations back to old, familiar patterns? Second, how might the deep structure of schooling reveal itself in the actions of the community served by the school? We live in a nation that has a tradition of local control of schooling. Despite growing evidence that this is no longer really the case, schools remain extremely vulnerable to both parent and community demands as well as dependent on their good will and support. First I explore the expectations and involvement of parents and then, later in the chapter, I take a look at how the collective attitudes and assumptions of the community can play a role in the support or defeat of new programs and practices in its schools.

A HISTORICAL NOTE

Parent and community involvement in public schooling has changed profoundly in the past 100 years. On the plus side, a society in which few teenagers completed high school has evolved into one in which almost all young people earn a high school diploma or its equivalent. On the other hand, a society in which the schoolteachers were among the best educated and most respected citizens in town has evolved into one that seems to distrust, even scorn, those to whom it entrusts its children for many hours each week.

In some places, such attitudes are leading to serious rifts between the community and its schools, including refusals to support education financially, resistance to changes initiated by educators, and a willingness to intrude upon and to override the professional judgment of teachers and school administrators. The board of education, as the structural link between a community and its schools, can become the adversary rather than the supporter of the community's schools, as citizens who think they see a great need to *fix* or even to *save* the schools are elected by other citizens who are inclined to believe the dire messages they hear.

PARENTS: EXPECTATIONS AND INVOLVEMENT

All parents may be said to *expect* certain things from the schools their children attend, but not many parents actually get *involved* with the schools. That is, they may not attend PTA meetings, serve as classroom volunteers, or participate in school-site decision-making. They may get involved sporadically—when what they see as a violation of their *expectations* becomes an issue. Such short-term, single-issue involvement might happen when there is a book censorship controversy, a change in the school attendance area resulting from a zoning decision, or a school board decision to eliminate a program the parents value for their children—or to add one with which they disagree (Bridge, 1978).

Consider a decision to move from a traditional to a year-round calendar. (Recall that the way we are accustomed to allocating *time* is one component of the deep structure of American schooling.) This change will never please everyone, no matter how conscientious the school board may be in soliciting parent input prior to making the decision. Parents who are unhappy with the change may organize around the issue and plan a campaign to have the decision reversed; and they may well win.

Or take another example—a decision by one school to adopt mixed-ability grouping. One might think that this would be a professional decision and, as such, that it should be made in-house and would not really concern parents. But so powerful (albeit unacknowledged by many) are the expectations that schools will maintain class distinctions that this internal organizational change can quickly become a public battle (Barnes, 1997; Brantlinger, Majd-Jabbari, & Guskin, 1996; Kohn, 1998; Kozol, 1991; Wells & Serna, 1996). It will play out with a full array of tactics—angry phone calls to the principal, the superintendent, and to board members if necessary; letters to the editor; parent delegations to board meetings; even TV coverage. It is a rare school administrator or board member who can withstand such pressure and successfully convince constituents of the benefits *to their children* of heterogeneous grouping. The plan will usually be tabled—indefinitely: The deep structure wins again.

When the principal of South Lakes High School in Reston from 1984 to 1994 was asked (in 1992) whether her parent community would support a new program or a change in how things were done at the school, she hesitated for a moment.

> Last year I would have said they would be very receptive to change, but this year I wouldn't, because something happened that makes me take another look at that. We instituted an attendance policy that was different, and we have an active group of about eight

parents who are heartily opposed to it. They wreaked a lot of havoc on the school by using the newspapers—our two newspapers take opposite views and vie with each other for headlines—and said all manner of things against it . . . their tactics have made it very, very hard. And this change wasn't even very big. I can't help thinking "My goodness, what if we really wanted to make a *radical* change?!"

These are examples of *sporadic* involvement by parents and community members. This kind of involvement is usually painful and often ugly, involving as it does the taking of sides, angry charges, defensive rebuttals, and hard feelings all round.

Getting Parents Involved

In an effort to minimize such sporadic events, school people sometimes deliberately implement policies intended to draw parents and community members more fully into the life of the school. At least two good arguments can be made for doing this, one strategic and one ideological. First, it is felt that if parents and others are closer to schools and understand them better, they will be less likely to set themselves up as critics and adversaries. Second, there is a genuine issue of democracy: Parents' voices *should* be heard. Excluding them would be antithetical to American values of citizen involvement in the public sphere—which certainly includes the public schools.

Each of these arguments is reasonable; and each is flawed. Just because a parent, grandparent, or guardian may be active in his or her child's school doesn't necessarily mean that on certain issues he or she might not oppose a school policy or practice. And although we all pay lip service to participatory democracy, it's pretty clear that only *some* parents' voices are heard. With these caveats in mind, let's explore parent involvement in a little more detail.

Parents, grandparents, and guardians can be involved with their children's schools in two ways: at the district or school-site level and as classroom helpers. At the district level, they may serve on committees, task forces, and advisory groups, or even on the board of education itself. At the school-site level, they may be active in the PTA/PTO, or with "band boosters" or other support groups; they may also be included on committees and involved in some school-site decision-making. In the normal course of events, this kind of involvement is healthy. It can be a model of a democratic community, and it may also serve to defuse potential crises, because parents who really know a school *can* be its advocates and can speak credibly on the school's behalf to the larger community.

Parent service as classroom helpers may be more problematic, especially if they want to work only in their own child's classroom. On one hand, many teachers welcome the help and can use it effectively. On the other hand, supervising a volunteer can drain time from other teaching tasks. Attending to parents' questions may be distracting. Opening one's classroom to continual public view is laudable, but one cannot be certain that the lay volunteer will understand why the professional educator does things a certain way; and taking time out to explain means yet more time away from the students and even then does not guarantee that the volunteer will understand and be supportive. Teachers may feel limited in the extent to which they can have important professional conversations with each other in an environment that is not private. And parent volunteers, helpful and well-intentioned as they may be, may intervene in inappropriate ways in student learning activities (Craig, 1998). Under such circumstances, and feeling exposed and vulnerable as they do (Blase & Anderson, 1995), teachers may be less than eager to try something new. In a variety of small ways that add up, parents' presence in the classroom can discourage innovation and inhibit professional practice.

These are important considerations, and deserve thoughtful discussion. Parents need to be welcome participants in the life of their children's schools, but given the nature of teachers' work, it may be more constructive to involve parents and other interested community members in site-level or district-level activities and decision-making rather than actually in the classroom.

What Parents Expect

Parental expectations of the school can run the gamut from very general assumptions about curriculum, discipline, testing, and other aspects of school life to very specific ideas about what a classroom should look like and when the school day should begin. Usually, however, expectations are framed in terms of "what I want the school to do for *my* child." A hypothetical middle-class parent might well say something like this:

> Generally, I want my child to be performing at grade level or better in what I understand to be the "basic" subjects; to be relating well to peers and cooperating with adults; to be safely looked after from roughly eight in the morning to three in the afternoon. Specifically, if I visit the school I expect to see quiet, orderly classes in clean rooms. I do *not* want to see youngsters unsupervised and out of class, walking the halls or gathering out behind the gym. I expect my child to be given homework. Report cards should use the A–F

grading system. A psychedelic mural in a classroom would make me uncomfortable, as would a certain noise level. Frankly, I do not know if the sight of a security guard would make me feel reassured or uneasy.

Whether general or specific, these expectations are grounded in the deep structure of schooling as we have known it for several generations. I have already made the point that when expectations are unmet or violated, parents may become actively—if temporarily—involved. As noted in Chapter 2, one of the strongest parent expectations is that the schools will play a custodial role, keeping children and young people safe for a good part of each weekday. Innovations that would alter this familiar schedule might meet with active resistance, and one of three things might happen. First, the parents might win and the change will not be implemented. Second, the change is implemented, but in a modified form as the result of negotiation. Third, a school *could* obtain parent support for a change in the use of time. However, one might predict that after a few years the school will return to a more conventional schedule. In the interim, the normal turnover of personnel (not to mention a changing parent population) will erode the original base of support and sooner or later someone will suggest another change—this time, back to a more conventional timetable.

Like the use of time, the use of *space* is also part of the deep structure of schooling: Parents and community members have certain expectations about what they will see when they walk into a school. During the years when open-plan schools were being built, the use of space could be a major battleground. In some cases, it became the platform upon which parents established their authority over the local school system. Gold and Miles (1981) documented a case of this kind, providing a detailed account of the first 2 years of an innovative new suburban elementary school. It is a classic example of the perennial tension, in our society, between school people and their clients:

> The central social process that took place during the development of the Lincoln Acres school was a prolonged, sometimes bitter conflict between professional educators—both teachers and administrators—and the parents of children attending the school. At the core, the issue was whether educators or parents had the right to determine the sort of education the school would offer . . . the conflict was in many respects one between expertise and democracy as a basis for decision-making. (p. 5)

Some parents were uneasy about open space and distinctly negative about "open education," but the teachers persuaded them to wait and give them a chance to show that it could be successful. When the school opened, however, modification began almost immediately. Parent pressure continued, and by the middle of the first semester teacher morale had dropped significantly. Visual barriers were dragged into place, creating enclosed areas more like what the parents considered "real classrooms." This made team teaching difficult, so teachers returned to using traditional self-contained instructional methods. Ultimately, as Gold and Miles (1981) observe, the parents won: "After a struggle, the school now fit the parents' image of education, not the educators'" (p. 300).

As an aside, it is worth noting that "adaptations" in an innovation, as described here and elsewhere (McLaughlin, 1978a), always seem to be made *in the direction of the traditional and familiar*, virtually never in the direction of increased innovativeness. They are negotiated agreements either to modify the original vision in the direction of the tried-and-true or to abandon it altogether and go back to business as usual.

It is discouraging to become aware of how often differences of opinion in the education field are framed in terms of winning and losing, and how often they seem to place professional educators on one side of an issue and the lay public on the other. Although it is true that there is a fundamental tension built into a system such as ours, which is based on the philosophy of "local control," most of the time educators and parents agree on what should be happening in our schools. To imply that they do not is a tactic that serves to further erode public confidence and, perhaps, to pave the way for a new—and less democratic—definition of schooling.

Powerful Parents

In every community there is a group of parents that has power and a larger group that does not. Powerful parents don't necessarily throw their weight around (though some do); most have power simply by virtue of their position in the socioeconomic pecking order, whether they choose to assert themselves or not (Thompson, 1990). Such men and women have learned how to work the system. They know whom to contact if they have a complaint, they aren't shy about making an appointment, and they know how to explain what they want for their son or daughter. If they are unsatisfied with the outcome, they know what to try next. "In the high-SES communities, parents . . . brought confidence, skill, and power to their relations with the schools," Metz noted in 1990 (p. 92). A Reston principal told me that because so many Reston parents work "across the river" in Washington, they are used to starting right at the top: "They start where they think the power is, not where the problem can be solved first. A lot of parents don't want to deal with the teacher, or with a counselor—they want to deal with the principal, or better yet, with the superintendent. They're used to start-ing at the top—with their general, you know, or their congressperson."

Sometimes working-class or minority parent groups have organized to *take* power within a school system—as, for example, in New York City during the 1960s. There have been times when power has been *given* to parent groups—as in Chicago during the early 1990s. Generally speaking, however, what I mean by "powerful" parents are those who don't have to *take* power or to *receive* it from someone else—they just *have* it. Relatively well educated and affluent, these citizens may not even be conscious of their privileged position or, if they are, it seems right and natural to them. They feel entitled.

This isn't about culture; it's about class. Middle-class second-genera-tion Mexican Americans who have been successful in the United States can be just as powerful and feel just as entitled as any fifth-generation WASP—and can be as intolerant of their poor relations, too.

According to Kohn (1998), powerful parents may get involved in con-troversies about pedagogy, placement, and competition. The first—and least problematic—is a concern about pedagogy. On the whole, parents are more comfortable with traditional methods than with active learning and problem solving. The second, selective placement, includes tracking and the separation of students by ability. It leads to differential access to knowl-edge, giving some students advantages that others do not receive. The third is a competitive evaluation system that produces only a few winners. These categories are extremely important to powerful parents, who want to see their own children given every chance for success and will go to great lengths to make sure that happens—even, sad to say, at the expense of other children who may have as good a claim—or better—on the prizes.[1]

There is considerable evidence that privileged parents are satisfied with the public schools attended by their children, and this suggests that they are getting what they want from their schools. The Gallup Poll of 1997, for example, found that about three out of every four of the parents who gave their oldest child's school a grade of A or B were college graduates and had children who were "at the top of their class or above-average aca-demically" (Rose & Rapp, 1997, p. 48). It follows, then, that these power-ful parents might tend to resist changes, especially in the three areas just mentioned. As far as they're concerned, nothing's broken (Frahm, 1994; Kohn, 1998).

The large comprehensive high school suits everyone, it seems. A dif-ferentiated curriculum allows everyone to believe that opportunities are equally available to all (Metz, 1989), while ensuring that the children of powerful parents get the GATE programs and Advanced Placement courses that they want. Moreover, access to these is kept carefully

limited—making them available to more than a small number would vio-
late the parents' expectations in the area of selective placement. One pioneer principal tells a story that illustrates this perfectly:

> When the new high school opened in 1957, we didn't have any
> grouping system. One of the things we wanted was that no matter
> which section the kids were in, they'd all get pretty much the same
> kind of program. Because our feeling was that the big job of the
> high school was civic education. The shift from a common curricu-
> lum, with just a few elective choices, to a more "shopping mall" or
> stratified system, happened pretty quickly after I left. They threw
> out the ungrouped classes right away, and the four-period day also,
> because that schedule didn't allow for enough different courses
> either.
>   And the last time I visited there, the current superintendent
> told me that in 25 years they've never lost a budget referendum
> (and you know in New Jersey there has to be one *every year*). He
> said, the reason we've never lost that vote is because we offer
> a whole range of courses *to keep the parents of the bright kids happy*.
> (G. Peterkin, interview by author, October 28, 1995)

That was in the late 1950s, but it hasn't changed. In the Study of Schooling in the late 1970s, a substudy of the data focusing on the lives of students found that students in any given "track" were unlikely to be friends
with students in a different track at their school (Benham, 1979a; B. B. Tye,
1985). Jeannie Oakes's (1981, 1985) substudy on tracking, later published
as a separate volume, reinforced this finding. And in the late 1990s, we find
the mainstream press documenting the internal segregation of schools, with
Honors classes populated by the children of affluent white parents (Barnes,
1997). If innovations designed to equalize opportunities and reduce such
internal differentiation were implemented, there is reason to believe that
many powerful parents would pull their children out and send them to
school elsewhere (Judis, 1997; Kohn, 1998). This is the ultimate veiled threat,
and because state funding follows enrollments, school administrators are
understandably reluctant to take such a risk.
     Powerful parents can support and protect as well as defeat change; it
all depends on what the change is. When the town of Reston was first built,
teenagers attended neighboring Herndon High School for a number of
years before the Fairfax County system felt that a new high school was
justified in Reston itself. Because the earliest residents of Reston tended to
be well educated and outspoken about the value of education for their
children, a high-powered, selective alternative program was established

at Herndon High. It served primarily—though not exclusively—Reston children.

This is the kind of change that powerful parents will usually support: Their own children will benefit intellectually, because the program is more challenging. Also, by clustering our youngsters with others who are "like us," we increase the chances that our children will have *the right kind of friends*. Indeed, were such an innovative program to be dismantled, those parents would likely organize to try to *save* it.

Powerful parents also made their voices heard in Columbia in 1985 through 1987, when a new principal at the high school tried to do away with the school's unusual no-fail grading system and cut down the time allocated for advisory period. They spoke up to defend the school again in the mid-1990s, when a redistricting battle turned ugly. In general, privileged parents seem to feel that they are getting what they want for their children, and when this is the case, they will fight to maintain innovations that meet their needs.

A discussion of powerful parents would be incomplete if it failed to acknowledge the hard work of two groups of parents and their supporters in the national community—the citizen movement for school desegregation in the 1950s and 1960s and its counterpart in the 1970s: unhindered access to public schooling for children with disabilities. These two movements, powered to a significant degree by parents wanting a fair deal for *their* children, changed the face of American schooling for *all* children.

Voiceless Parents

Whose voices are not heard, as a rule? Those of parents whom society labels blue-collar, unskilled, or unemployed; those who did not experience success in school themselves and never want to set foot in a school building again; undocumented immigrants afraid of deportation; those who are not educationally ambitious for their children, or who are intimidated by school people and others with more formal schooling than they have. The result, as Bridge (1978) pointed out over 20 years ago, is that "advantaged clienteles will have the largest impact on school innovations unless extraordinary efforts are made to involve others" (p. 113). The squeaky wheel, as we say, gets the attention. Voter registration drives, community action efforts, and outreach by school people can start those wheels squeaking.

Pioneer Parents

In the planned communities of Columbia, Irvine, and Reston, were pioneer parents different from parents living there 20 to 25 years later? If so, in what ways? Were they more—or less—likely to support educational innovation? Did they take action to pull back innovative programs to something they considered more like "real school"?

As I visited each of the three planned communities several times during the mid-1990s, I found longtime residents (both parents and school people) eager to share their views of the early years. Many of the people I interviewed felt that a certain trailblazing spirit characterized the pioneer parents who chose to buy homes in these new towns. That seems to have been especially true in the case of Columbia, Maryland, which was a more dramatically different community—a cosmopolitan *ideal* of a community set down smack in the middle of conservative farm country—than either Irvine, California, or Reston, Virginia: "The first people who came here— to Columbia—were more of a revolutionary kind of people," said one early resident.

"The people who were coming into Columbia were the kind of people who immigrated from the Old World to the new country. They had the guts to move into an entirely new situation," a former Howard County board member told me. "Pioneer parents, if they came here with children—and most of us did," said another board member, "certainly looked at the schools and knew what they were getting into, and approved of it or they wouldn't have come."

It is also true, however, that despite that spirit, parents in all three communities were sometimes dismayed by the extent to which the new schools were different from anything they had encountered before. "Multi-age grouping disappeared in a hurry; there was a lot of resistance to that. Then there was some resistance to the open space. I mean, just the idea of having kids sit on the floor to learn was appalling to some parents—they were so sure that if you're going to learn you need to sit in a chair! I don't know if there is any way you could have proved to parents that it worked—" observed one Reston parent. "It was a far cry from their own experience as children, when you didn't dare raise your voice. You sat in a seat and you didn't talk unless the teacher asked you a question," recalled another.

"There was a sense of community and common purpose and we're-all-in-this-together, but there were a lot of parents who were not all that sure about what was going on. After all, this school building just blew their minds—education went on here in a way unlike anything they had ever experienced and it was far more different then than it is now in appearance," said the Wilde Lake High School principal in 1993. Her perspective is especially useful because, as readers may recall, she had been a classroom teacher when Wilde Lake opened in 1971.

A few interviewees felt that pioneer parents were *less* supportive of their schools than are today's parents—but perhaps that's because the communities have become accustomed to the way their schools are. And because the Columbia, Irvine, and Reston schools have a good track record of getting their graduates into college, the parents have few complaints.

"If the school looks unusual, if it has an unusual bell schedule or a unique curriculum or a teacher-advisor program, well—so what?—it seems to work. And it's not an *experimental* school; in most ways it's very like the one I remember when I was a youngster . . . I'll overlook a few eccentricities as long as my child is on the inside track to the good life," one Reston parent said.

Indeed, families who have moved in more recently often do so precisely because they want *those* schools for their children. One of the original principals in Irvine pointed out that "pioneers skew the curve" because they are taking a chance on a new thing. "But with time, you get a community that is a more normal distribution of values and expectations for education." He suggested that regression of innovative schools to the mean is inevitable as new people move into town and add a wider array of voices to the conversation about the schools.

Burby's (1977) research on schools in planned communities provides some support for the perception that pioneer parents may have been distinctly less supportive of their innovative new schools than the educators originally hoped:

> Although new community development has been viewed as an opportunity to experiment with new educational methods and techniques and to achieve racially integrated suburban communities and schools, these expectations were not shared by the parents . . . who seemed to prefer more traditional schools and racially homogeneous enrollments. (p. 12)

This finding lends credence to the notion that those pioneer parents might have been happy to support changes that would render the schools less innovative and more traditional. During the intervening years many of the original differences *have* in fact been scaled back to more familiar contours; as we have seen, in each community the original vision was modified in a variety of ways over time. All things considered, then, it's little wonder that the parents of Columbia, Irvine, and Reston today are quite happy with their good, typical American schools.

THE COMMUNITY

Let's turn our attention now to the impact of the community at large: anyone who, either at the ballot box or by some other means of expression, participates in exerting pressure on the local school or district to change—

or not to change. At this point in our history, such community pressure for change is nearly always in the direction of more conservative and traditional practice rather than toward increased innovation.

Expectations of Familiarity

"As long as you are part of a larger system, which is relatively slow and conservative by definition, you can push the envelope for awhile; but eventually the larger system is going to push back, *and it's not going to push back in the direction of innovation,*" one pioneer principal told me.

It sometimes seems as if our schools have grown away from the communities they serve. Large intermediate and high schools, especially, have become more bureaucratized and impersonal. The professionalization of teachers, too, may contribute to feelings of distance. It is ironic that this growing separation is increasingly felt just when our society is asking its schools to do many of the things that used to be done by parents.

In small towns across the United States, the schools (especially the high schools) still serve as a focal point for the community, with nearly everyone turning out for the football games in the fall and with good turnouts, too, for the Christmas concert and the senior class play. When it comes to the substantive mission of the school, however, community involvement is, for the most part, episodic and triggered by specific contentious issues. Citizen interest tends to be expressed first by recourse to the board of education, the superintendent, or by direct pressure on teachers. If none of those tactics work, more public tactics may be used. On the whole, in most communities, citizen interest, awareness, and active involvement in school issues is usually pretty low (Martin, 1969).

Heckscher, Eisenstadt, and Rice (1994) have pointed out that in any organization, there are constituencies who expect people to act in familiar ways. Members of a community certainly expect their schools—and those in charge of them—to act in familiar ways; in fact this *expectation of familiarity* is one reason why selling the community on a change in its schools is so often a challenge. Community resistance to a change may be ignited when this expectation of familiarity is violated. On the other hand, when schools are functioning according to expectation, the community will see no need for intervention and this may account for the low citizen participation when things are going along "normally."

What is the substance of these expectations that the community holds and will rise to defend? We expect young people to emerge from 12 years of schooling ready to function as responsible adults, to manage adequately in higher education or the workplace (or at least, to be trainable), and to be law-abiding citizens. These are the values imposed on the emerging educational system during the 19th and early 20th centuries by the growing middle class (Gutek, 1972). They are an integral part of what I am calling the "deep structure" of schooling. We have been living with them for a long time now and, as Eisner (1992) has observed, it is precisely that segment of the population for whom the schools have worked well that now will defend the traditional structures that made *them* successful:

> School reform efforts that challenge tradition can be expected to encounter difficulties, especially from the segment of the population that has done well in socioeconomic terms and has the tendency to believe that the kind of schooling that facilitated their success is precisely the kind that their own children should receive. . . . The point here is that educational consumers can exercise a conservative function in the effort at educational reform. It is difficult for schools to exceed in aim, form, and content what the public is willing to accept. (p. 394)

Effects of Hard Times

One macropolitical influence that clearly affects communities is the state of the national economy. Though at first glance it may seem that this discussion should be in the earlier chapter on fiscal realities, it is included here because it connects to the ways in which communities respond to their schools. For example, in the early 1990s, across the nation some communities seemed to be more stressed financially than others. These were often middle- and upper-middle-class areas that were feeling the pinch of corporate downsizing rather than the chronically poor areas that had little left to lose. A principal in Irvine, California, said he sensed that " . . . people have to work harder to keep okay financially. We're seeing more bounced checks, more questions about materials fees and so on. Less parent volunteerism because in more families, both parents have to work." A principal in Fairfax County, Virginia, made the direct connection between the economic climate and its impact on the schools in his district:

> They've managed to cut back by giving no salary increases, no cost of living increases, and by taking away benefits, by increasing class sizes. There's no sign of any community concern—yet—because they've done a very good job of not affecting the kids. They haven't cut the GATE programs, they talked about taking away late buses earlier this year but of course they brought them right back. They were talking about cutting the sports programs and of course that got put right back in. If they have to go another 39 million next year, my guess is that they're not going to be able to put it on the backs of the employees for a third year in a row. They're going to have to cut

some significant programs, and *then* we'll see how the community reacts.

One popular solution in this type of community has been the formation of independent "community foundations" expressly for the purpose of raising money to provide things for the schools that the school district budget can no longer cover. This works in affluent communities; even when such families have to tighten their belts, most still have the luxury of *some* discretionary income and most are determined that the schools continue to provide the advantages they believe their children deserve. It doesn't work, of course, in communities where families barely get by from one paycheck to the next—or worse. As a solution, therefore, it further separates one community from another and exacerbates the national loss of common purpose.

Differences of Opinion

Not only do communities differ one from another, but there often may be significant disagreements *within* communities. "The community is a fickle master," Bruce Joyce (1982) has observed. "Because the community does not agree about education, almost anything that is done will be criticized by some sizable (or at least vociferous) group" (pp. 57–58). A seasoned principal understands this well: "I've come to the conclusion that you do all you can do and then you've just got to let it go and know that there are some people who are not going to agree with you and that's alright. I mean, that's going to be the way it is."

Hargreaves and Fullan (1998) have documented how different the school environment was by the end of the 1990s when compared with the beginning of that decade. They show how permeable the walls of the school are now and how, to a perhaps unprecedented degree, the outside world intrudes upon the life of the school. "Government policy, parent and community demands, corporate interests, and ubiquitous technology have all stormed the walls of the school," comments Fullan (1998, p. 6).

There are a number of ways in which the local community exerts influence on its schools (Rosenthal, 1969). First, local elections can reveal citizen attitudes and preferences. Did the school bond issue pass? Who was elected to the school board? During the 1990s, there was a concerted effort by the religious right in some American communities to get its slate of candidates elected to the school board and in that way to control local education policymaking. This movement suffered a setback in the spring of 1999 when a number of its leaders withdrew their support for such political strategies. Nevertheless, it remains true that any organized special interest group may, in an open society, take similar action to influence what happens to our schools. Even if their own numbers are relatively small, their impact can be enormous.

Second, there may be local groups who make demands outside the framework of elections. Initiating a recall petition (rather than waiting to unseat a board member at the next election) is an example of this type of pressure, as is organized opposition to a textbook series. Third, the preferences of the local elite can be communicated informally. In a small town, this may extend to who gets hired as the new middle school principal— and who doesn't—or whether the coach is fired after a losing season. In the case of a hiring issue, such informal pressure is exerted *outside* the official search process, but a savvy director of personnel will take it into consideration nevertheless.

Finally, local interests may also be *indirectly* represented by school board members. After all, presumably they were elected in part because they successfully articulated locally popular positions regarding school policies and practices. Some voters might have chosen a particular candidate simply because of *who he or she is*—selecting a well-known civic or business leader, for example, over a housewife or a plumber. There is a considerable literature on the makeup of school boards historically, and that they have tended to be dominated by business interests is well documented (Callahan, 1962; Counts, 1927; House, 1974; Kimbrough, 1969; Martin, 1991). As board members serve their terms, they may cast their votes in line with the wishes of individuals or groups who have come to them with a specific position in mind but present it as *their* position rather than that of their constituents. This is one example of indirect representation.

School people, particularly site- and district-level staff whose roles require contact with parents and community, learn to keep their ears open for rumblings. A Reston administrator said he believes that there is some room for experimentation in the schools, "unless there's an uprising in your community. *Then* I think the bureaucracy would step in and say, 'That's not the way we do things here.'" "Right now we have no delegations coming in to complain," said an Irvine principal, "but we know how far we can go—and we keep a finger in the wind."

Playing It Safe

In the final analysis, schools have to protect their base of community support. Even charter, experimental, or alternative schools can't vary too much from what the community recognizes as legitimate and familiar (Meyer & Rowan, 1977). After all, as Paul Mort noted in 1957 and it's still true today (in some places, maybe *more* so today), "It is the community as a whole,

including the school, that is the adapting organism—not the school system alone" (p. 183).

This being the case, failure to keep the community informed and involved when an innovation is being considered can create problems later
on. These may range from passive resistance to active hostility, but whatever develops, it cannot help but alter the change effort. Negative community reaction can kill a new program or practice, or it can lead to negotiation that will result in modifications. These, as I've said before, will always
be in the direction of *a return to the conventional*. It is interesting to note that
one of the reasons some of the schools that participated in the Eight-Year
Study failed to maintain the changes that they had achieved was that they
had *failed to include their communities* (Aikin, 1953; Redefer, 1950).

Like many restructuring schools of today, the Eight-Year Study schools
weren't just making small internal changes. They were attempting to alter
long-standing patterns of behavior and to implement changes that would
make the schools quite different from what the parents and wider community had experienced when *they* were in school. Without the vigorous
and *continuing* support of community leaders, parents, and the general
citizenry, changes in what Americans take for granted about how schools
should look and be run are bound to falter.

Tyack and Tobin (1994) tell of the formation of a new high school in
Portland, Oregon, in 1970, and of the outrage expressed by the surrounding community when its members began to understand what was being
planned. Flexible modular scheduling, including a considerable amount
of discretionary time for the students, seemed to be especially unpopular.
Parents whose children did not perform well blamed the modular scheduling, and—rightly or wrongly—many community members connected the
innovative schedule to lax discipline and lowering of standards. This happened not only in Portland but in other communities where foundation
grants were supporting educational change in the late 1960s and early
1970s. "Many communities grew tired of boat-rocking leaders and instead
wanted the comfort of stable old patterns of schooling. Most of the high
schools of tomorrow reverted back to the familiar grammar of schooling,"
Tyack and Tobin concluded (p. 474).

In assessing the impact of the Chicago reform efforts of the early 1990s,
Anthony Bryk et al. (1994) warn that during a period of transition, "a
school may look even worse when judged by old standards" (p. 78). This
is difficult for parents and community members to accept, and it isn't unusual for them to urge that the planned change be abandoned: The risk just
doesn't seem worth taking. Even school people may want to return to the
security of the old ways rather than continue to take tentative steps into

new territory. If they do so, the inhibiting forces of the deep structure will have won the day—again.

SUMMARY AND CONCLUSION

In this chapter, I have tried to sketch a picture of some of the ways in which parents and members of the community can have an impact upon efforts to introduce change in schools. A certain familiarity is expected. Therefore, even when a change proposal has included input from parent and community representatives, continuing acceptance of the change by the rest of the community is far from assured. After a few years a reaction may set in and, sooner or later, the change may be modified back toward the old, familiar practices.

Communities occasionally rise in contentious debate over a school-related issue that captures the attention of parents and nonparents alike. These episodes pass but can leave the school weakened. On the whole, however, observers find that citizen interest in the schools has been diminishing and that parents are not as involved in the life of their child's school as they used to be (Elam, 1996; Weil, 1997). Low voter turnout and other signs of popular disengagement from the processes of self-government are complex phenomena and become even more so when one begins to grasp the myriad ways in which they are related to seismic shifts in the national psyche (Elkind, 1995).

On a hopeful note, new models for public discourse around educational and other civic issues seem to be emerging. Danzberger and Friedman (1997), for example, describe a partnership between the organizations Public Agenda and the Institute for Educational Leadership. The development phase led to the identification of six "discussion-starter scenarios" such as those used by Paulo Freire, as well as a plan to use the "choice work" approach and a small-groups format within a time frame of about 4 hours. Pilot events were held during the 1996–97 year in 12 locations around the country, and it was clear from the follow-up survey responses that *people want to talk with their neighbors about important issues concerning their schools.*

Similar community forum models are being tested under the aegis of other organizations (Fishkin, 1995; Mathews, 1997). The Kettering Foundation and the National Issues Forums Institute, for example, each have been sponsoring such forums for some time. Annual summer institutes on how to engage in community dialogue and choice work have been offered by the Graduate School of Education at the University of Pennsylvania

(Sokoloff, 1996). Though supported by different agencies and not always explicitly focused on schooling issues, these models are quite similar in that they all seek to promote dialogue among the various groups in a town, municipality, or neighborhood. In this age when so much about our lives seems to separate us rather than bring us together, these conversations with our neighbors may help us rediscover the value of democratic discourse while we feel our way slowly toward a reaffirmation of a shared commitment to public education.

NOTE

1. "Americans are not really very enthusiastic about class education, but as parents we do want our children to get ahead whatever the cost: principles and other people's children be damned" (Bullough, 1988, p. 16). A 1990 study of middle-class mothers and how they justified the advantages they wanted schools to provide for their children found that "Most were attracted to socially inclusive, integrated ideas of education, but *were intent on having advantaged circumstances for their own children.* . . . Subtle ideological operations allowed them to deny advantage and explain the accomplishments of their offspring in a way that legitimated class privilege" (Brantlinger et al., 1996, pp. 589–590).

6

The Complexity of Teachers' Lives

Precollegiate teachers are caught in a system that keeps them on the run, overwhelming them with competing demands that often prevent them from having enough time and energy for the extra work involved in learning to practice their craft in different, more creative, and more satisfying ways. Under the circumstances, it's astonishing that so many teachers *do* manage to find spaces within which they can function, trying this way or that to help students learn more effectively. Despite all the barriers to success, many teachers do implement useful classroom-based changes. These are rarely changes that challenge the deep structure, however. And—partly for that reason, and partly because they *are* hidden "behind the classroom door"—they seldom draw public attention. Modest and unheralded as they may be, such successful changes can improve job satisfaction. That's important, because happy teachers who look forward to going to work each day are likely to have happy students who enjoy being with those teachers and learning from them (B. B. Tye, 1985).

The complexity of teachers' lives is mind-boggling. Not only that, but trying to describe it is like trying to hit a moving target—the daily life of a teacher is never static but is always emergent and dialectical (Davies, 1990). That acknowledged, nevertheless I shall try, in this chapter, to identify some of the pressures—both externally imposed pressures and those inherent in the nature of the profession—that inhibit changes that would alter the deep structure of schooling.

These can be roughly grouped into four categories. First are the characteristics of those who are attracted to teaching as a career. Second are the daily realities of the job itself. The norms and assumptions of the culture of teaching form a third category, and the related issues of personnel turnover and induction of newcomers is the fourth. The remainder of this chapter examines each of these and concludes by identifying some of the ways in which teachers, by employing resistance strategies as a matter of self-defense, can undermine even change efforts with which they basically agree.

125

HISTORICAL PERSPECTIVE:
WHO DECIDES WHAT TEACHERS CAN DO?

There have always been limitations to what a teacher can do. Much of this has been due to the public nature of the work: Being a teacher has always meant that, to some extent, both one's personal life and one's professional behavior were open to scrutiny. Every community kept an eye on its schoolmaster (Stuart, 1949), and the watchfulness intensified as women gradually replaced men behind the teacher's desk. Limitations were always there; what changed over time was who had the right to decide what they would be and the power to impose them.

As deep structure theory would suggest, this shift in the locus of educational decision-making was tied to changes under way in the society at large. It is not merely a coincidence that the industrial revolution, with its accompanying ethos of standardization and centralization, was happening at the same time. As we've seen in earlier sections of this book, both the efficiency of the assembly line and the emergence of the bureaucratic organizational structure had an inevitable impact on the still-malleable public schools. Beginning with the successful mid-19th-century campaign for the establishment of state and local boards of education and the regulation of normal schools for teacher training, many decisions about teaching have for at least the past 150 years been made by people other than classroom teachers. Today, when teachers in a school may not even know each other, let alone know or be known by the parents of their students, social vigilance has been replaced by formalized, standardized rules made by centralized authorities (Anderson, 1968).

The feminization of the teaching force that accompanied the growth of bureaucratic structures in the early 20th century exacerbated this trend to move decisions away from the grass roots. It was seen as inappropriate for female teachers to make substantive decisions; rather, they would follow orders generated by men in the superordinate system (Anderson, 1968; Darling-Hammond, 1997). In any case, historically teachers have been viewed as *employees*, not as autonomous professionals (Stiles & Robinson, 1973).

Classroom teachers, both male and female, are still living with this legacy, despite the increasing proportion of women in administrative positions: The bureaucratic structure of schooling tenaciously holds the old, paternalistic patterns in place. Indeed, as we saw in Chapter 3, that bureaucratic structure is one of the inhibiting forces that prevents significant change in how schools are run and, in this case, in who makes the decisions. A former student—now a teacher educator himself—reflecting upon his experiences teaching in an inner-city Los Angeles junior high school, commented that "virtually every facet of a teacher's life at the school [was] mandated by state or local education bureaucracies" (Yeo, 1997, p. 86).

TODAY: DESKILLED AND MARGINALIZED

In the context of our history, it comes as no surprise that today's teachers often feel marginalized; there is ample evidence that their experience and knowledge are devalued. The popular belief that teaching is a job that anyone can do has roots in our history. Not so long ago, it was literally true: In the early 1800s, anyone who *completed* elementary school could *teach* in an elementary school, with no additional schooling or training. A generation or two later, it was something that *even a woman could do*.

In the 20th century, the nation reached the point where almost all of its young were in school for 12 years, with the result that all of us have had plenty of time to watch various teachers at work: Now we're all *sure* that we know what it takes (Labaree, 1999). In addition, the media are fond of reporting studies showing that the "best and brightest" aren't entering teaching any more. In the public mind, the message is surely that today's teachers' views—even concerning their own work with our children—aren't very important. If anyone doubts this, he or she has only to reflect on the fact that whereas most Americans would accept their doctor's advice with no argument, they wouldn't hesitate to overrule the advice of their child's third-grade teacher.

Furthermore, Americans aren't sure if teaching is really a profession or not. Many educators seem to share this uncertainty, which amplifies the doubt in the public mind. Wasley (1991), in fact, considered the commonly accepted definitions of "professional practice" point by point and concluded that "Current research demonstrates that it is difficult to describe teaching using these definitions" (p. 17). Hargreaves (1994) suggests that teachers' work is becoming more *intensified*—more demanding, routinized, and time-consuming—but this doesn't necessarily mean it is becoming more professionalized. Meyer and Rowan (1983) acknowledge the *appearance* of professionalism, attributing it to the fact that teachers do have "much discretion within a loosely-coupled system," but argue that it is a myth (p. 81), and maybe they are right.

Whether teachers see themselves as professionals or not, and whether or not their work lives fit popular definitions of what it means to be a professional, there's no denying that they often aren't treated as professionals. Tyack and Cuban (1995) note that teachers are frequently left out of the loop when it comes to designing reform efforts. Hong (1996) tells the story of a school in which teachers were "excluded from the evaluation process as a matter of policy." Lieberman (1995) notes that traditional staff development that is top-down and unconnected to classroom life is both demeaning and inadequate to the challenges of contemporary schooling. In her 1994 report on teachers' working conditions for the Council for Basic Education, Harriet Tyson observed that even well-intended "teacher recognition" programs are condescending and serve to reinforce the low status of most teachers as they single out a few stars.

McLaren, Giroux, Apple, McCutcheon, and other critical theorists have been diligent in identifying ways in which the system deskills teachers and renders them voiceless. Not only are they voiceless within the context of their own work environment, but as they interact with the world beyond the school they are similarly silenced. Rob Weil (1997), a high school math teacher in Colorado, captures this perfectly:

> When teachers are asked to participate in discussions on school reform, they are frequently treated as foxes assigned to guard the henhouse. Perceived as thoughtless amateurs defending the status quo, teachers often find themselves the targets in these discussions rather than active participants. (p. 763)

As a nation, we pay a price for our mistreatment of teachers. "By silencing the voices from the field," notes Deborah Meier (1996), "we both undermine the growth of professional judgment and starve our public debate of the real stuff. We leave public discussion to public policymakers on one hand, and the often irritated anecdotes of dissatisfied customers on the other hand. Myths and rumors replace reason" (p. 188).

Taking a wider, more macrosocietal view, Martin (1991) proposes that teachers "are undergoing a process of proletarianization similar to that of other skilled workers in industry organized within the capitalist mode of production" (p. 354). Such an analysis suggests not only that teachers are *not professionals* but that their marginalization is an inevitable consequence of the type of socioeconomic system we have in this country. Other contemporary analyses imply that the system *intentionally* deskills and demoralizes teachers as a way of rendering them passive. Fatalism—the feeling that "nothing I could do will make things better"—may be *culturally constructed to serve the dominant order of things* (Leonard, 1990). Many see this as part of an ideological shift now under way in the United States to a libertarian viewpoint that defines the purposes of schooling almost exclusively in terms of the logic of the marketplace. Seen in this light, "the increasing adoption of management-type pedagogies has resulted in policy proposals that promote the deskilling of teachers and the creation of a technocratic rationality in which . . . the dominant model of the teacher becomes that of the technician or white-collar clerk" (McLaren, 1998, p. 6). Darling-Hammond

(1997) warns that "the further we push the twentieth-century model of educational management, the less well-served many students will be" (p. 21).

One could argue that no matter how marginalized teachers might feel, there is strength in numbers and power in collective action: The downward spiral can reverse, and morale can rise. Indeed, our own history shows us what *can* happen when educators act strategically and in concert to promote an innovation. For example, backers of the common school movement worked through groups and organizations, made use of the press, and held key leadership positions—and ultimately, they *won* (Cremin, 1951).

Could something similar happen today? On one hand, of course, the teachers' unions come to mind: A useful mechanism for collective action exists. Where teachers feel well represented by their local chapter, they may come together in common cause over a local issue. On the other hand, as Bruce Joyce (1982) has pointed out, some collective bargaining agreements can actually *serve the bureaucracy's purposes*. Clauses that limit the number of after-school meetings, for example—though they may protect teachers' health and sanity—also make it less likely that teachers will voluntarily stay after school to talk with each other or to organize a collaborative effort.

A final observation I want to make on this whole problem of the silencing, deskilling, and marginalization of teachers has to do with the responsibility/authority equation. In many organizations, as an employee I might accept responsibility for an added task, but I would expect to have the authority to make decisions about how and when the task would be completed. In fact, without that authority, I would refuse to accept the additional responsibility.

The same is not true of teaching, however. In recent years, the responsibility for student learning has shifted from the student to the teacher; but the teacher has not been given the authority to go along with this responsibility. Teachers are now to be held *accountable* but are not given the tools with which to produce the results—student success—that society desires. One of those tools would be the authority to use their own judgment in doing their job without interference. Ironically, then, holding teachers "accountable" lets students *off the hook*. Increasingly they tune out and assume less and less responsibility for their own education. This further undermines the teacher's authority in the classroom (Anderson, 1968; Tyson, 1994).

It's worth noting that the same dynamic applies to parent involvement: If student learning is seen as entirely the *teacher's* responsibility, parents are off the hook too. Teachers are left with no authority in their classrooms (beyond what they can muster by sheer force of personality) and little support from home. It's a recipe for a demoralized teaching force, guaranteed to produce exactly the opposite results from those we would all like to see in our schools.

TEACHERS' WORK LIVES

Our task is to understand the characteristics of the daily lives of teachers that, singly or in combination, act to obstruct the permanent adoption of innovation. We need to keep in mind, however, that the *kinds* of innovation we are addressing here are specific: They are attempted changes in elements of the deep structure, such as the traditional use of time and of space, mechanisms for sorting students, the subject-centered curriculum, the bureaucratic administrative structure, and so forth. As we see in Chapter 7, many changes can be successfully made that are local and well suited to a specific school and its community and that do not attempt to alter the deep structure.

Who Chooses Teaching?

It is beyond question that there are many, many wonderful dedicated and conscientious teachers in our elementary and secondary schools. As we shall see, they are doing vitally important work, in difficult conditions. All the same, research has revealed some characteristics of people who choose to become teachers, and these characteristics can, when mixed with the right blend of contextual features in a school, create a climate that protects rather than challenges the status quo.

A profile of the American teacher released in 1997 reveals that 87% of our teaching force is white; 73% is female; and the mean age in 1993–94 was rather high at 43 years. Nine out of ten were teaching in their proper fields of certification, and eight out of ten teachers expressed high satisfaction with their work (Henke, Choy, Chen, Geis, & Alt, 1997; Meek, 1998). What appears to be a contradiction—that 80% of American teachers express high satisfaction while at the same time feeling marginalized—may well be a function of how the questions were asked. Possibly, when asked about "job satisfaction," most teachers think first of their work with children. If the questioner were to dig deeper, perhaps defining "your job" as the whole array of tasks a teacher must do, my guess is that many teachers would want to qualify their original responses.

Then there is also the disquieting possibility that teachers can feel marginalized and voiceless *but not feel too bothered by it* as long as they can close that classroom door. To many, it simply might not matter that they aren't involved in school or district decisions, or even that the community doesn't hold them in very high regard. This would be an interesting area for further study.

Statistics, as always, tell only part of the story. We know that our images of what a teacher is and does are formed early in our lives, from our experience as students (Eisner, 1992). Without even realizing it, we all formed a pretty clear idea of both the routines of teaching and the behavior considered appropriate for teachers not only in the classroom and the school but in the community. It is this internalized set of images that permits the too easy popular assumption that "anyone" can teach. But that understanding is based only on what we were able to *see*, as students; and that, as it turns out, is also only part of the story. Decades of research into this subject, much of it by sociologists, provides us with additional insights (and food for thought). What are some of these insights about who chooses to become a teacher?

First, generally speaking, teaching appeals to those who were successful as students. One might consider this a benefit, because common sense suggests that such people will be happy to return as adults to an environment that they enjoyed as youngsters. But it could also be seen as detrimental, because such people may also be unwilling to make changes in a system that worked well for them and that they believe they understand (Lortie, 1975). In other words, we educators, by and large, are people for whom the deep structure of schooling is *not problematic*.

Second, four out of five teachers today are women (Goodlad, 1990). When women first began to enter the teaching force, the mores of society were such that, in most communities, female teachers were not permitted to marry. Therefore the majority only stayed a short while, and a pattern of short tenure became taken for granted, even after the marriage restrictions were abandoned. Teachers who do not see themselves as *permanent career professionals* may have little interest in investing time and energy in making changes for a career future they are unlikely to see; rather, they focus on the daily challenges of their work.

Third, it has long been recognized that most men who go into teaching do not intend to remain there (Mason, 1961). If they remain in education at all, they want to move into administrative roles where they find increased rewards in the form of higher pay and status and a different set of responsibilities. Interestingly, this entails a move from the loosely coupled environment of teaching to the tightly coupled, bureaucratic structure of administration. If they find that environment congenial, they are unlikely to want to change it much. As Lortie (1975) also noted, male teachers have a vested interest in preserving the administrative hierarchy into which they hope to move eventually. I would extend this to include those elements of schooling that form the bulk of the administrator's work: scheduling (use of time and the sorting of students); room assignments (use of space); and discipline (control of students). In a nutshell, the administrator is charged with operationalizing and defending the deep structure of schooling. Male or female, the person hoping to occupy that role is unlikely to support changes that will significantly alter those aspects of the enterprise.

Fourth, researchers who have studied career choice and personality point out that as a type of work attracts certain kinds of people, a typical "career atmosphere" is created. It, in turn, attracts more of the same kinds of people (Bowles & Gintis, 1976; Guba, Jackson, & Bidwell, 1959; Osipow, 1973; Stern, Stein, & Bloom, 1956). A number of characteristics commonly found in those who elect a life of teaching include some that tend to create a conservative, rather than an innovative, career atmosphere. Although there is no single personality that can be said to be that of *all* teachers, some traits seem common enough to be considered modal for the profession. For example, Jackson and Guba (1957) found that teachers as a group score high on need for deference, need to yield to others' judgment and leadership, need for order, avoidance of change, conformity to custom, and avoidance of the unconventional.

As long ago as 1932, Waller observed that the nature of the work culture of teaching discourages the energetic and creative and encourages the reticent. Stiles and Robinson (1973), likewise, propose that change-oriented people are unlikely to be attracted to teaching because they see the adult work environment of the school as too limiting and static. Giroux (1985) contends that teacher training programs fail to produce reflective practitioners, instead producing teachers who are most interested in how-to-do-it and what-will-I-do-on-Monday. If Waller and the others are correct, however, the problem may be that most of the people who enter the teacher training programs in the first place simply aren't reflective by nature.

It is important to recognize that the teaching force did change somewhat during the early 1970s, as new teachers shaped by the idealism of that time entered the schools. Those who stayed are now the veterans, and many have remained fairly liberal through the years. Indeed, some have told me that they often find the new teachers of the 1980s and 1990s depressingly conservative as compared to their own generation. It appears that the more innovative teachers of the 1970s did not represent a permanent change in the characteristics of those attracted to a career in the classroom.

This may be somewhat less true in urban areas than in the rest of the nation, however, as more minority teachers have entered the profession in the cities and may bring a more critical perspective to their work (this would be an area for further study, particularly in view of some sociological evidence to suggest that upward-bound minorities are often—though not always—surprisingly conservative). Nevertheless, overall the teaching profession remains overwhelmingly (92%) white, reported Goodlad in 1990. White, middle-class women dominated the profession all through the 20th century.

Fifth, the matter of workplace autonomy is pertinent. After analyzing the data that he had collected in his study of teachers in five towns in the Boston area, Lortie (1975) speculated that people who choose careers in teaching are attracted by the autonomy inherent in the job. From the days of the one-room schoolhouse to the present, teachers did not *have* to work together: Given a group of students and a more or less quiet place, we can do our job by ourselves. This "separation and low task interdependence," to use Lortie's terminology, may actually attract people who would *rather not* work collaboratively (p. 15). I suspect that this may be even more true of secondary than of elementary teachers. Grant and Sleeter (1996), for example, found that the junior high teachers in their study did not discuss teaching with each other, and "viewed teaching as something one does and learns about alone" (p. 131).

To conclude this section I refer to a 1977 essay by Charles Weingartner, in which he takes a broader perspective on career choice. Weingartner reminds us that language and its metaphors shape the policies people conceive; that educational policy has been shaped by the systems language of 20th-century industrial management; that personalities who crave certainty find this kind of language attractive; and that many such types can be found at all levels of educational decision-making. There is some evidence that we teachers are comfortable in our assigned roles and are quite willing to leave the decisions to the bureaucrats—if they will leave us alone to do our work with children.

The Daily Realities of the Job

What Lieberman (1995; see also Lieberman & Miller, 1984) calls the "dailyness" of teachers' work is shaped by, among other things, structural factors, resource issues, the press of competing demands, and interactions with administrators.[1] In order to cope, teachers make use of a number of defense mechanisms. A few of these are healthy and constructive; others are less so. Some, while physically or emotionally necessary, have the effect of stifling change efforts.

Structural Factors. Structural factors are those aspects of schooling that form the framework within which teachers work. Waller (1932), for example, identified the *rhythms* of the teacher's life—and it's quite true: For an educator, the new year begins in September, not January 1. As it unfolds, it has a beat all its own (distinctively different, I suspect, from that of other careers). The rhythm of the academic year can inhibit deep structure change simply because the times of relative calm and receptivity to trying something new alternate with longer periods of frantic activity and absolute overload. This leads us to the reality of competing demands, to which we turn in a moment.

Another structural reality that shapes a teacher's day is the nature of the student body with which he or she must work. It may seem odd to think of students as a "structural" element, but the term is appropriate in terms of demographic characteristics. There is some evidence to suggest, for example, that teachers' lives differ depending on the social class of the community in which they work. Student attitudes, shaped by their socioeconomic status and related visions of their probable futures, greatly affect the adult work environment of the school (Metz, 1990). Schools that have a large proportion of students who see no hopeful future for themselves are likely to be difficult places to teach (and may attract a different kind of person from the more typical teacher described in the previous section). As Apple (1995) has observed, teachers in *any* school have to deal with some students who simply reject everything the school stands for, but there are more of them in poor communities: Poverty has a way of making hope seem far away. According to Anyon (1995), many teachers in such schools *recognize* the structural basis that promotes the failure of their students, so they are skeptical of reform proposals that all too often fail to get at root causes and focus only on alleviating symptoms of the problem.

The very *size* of a school, regardless of its relative poverty or affluence, is a third structural factor that affects the daily experiences of all those who spend their days in that building. Not everyone agreed with Conant when, in the 1950s, he traveled the country promoting the consolidation of schools and districts. Within a decade, the strengths of large schools were acknowledged, but their weaknesses were also being identified (Anderson, 1968; R. G. Barker & Gump, 1964). More recently, Bruce O. Barker (1986) reminds us that not only are smaller schools more humane and personal environments where students (and adults, for that matter) are less likely to feel isolated but also change is easier to implement in such environments. There is "less red tape and fewer regulations. . . . Bureaucratic layering is at a minimum, allowing relatively easy access between students, teachers, and administrators" (p. 7).

Deborah Meier (1998), founder of the Central Park East Secondary Schools in Harlem and subsequently principal of the Mission Hill School in Boston, would agree. Linda Darling-Hammond (1997), writing about a high school in New York City, observes that the school's teachers believe that its small size is one of the reasons it has been successful. Smaller schools may have problems, but those problems are more visible and easier to solve because such schools are, by definition, less complex organizations. There is no comparison—in terms of organizational complexity—between the

Ohio high school of 400 students where I taught in 1971 and the California high school of 2,000-plus where I taught in 1989.

Finally, one of the findings of the Study of Schooling was a connection between teachers' job satisfaction and the amount and intensity of problems they perceive their school to have (Goodlad, 1984; Overman, 1980; B. B. Tye, 1985). This is a correlation that seems almost too obvious. Every teacher who has worked in a troubled school intuitively understands how hard it is to focus on one's work—let alone love it—if a steady barrage of problems, many unrelated to the teaching/learning process, claims one's constant attention. I view this as a structural factor insofar as it shapes the teachers' daily lives in significant ways and is *always there, needing to be dealt with*. There is little doubt that the pull of coping with problems distracts teachers from becoming fully involved in school improvement efforts. We return to this in a moment, when we consider the reality of competing demands in more depth.

Before leaving this topic, however, I want to make it quite clear that it isn't only poor schools that have distracting problems. Even an elegant, affluent suburban school can be a troubled place. It's interesting that the teachers who were a part of Lortie's 1975 "Five Towns" Study, when interviewed again 20 years later, reported that the problems at their Boston area schools are worse now: more numerous, more intense, and more serious (Cohn, Kottcamp, McCloskey, & Provenzo, 1987).

Resource Issues.

It is not that American teachers and students cannot succeed when they are well supported, it is that the system fails to support so many of them.
                                                Darling-Hammond (1997, p. 27)

If any reader doubts Darling-Hammond's charge of nonsupport, he or she has only to read the discouraging chapter on the working conditions of American teachers in Harriet Tyson's 1994 report, mentioned earlier. Tyson lists, among other things, the perennial problems of low pay, large classes, lack of supplies, absence of administrative support, no telephones, no quiet place to work, unsafe school buildings, and mundane chores that are "more galling than yesterday's (chopping wood and stoking the stove)" (p. 120).

The fundamental question about resources as they relate to educational change is this: When teachers fail to get even the most basic materials they need to do their regular job on a day-to-day basis, how can policymakers, ordinary citizens, or anyone else ask them to do the *extra* work required to

implement a new project or make a change in how something is done at
the school? Two teachers at an Irvine middle school confessed when I
visited their campus that they often feel frustration and anger when they
see funds going to new "reforms" when worthwhile efforts already in place
aren't getting the support they need. I have every reason to suspect that
such feelings are fairly widespread among American teachers.

At the beginning of this chapter I mentioned the connection between
happy teachers and happy, productive students and raised the question
of why our society invests so little in making our teachers feel valued.
Being sure they have what they need in order to do good work—not only
materials and equipment but space and time as well—seems a logical
starting point. Of course, that is a normative statement (what *should* be);
the descriptive reality is—unfortunately—much different. And it is to the
real, rather than to the ideal, that we must address ourselves in understanding how the deep structure actually works to defeat change in our
schools.

When the Howard County, Maryland, School District got its very first
planning grant to develop new schools for Columbia, it sent a team to visit
innovative schools in other parts of the country. One of the things they
noticed was that where teachers were treated well, they were happy and
very productive. So the team came back and recommended that the planned
high school include a partial third story basically for the teachers—a lounge,
a lunchroom, and work space. The architects drew up blueprints that included these spaces. Four years later, when two showcase elementary
schools and one innovative middle school had been built and it was time
to construct the high school, those spaces were the first to go. Investing in
teacher satisfaction wasn't high on the board's list of priorities by then. The
new high school was still an exciting building. But deep structure assumptions about the appropriate use of space in a "real school" had effectively
prevented anything truly innovative from being done for the teachers.

Competing Demands. The school day hasn't changed a great deal since
midcentury—the "official" day is still around 6 hours long. What *has*
changed is the extent of society's expectations as to what will be included
in that 6 hours. The role of the school has expanded enormously in the
past 50 years. There are more demands competing for teachers' time,
attention, and energy than can possibly be accommodated in the hours
available. New tasks and responsibilities are being assigned to the schools
every year.[2]

Consequently, most teachers spend more than 7 hours a day at school
and more than 40 hours a week on the job. Some teach an "x period" early
in the morning, some supervise extracurricular activities after school, many

stay late to prepare lessons, grade papers, attend meetings, give extra help to students who need it, or meet with parents. Unable to complete everything even within an extended workday, a great many also take hours of work home. Here are just a few of the teacher voices I heard during my visits to schools in Reston and Irvine:

> The meeting was to take place at 2:45, but only Barry was able to be there. Santos explained that he and Edna had unexpected things to take care of.

> We have two weeks of parent conferences coming up, so no time for extra meetings until after that.

> International Awareness Day might not go this year because of the number of additional activities going on at the school. . . . Part of the problem is that Maggie and Eva don't have the same conference period, and they have too many additional responsibilities after school.

> We were told that Gary, who was really interested in the project, was not there because he is a track coach and was at a meet.

It is within this high-pressure context that somehow time must be found for implementing changes. The very situation renders success unlikely. The deep structure of schooling prevents radical restructuring in the use of school time. For example, in some parts of the country year-round schools are taking hold, but not without controversy. Efforts to include student-free or early-release days at regular intervals have likewise been unpopular with parents. A logical solution—the 11- or 12-month contract, with nonteaching time for professional development, site-based improvement projects, and the like—has never been seriously considered by policymakers (Goodlad & Klein, 1974; Goodlad, 1990). So powerful is the press of time on school people that even if no other deep structure forces were involved (conventional wisdom, bureaucratic structures, fiscal constraints, parent expectations, the culture of teaching), the *lack of time alone* is often enough to bring down a promising new program.

> School reform takes more time than is typically allotted to it. . . . Our study has found that most mainstream administrators, school boards, and taxpayers underestimate how much time is needed for school faculty members to [try, evaluate, and incorporate new processes and methods] . . . and to maintain simultaneously the daily functioning of the school. (Adelman & Pringle, 1995, p. 29)

Interestingly, it isn't enough to say that if teachers get more discretionary time in the school day or week to use for planning and preparation, the problem of competing demands will be alleviated. Hargreaves's (1994) study of increased preparation time shows that more time can sometimes have the opposite effect. It "created a proliferation of meetings and additional work that intensified teachers' work still further, and subjected them to further administrative control instead of releasing them to develop things themselves" (p. 137). Damned if we do, damned if we don't—when it comes to time, it almost seems we can't win. Usually there's not enough; if somehow more is found, it quickly fills up with the regular work overload. Only very rarely is it used for new initiatives, and when it is, after a year or two even that slips away.

The Front Office. How a teacher feels about his or her principal and the other administrators in the building forms the fourth and final reality of the teacher's daily work life that I want to discuss in this section. As was mentioned in Chapter 3, studies show fairly definitively that much of the tone and nuance of a school can be directly attributed to the leadership style of the principal. The ambiance—whether supportive or tyrannical—pervades the workplace and affects the day-to-day interaction of teachers with each other, with other adults, and with their students.

As a rule, the principal does not play a personally active role in the work of teachers, who feel that they get most of their ideas from their colleagues and monitor their own job performance themselves. They don't rely much on the judgment or suggestions of site administrators (Lortie, 1975).

Teachers don't go their own way entirely, however. There is ample room for disagreement and interpersonal friction between teachers and administrators, and when things are not working smoothly in a school, personality differences that ordinarily would be overlooked emerge to exacerbate the situation (Cusick, 1992). Adding to the dissonance is the likelihood that teachers and administrators actually *see their world quite differently* (Kleine-Kracht & Wong, 1991; Shen, 1998). This is important insofar as attempts to innovate are concerned, because what looks like an attractive new program to an administrator may not look all that promising to those who will have to implement it (House, 1974). At that point, whether reluctant teachers will agree to give it a try or will resist adoption of the new program may depend on how they feel about the administrator as a person and as a legitimate authority figure in the school. From the work of Raven and French (1957, 1958a, 1958b) in this area, we know that teachers do what the principal asks of them for a variety of reasons, some more constructive than others.

Of course, the opposite can also happen: Teachers may be enthused about a new program, but the principal is not. In such a case, the principal might make use of language that casts doubt upon the program's value, workability, or cost, or the likelihood that it will be approved by the board of education. Such disparagement sets the boundaries of what the administrator considers acceptable and effectively dampens teacher enthusiasm (Hargreaves, 1984; Joyce, 1982). Whether resistance originates with the teachers or with the principal, the move to abandon a change can sometimes be traced to the nature of the relationship between the faculty and the administrators.

The Culture of Teaching

The field of sociology has established that every culture and subculture has explicit and implicit norms that guide behavior for that group, and the culture of teaching is no exception. Blase and Anderson (1995), for example, have cited studies that yield the following list of norms within the culture of teaching: friendliness, sociability, mutual support, faculty loyalty and solidarity, noninterference, and control of students. However, they also remind us that although values and norms can be identified, they are not neat conceptual boxes containing discrete behaviors; rather, there is a continuum of variation for each.

I concentrate on just four areas in which normative expectations clearly shape the lives and actions of teachers—conservatism, collegiality, egalitarianism, and autonomy—and will try to show how each of the four can discourage innovation. Strange as it may seem, the deep structure also acts through the behaviors of teachers themselves.

Conservatism. Teachers are people who can be liberal or even radical politically and still be very conservative when it comes to their work.[3] We don't usually think of ourselves in these terms, although most of us are aware of the work of others who study and write about teacher behavior. It doesn't surprise us to be reminded that we tend to teach as we were taught and to replicate the learning experiences our own teachers used successfully with us (Cuban, 1984). Nor are we very disturbed to be told that our teacher training programs, for the most part, prepared us to fit into the system and do our part to maintain it. And finally, we know that the culture of the school reinforces what we learned in our teacher training programs (Sarason, 1991) and inhibits deviation from deeply rooted norms. We are rapidly socialized into this environment (Joyce, 1975), the more so precisely because it *is* familiar to begin with.

What we are less eager to consider is the possibility that we may have a conservative streak in our own personalities, which is part of why we were attracted to this profession in the first place. We knew what we were getting into, and we didn't want any surprises.

> The system is geared to self-preservation, not to self-renewal . . . challenging the behavior patterns of adults is a task of formidable dimensions, especially when present patterns have been carefully taught through a long, structured system of schooling and are endorsed and protected by the system. (Goodlad & Klein, 1974, pp. 100, 102)

One of the reforms now being tried in many parts of the country involves the establishment of professional development schools (Darling-Hammond & McLaughlin, 1995). These are elementary and secondary schools that collaborate with a local teachers college or university school of education in the induction of new teachers. The very best veteran teachers the system can offer are matched with newcomers and, in theory, their collaborative efforts are expected to yield improved teaching for both, not simply a routine introduction to the status quo such as happens in the usual student teacher / master teacher relationship. The necessary keystone of this edifice, however, is the willingness of the veteran teachers to define themselves as ongoing learners and that, I suspect, is much more easily said than done. As one of the Irvine district administrators put it, "Our veteran teachers are more interested in stability than in shaking the tree."

Venturing into new ways of preparing lessons, managing the classroom, and relating to students and colleagues would be, by definition, uncomfortable for most of us if we are, indeed, fairly conservative about our work. Wilford Aiken (1942), director of the Eight-Year Study, observed that not all teachers in the participating schools were happy about the experiment. To some, he noted, "the Study was an unnecessary and dangerous innovation." He added, "No school is ready to advance until teachers have a sure sense of security in adventure. They are safe in following tradition; they must be sure that they will be equally secure in departing from tradition" (p. 130).

Lieberman and Miller (1984) make the point that "teachers must be able to use innovations in a practical way. Their cry that ideas are 'too theoretical' speaks . . . to the complexity of keeping the classroom operable while incorporating new ideas" (p. 102).

The conservatism of the profession, then, can legitimately be seen as a function of contextual pressures as well as early socialization via schooling, the nature of teacher preparation programs, and induction into the norms of the profession. Together, these realities present a formidable barrier to the adoption and successful, *permanent* implementation of change.

Collegiality. Collegiality, "those behaviors appropriate among people who work together," can be an important source of teacher satisfaction. In the case of K–12 teachers, the term implies friendliness and mutual support, including sharing, helping, advising, giving praise and recognition, and empathizing. Another definition includes talking about practice, observing each other teach, working on curriculum together, and sharing what we know with each other (Little, 1981). Collegiality also includes self-control, an important part of what Blase and Anderson (1995) call "diplomatic" behavior among teachers. Their choice of the term *diplomatic* underscores the fact that teaching is a job and schools are a work environment. Although friendships among teachers are not discouraged, neither are they necessary for the work to continue in a harmonious way: It is enough that everyone behave tactfully, diplomatically, and with self-control.

Little's (1990) comprehensive analysis of the literature on collegiality provides two useful frameworks for thinking about this aspect of the culture of teaching. The first involves making a distinction between *weak* and *strong* ties between colleagues, as a way of examining the degree to which they do or do not influence each others' classroom practices. From this angle, it would seem likely that most collegial ties between teachers are likely to be weak.

The second presents a continuum from *independence* to *interdependence*. Little (1990) concludes that independence is the dominant pattern and that "individualism, presentism, and conservatism" are the prevailing cultural norms. She points out that teachers don't see each other as essential to their work in the same way that, for instance, brain surgeons, baseball players, or symphony orchestra musicians must. In the final analysis, she challenges the assumption that collegiality is always desirable and constructive:

> Closely bound groups are instruments both for promoting change and for conserving the present. Changes, indeed, may prove substantial or trivial. Finally, collaborations may arise naturally . . . but often they appear contrived, inauthentic, grafted on, perched precariously (and often temporarily) on the margins of real work. (pp. 509–510)

Hargreaves (1991, 1992) provides a similar insight in suggesting that "collegiality" can be used to co-opt teachers into supporting goals or programs, or both, imposed by others. It can, in fact, be "contrived," in much the way that Little describes: imposed, regulated, monitored, bounded as to acceptable topics and initiatives, and implementation-oriented. Surface issues and one-shot events can characterize efforts at "collegiality." And that's fine with most teachers, who ask only for an upbeat and mutually supportive workplace within which to do their job—mostly by themselves, as we shall now see.

Autonomy. Arguably the strongest norm in the culture of teaching is the norm of autonomy. It is deeply entrenched for historical, structural, and psychological reasons. "Throughout the long, formative decades of the modern school system," observes Lortie (1975), "schools were organized around teacher separation rather than teacher interdependence" (p. 14). Images of the one-room schoolhouse and the durable "egg-carton" school design come to mind. Physical isolation was reinforced by a schedule that tended to limit the time teachers had for talking with—let alone working with—each other.

Psychologically, the attraction to a career that promises a degree of independence has already been mentioned. "Like most people who work, teachers want control of their working lives . . . there is a strongly-held belief in the right to close one's door and do whatever one thinks is appropriate with a particular group of students" (Parish & Aquila, 1996, p. 300). However, as Cuban (1984) reminds us, the degree of true autonomy that teachers have is actually quite narrow. Many basic decisions about instruction are made by others, and those that remain for individual teachers to make are extremely limited: the arrangement of furniture, how students will be grouped for instruction, who should talk and when, what learning activities will be used, and the like. One might speculate that this is why, although teachers sometimes complain about what we perceive as isolation, we nevertheless "struggle fiercely to maintain it" (Joyce, 1982, p. 48). What little room we have to see ourselves as active, independent professionals must be guarded against any further encroachment, even by our colleagues.

Speaking of colleagues, Hargreaves (1992) suggests that there are four broad types of teacher culture that might be found in any given school: individualistic, balkanized, collaborative, and what might be termed contrived/collegial. Of these, two—the individualistic and balkanized—involve high levels of autonomous behavior. Only the collaborative culture is truly constructive, says Hargreaves, and unfortunately it is both rare and difficult to sustain over time because it "goes right against the grain of all the pressures and constraints that normally come with teachers' work" (p. 227). The culture of individualism is far more common. A later analysis by Hargreaves (1994) proposes that the individualistic culture is complex, and includes not only the structural constraints already mentioned (architecture, overcrowding, and scheduling) but also "strategic" individualism—when teachers use whatever extra time they have to attend to their own classroom tasks rather than to attend meetings or work collaboratively—and "elective" individualism, which he calls "the principled choice to work alone" (p. 172).

Hargreaves's (1994) use of the word *principled*, however, suggests a level of reflective self-awareness that may be uncommon among American teachers. Remove that word and one is left with, simply, the "choice to work alone." It is more comfortable not to be watched while one does one's job. Free from scrutiny, each of us is left to rely on our own experience and knowledge base in running our classrooms. Our self-selected isolation separates us from sources of new knowledge, be they contact with other educators or with new ideas in the literature, at conferences, and so forth (B. B. Tye & K. A. Tye, 1984). Eisner (1992) calls this "secondary ignorance"—when you don't know that you don't know (p. 393). Tyson (1994) suggests that the norm of autonomy prevents teachers from knowing about the successful practices of their peers because "An unwritten rule in the . . . American school culture is that teachers should report neither their successes nor their failures to others" (p. 178). No wonder that what works well in one classroom is almost impossible to replicate in others (Pauly, 1991).

Although the system of extrinsic rewards in the teaching profession discourages teacher solidarity and strengthens individualism, it is really the intrinsic rewards of teaching that cement the norm of autonomy into place. "Many teachers gain their deepest satisfaction from their own classroom. . . . They are not particularly interested in collaboration" (Eisner, 1992, p. 395). As a result, teachers—especially at the secondary level—tend to live by an educator's version of the Golden Rule: I'll give you your space if you'll allow me mine (Grant & Sleeter, 1996). Noninterference is the inevitable companion of autonomy in the culture of teaching.

We purchase this freedom with occasional displays of teamwork. Sensing that the system wants a show of collaboration—for example, to demonstrate that a particular innovation is working—we play the game, giving some time to site-based management, shared decision-making, and other cooperative efforts. But given a choice, few of us would abandon our professional independence, limited as it may be.

> *Sporadic and superficial interchange may be sufficient . . . to sustain the "logic of confidence" that both enables teachers' largely independent existence and warrants the absence of scrutiny.*
>
> Little (1990, p. 531)

This may be part of the reason so many innovations that rely on collaboration fade after awhile. For example, the norm of autonomy underlies teachers' reluctance to engage in peer coaching on a sustained, permanent basis. Observation of other teachers may be fine while one is a trainee, but once credentialed, the urge to observe and be observed quickly fades. Peer coaching has been tried on and off over the years and, in many districts, has been popular—for awhile. Given a choice, though, most teachers would probably be just as happy to use their time for what they see as more urgent matters. Even the most enthusiastic teachers let it go after awhile.

Other forms of professional collaboration, too, give way eventually to the norm of autonomy. As Fraley (1981) noted in her study of democratic classroom projects,

> Team teaching or any other plan for integrated curriculum means only that the teacher no longer can simply teach as individual conscience directs but must, in effect, merchandise all ideas and plans and justify them to the other members of the team for approval before work can proceed. . . . Little wonder that attempts to integrate studies are soon reduced to live and let live arrangements. It has been tried in many forms, from teams of two to whole schools, and the institution of school could not accommodate it as an ongoing program structure. (p. 174)

Teachers are well aware of the hidden costs of collaboration, particularly of the added time and energy required to work in teams. Goodlad (1975) and his team of researchers found in the mid-1970s that teachers in the League of Cooperating Schools "spoke favorably of principals who placed no demands on them for matters beyond the confines of their own classrooms . . . improvement activities of this kind apparently threaten certain regularities in schools; those involved are regarded as rate busters whose efforts, if institutionalized, will create new expectations for everyone else" (p. 62). Goodlad (1990) also blames the regularities of teacher training programs—which fail to prepare future teachers to work collaboratively or to instill any sense of group identity—for reinforcing the norm of autonomy.

Finally, the norm of autonomy reinforces and is reinforced by the loosely coupled nature of schooling at the instructional level, which was explored in Chapter 3. "Classrooms are loosely connected, and the schools in many districts are loosely joined to one another. Instruction is the least controlled activity," Lieberman and Miller (1984) remind us. "This is a key understanding . . . for it is at the heart of most school improvement projects" (p. 101).

Egalitarianism. One of the distinctive characteristics of teaching as a career is its pervasive and deeply rooted egalitarianism. Tyack and Cuban (1995) tell the story of the early 20th-century battle for the single pay schedule for teachers, a useful case study of the egalitarian ethos in K–12 education. Prior to World War I a teacher might have been hired, fired, and paid based on arbitrary or locally idiosyncratic criteria. Lobbying efforts in the 1920s and 1930s, however, resulted in laws mandating equal pay for elementary and secondary teachers and for male and female teachers as well. Educators discovered that "equal pay improved morale and eliminated or decreased what they called 'class distinctions' between secondary and primary teachers" (p. 128).

Today, although novice teachers express dismay at the low beginning pay and veteran teachers sometimes grumble about the low salary ceiling for even the most experienced, few would be willing to abandon the single schedule that equalizes pay for elementary and secondary levels and by gender. Similarly, there is little support for periodic efforts to adopt systems of "merit" pay for exceptional performance. Because the water level is low everywhere, most teachers feel that if one boat is to rise, all boats should rise. Outsiders, to whom merit pay seems to make perfect sense, fail to understand the dynamics of teaching. In particular, they cannot see how competition—so valued in other aspects of American life—can be distinctly counterproductive in the teaching-learning context. "Promoting competition among colleagues," Johnson (1990) has observed, "would reduce rather than increase the productivity of schools because teachers would conceal their best ideas and pursue their own interests rather than the general good" (p. 125).

Teachers resist being pitted against each other; and they also are sometimes uncomfortable when colleagues step outside the fraternity by being put in the spotlight or by taking on semi-administrative roles (project coordinator, teacher-in-charge, consultant, or the like). "I have concluded that the egalitarian ethos of teaching," comments Wasley (1991), ". . . makes it problematic for teachers to perceive their colleagues as experts" (pp. 166–167). Wasley concludes that the role of teacher leader *can* work, but only in site-specific, "contextually bound" ways—in other words, it can be successful in one school but not in another. This is likely to be frustrating to reformers, who assume too readily that what works in one place can work elsewhere.

The norm of egalitarianism causes good ideas and successful practices to spread erratically rather than systematically, because there is no way to ensure that an innovation will be implemented on any but an individual, trial-and-error basis. As a teacher at a school in Reston, Virginia, told me, "Teachers would rather 'keep their light under a bushel,' as the saying goes, than seem to be uppity or 'better than the next guy.' If I've got something that works well, I'd better be careful about how I talk about it in the teacher's room . . . if I seem too proud of it, I'll be stepping over that line to where I'll be considered a show-off. And then *nobod*y will take a look at what I'm doing, even if it's just great."

Loss of Leadership and the Induction of Newcomers

What happens to a new program or a new way of doing something when those who initiated and supported it move on? The closely related issues of teacher turnover and the induction of newcomers are the fourth and final aspect of the work lives of teachers to be explored in the context of this study. It's a familiar story: The charismatic leader leaves—often wooed away, to weave his or her magic elsewhere. Time and again the loss of leadership has weakened a project's chances of becoming institutionalized. If the one who leaves is a teacher, the total energy and time devoted to the project decline—even if other teachers remain to tend the flame. If it is an administrator, the project loses its public advocate, its spokesperson to the superordinate system and the community.

Readers will recall from the community profiles in the Introduction that when the town of Columbia was taking shape, teachers for the first school were hired 6 months before the school actually opened. A particular kind of teacher, one who welcomed the chance to work in an innovative setting and was something of a risk-taker, was sought; the district even recruited out of state. Then, there was plenty of time to prepare together to implement the new approaches. Consequently, the members of that pioneer faculty formed a lively sense of ownership and were conscious of being trailblazers. In the years since then, as one of them described to me in a 1994 interview,

> When the first of us left, the new teachers who came must have felt sort of "out of it," because most of us were still devoted to what we were trying to do. A bit further on, when it got to about half and half, it was unfortunate because there was kind of an "us and them" feeling. I must say, we—the oldtimers—contributed to that too because we felt that the original vision belonged to us, not to them. And now, with only a few of us left, most everything has been modified somewhat and some of the things we used to have — differentiated staffing, for instance—are completely gone.

Sometimes people can "leave" without actually going away, as Stan Corey, the first superintendent in Irvine, explained when interviewed in 1995:

> The dynamic development of programs depends on extraordinary human effort on the part of the key people who are leading or moving the effort. Ultimately, all people get tired. Which may be one of the key factors in regression to the mean in institutional life: people get old and people get tired. The exceptional people wait a very long time to get old and tired, but . . . it happens.

What Corey didn't say was that even young people can get tired, and that educators of any age who give 100% to their work and another 100%

to implementing a new program can reach the point where they simply must pull back: In that sense, they "leave."

Teacher leaders also leave as a result of a district's policy of letting a transferred principal take some teachers along to the new school. At one fell swoop an innovation can be stripped of some of its strongest supporters. That might not be so bad, if mechanisms are in place to enlarge the support base among the remaining teachers and to systematically initiate new faculty members into the project or practice. Too often, however, this doesn't happen. The induction of newcomers may be the very weakest link in the implementation and institutionalization of educational change.

One of the original teachers in Reston, reflecting on the absence of appropriate initiation for newcomers, had this to say about the teachers who were hired after the first few years:

> The new teachers did what any new teacher would do, which is to fall back on what you know: traditional methods, themes, all the stuff that's comfortable. If the kids are lucky and there's enough pressure and some sort of training, you might gradually learn to do the new things. But that has to be part of what's going on or you will be the traditional person in the innovative program.

Ever since I learned about the Eight-Year Study, I have heard that its findings were a casualty of World War II. The conventional wisdom among educators seems to be that if it hadn't been for the war, the implications of the study would have reached the popular press and made more of an impression—perhaps even changing the way universities screened applicants for admission. It's impossible to say what *might* have happened. But now I know that the failure of the Eight-Year Study to make even a small dent in the stranglehold of university admissions requirements over the high school curriculum wasn't due only to the distractions of the war: According to one of its original staff members, *no provision was made for the induction of new faculty into the innovative programs developed in any of the study schools—even those that were the most successful* (Redefer, 1950).

TEACHERS' DEFENSE MECHANISMS

Thus far, we have reviewed the history of teaching as a career, considered deskilling and marginalization, and analyzed the daily work lives of teachers. One last angle remains for us to ponder: the ways in which the defense mechanisms and coping strategies used by teachers to deal with the pressures of their work can also act as barriers to the success of new initiatives.

Coping with the Pressures of the Job

Behaving defensively is nothing new for American teachers: Willard Waller, in his classic 1932 study of teaching, identified a number of coping mechanisms used by educators in dealing with pressure and in adjusting their own behavior to the norms of the culture of teaching. A typology of teacher defense mechanisms that emerged as an outcome of a study of change with which I was involved included burnout, refusal, avoidance, withdrawal, and selective participation (B. B. Tye & K. A. Tye, 1992). The latter three, although defensive in nature, are not necessarily negative. They may even be seen as constructive, if one accepts the premise that each of us must make judgments about the allocation of our own limited time and energy.

Blase and Anderson (1995), exploring teachers' defense mechanisms, found that they "develop an acute sensitivity to both positive and negative forms of control and manipulation by others" (p. 68). They further proposed that teachers, feeling vulnerable as they do—the familiar "fishbowl" imagery is used—employ both *reactive* (protective) and *proactive* (efforts to influence others) defense mechanisms. When a colleague says, "I've learned to be careful about what I say about other teachers because it can get twisted so easily and it always gets back to them and we do, after all, have to keep on working together," this is *reactive* or *protective* behavior. At some other time, that same person might confide that "I've been able to get some extra materials for my science class by reminding the principal that our students will be better prepared for the state standardized tests coming up next semester." This is what Blase and Anderson call *proactive* or *influence* behavior. Both are defense mechanisms used in response to the micropolitical dynamics of the school in which that teacher works.

Another way in which teachers deal with the pressures of their work is by reacting fairly conservatively to proposals for reform. The public routinely mistakes this behavior for stubborn resistance to good new ideas, when in reality it may be simply a way of conserving energy for one's classroom responsibilities and other projects. Louis (1990) points out that the American penchant for educational change—some would say a never-ending search for a quick fix to each perceived problem—means a never-ending demand for energy, with the accompanying stress and possible burnout. And because the system seldom provides the necessary support for implementation—including time for reflection and adaptation undertaken by the whole group—there can sometimes be a feeling of being out there all alone. In this untenable position teachers may withdraw from active involvement, and the change slips out of sight. After enough such experiences with unsupported change efforts, it's little wonder that feelings of disillusion set in. All of this reinforces an understandable tendency to be very cautious about becoming too involved with the many new initiatives that appear every year.

Bliss and Mazur (1998), who studied change efforts at the intermediate level using a case study approach, found that *even teachers who are quite receptive* to a new program (in this case, the pilot-testing of a student-centered unit) can be anxious about trying something new. The quotes they cite reveal people who feel that the new program doesn't use their strengths, is too unstructured, puts their job security in jeopardy ("I have to think about my first-year evaluations," says the new teacher), and may not provide enough assessment data "to show parents if they ask." Some teachers may see a suggested innovation as a threat to their professional autonomy (Stiles & Robinson, 1973). These are not unreasonable concerns, and they may lead to "reasonable refusal."

Reasonable Refusal

> *Teachers are often reluctant to relinquish teaching repertoires that provide an important source of security for them. . . . Given the overload that teachers typically experience . . . economy of effort is an important value.*
> Elliot W. Eisner (1992, p. 611)

Of course, not all teachers respond conservatively. Robert H. Anderson, one of the consultants brought into the early stages of planning for the new schools in Howard County, Maryland, in the 1960s, recalls the meetings that were held to introduce the new vision to teachers already employed in the district: "Some just sat and watched, with their arms folded; but many of them were entranced by what they were hearing."

It would be a mistake to assume that teachers are always negative about proposed changes. In fact, most teachers try very hard to be positive, to give new initiatives a fair hearing, and to implement them if they possibly can, adapting as necessary to make them work in their own particular classrooms. According to Corcoran (1990), optimistic and constructive attitudes are more likely when teachers feel good about their work environment. That being the case, he concludes, "Policymakers need to listen carefully to what teachers are saying about their working conditions" (p. 162).

Although teachers are not always negative, conservative, or reluctant to try something new, it is also true that changes are not *always* good or desirable. Some are poorly thought out or badly designed, many leave key stakeholders out of the planning process, and many more (especially when mandated from policymakers distant from the school site) are incompatible with a school's real needs. Innovations bear the burden of proof: Why fix something that isn't broken? Viewed in this light, refusal might actually be an *appropriate* response to some of the bandwagons that come rolling through town:

> Across the nation there are teachers who have the wisdom to reject fashionable innovations that violate their sense of what their pupils need and instead to experiment on their own terms with reforms they believe in. (Tyack & Cuban, 1995, p. 132)

It is important to distinguish between resistance to change in general and resistance to a *particular* change. Resistance by teachers may well be specific to certain proposed reforms rather than a chronic negativity toward change of any kind (Hargreaves, 1992; Poole, 1991).

Not only must a judgment be made about the value of the change itself, but those responsible for implementing it must also assess the degree to which the necessary resources are likely to be forthcoming. This point has been made earlier, but it is also pertinent here: Teachers may in fact be eager to implement the change but still decide not to participate because the resources and the support that would be needed in order to do it well simply aren't there (McLaughlin, 1990). Once again, refusal may be reasonable.

Then, too, one must consider the matter of *time*. There simply isn't enough time to do everything: Choices have to be made. As Fullan (1991) reminds us, however, lack of time shouldn't simply be used as a convenient excuse: "It is not acceptable to say 'I cannot implement X' unless we can continue the sentence by saying 'because I am bringing about improvements in Y and Z'" (p. 347).

If it's a good change, if the resources and support are provided, and if it seems to require what the teachers judge to be a reasonable time commitment, a new project, program, process, or structure may stand a chance of being adopted. Teachers are also interested in whether it can be made to *work*, and whether it will be likely to *last*. These are some of the criteria used by teachers in determining whether to make a commitment to a specific change. Unfortunately, the criteria used by policymakers are seldom even in the same ballpark. "Problems that frustrate teachers on a daily basis . . . are being neglected as reformers focus on the big issues," observes Corcoran (1990, p. 160). "What people talked about downtown often failed to reflect the reality of schools or to have meaning for the people who worked in them," note Katz, Fine, and Simon (1997), who studied the Chicago school reforms of the 1990s (p. 136). Indeed, school improvements are often seen by practitioners as being political or in danger of becoming politicized (Lieberman & Miller, 1984). This alone could make teachers wary and kill an otherwise promising program.

Another reason teachers respond with caution to calls for change is that they understand that the problems of schools are chronic and systemic, whereas the proposed solutions often treat them as acute—that is, as amenable to a short-term treatment. It's as if one attempted to cure cancer with lots of liquids, a big dose of vitamin C, two antihistamine tablets, and a box of cough drops. In a day or two, your head cold would be gone, but you didn't have a head cold, and the cancer is still there. In a school, although a new program may be implemented, the underlying problem that it was designed to ameliorate may persist.

Against this reality—that the most serious problems of our schools are both chronic and systemic—policymakers nonetheless continue to press for quick results. When these are slow in coming, or do not resemble the outcomes that had been envisioned, school people are blamed. I really believe that Hord and Hall (1986) are right to warn that innovations should not be evaluated too soon—not, in fact, until teachers are using them *routinely*.

Forms of Resistance

An eager crusader may have announced, "We'll go this way!" but others stood calmly and patiently at the gate asking, "Why? What's over there?"
Hong (1996, p. 167)

Various studies over the years have shown that people go through discernible stages as they move toward adopting a change and making it part of their lives. One classic typology is that developed by Everett Rogers (1962) and refined by Ronald Havelock (1971). They propose that a group such as a school faculty consists of *innovators*, who are often in the forefront of any new project and who are recognized risk-takers; *early adopters*, also open to trying something new; and an *early majority*, who wait in the wings to see how their more adventurous colleagues are doing or if the change seems likely to stick. The *late majority* are resisters, and the *laggards* simply refuse to participate, and may even attempt to sabotage the program.

Although it might seem on the surface that educational change depends on the leadership of the innovators and the early adopters, that alone is not enough and, in fact, may do more harm than good. In more traditional schools, innovators and risk-takers aren't looked to by their peers as exemplars but as deviant (Rogers, 1965). Their support for a proposed change is sometimes the kiss of death, or it may provide the late majority and the laggards with an excuse not to participate: The change can come to be seen as "belonging to" a relatively small in-group (B. B. Tye & K. A. Tye, 1992).

Simply *not acting* can also be a form of resistance to change, and it can be used at any level of the system. New York City Schools' Experimental Elementary Program (EEP), which devoted $40 million to just 11 schools between 1969 and 1973, disappeared at the end of the funding period—as so many reforms seem to do. Warren (1978), who studied this project, reached the following conclusion:

> Those individuals and groups involved were professionals who knew well the resistances to change in the school system, and who saw them demonstrated repeatedly in EEP. Their choice NOT to act constituted a decision to let EEP die without ever having to call openly for the program's failure. . . . Those in positions of power did not overtly use their power to destroy a policy they did not want, but instead allowed the existing political bias as institutionalized in current practices to defeat the policy for them. (p. 161)

Joyce (1982) captured the spirit of resistance-by-inaction perfectly when he noted that "In education, teachers (and administrators) operate through unorganized passive resistance. They *just don't do it*"(p. 61).

Anyone who has ever become involved in trying to put a new program into place in a school has probably encountered the two-sided response of colleagues: Although both teachers and administrators express overt *support* for the project, they engage in covert resistance and inaction at the same time (Wasley, 1991). Tyson (1994) observed another way in which this happens: "The faculty studies the situation to death and keeps on doing what it was doing before" (p. 183).

Eicholz (1963) developed a typology of rejection that can be used to classify and understand different forms of resistance to the implementation of a new program, process, or structure: Some resist out of ignorance of what the proposed change involves; others suspend their judgment; and others may refuse for situational or personal reasons. Maurer (1996) identified additional signs of active resistance, some of them quite unpleasant but all of them familiar: confusion, denial that a problem exists, malicious compliance, sabotage, too-easy agreement, changing the subject, silence, and in-your-face criticism. It has been my experience that usually resistance, when it does occur, is passive and fairly quiet because such behavior is more in keeping with the culture of the teaching profession.

SUMMARY AND CONCLUSION

We have examined the work lives of teachers in our elementary and secondary public schools in some detail. Within its historical context, the relatively marginal role of teachers in contemporary society was acknowledged. We found that, on the whole, the teaching profession in the 20th century has been composed primarily of fairly conservative people—mostly white, middle-class women—whose chief source of satisfaction comes when they can close the door and work with their students without interference. The day-to-day press of structural factors, limited resources, competing demands, and relationships with administrators was found to limit the amount of reform that most teachers will tolerate.

Four powerful norms within the culture of teaching—conservatism, collegiality, autonomy, and egalitarianism—can dramatically affect the success or failure of reform efforts. Teachers are cautious (often rightly so), concerned about the reaction of colleagues to any step toward the new and untried; and uncomfortable about being observed at work. There seems to be a very strong feeling that one mustn't place oneself too far outside the group or be too adventurous in trying new things.

Personnel turnover can have a devastating impact upon the continuation of a new program or practice, and a viable mechanism for inducting newcomers into the effort to keep the flame alight is seldom found. Finally, we saw that various defense mechanisms and coping strategies used by teachers to deal with the pressures of their work can also act as barriers to the success of new initiatives.

Looking at our profession using descriptive lenses, and making an effort to avoid speaking of how things *could* or *should* be, is difficult. But it enables us to see ways in which the culture of teaching contains, within itself, forces that prevent any significant alteration in the deep structure of schooling as it exists today.

I trust it is clear that I view teaching as an incredibly demanding job, more often than not performed in difficult circumstances with a myriad of context-specific challenges. Within this daily reality, educators are forced to be selective about how they allocate what little spare time and energy they may have. Whatever the dynamics at work in any given setting, the work lives of K–12 teachers contain many elements that can and do serve to preserve the deep structure of schooling and defeat attempts to change any of its component parts.

NOTES

1. A perfect example of the way in which the realities of daily life can prevent a new practice from taking root is provided in the description by Ferguson, Forte, Regan, Alter, & Treacy (1995) of an effort at a San Francisco middle school to train teachers in the use of cooperative learning techniques. The inhibiting factors that were identified all relate to the "daily-ness" of teachers' lives: The school

had many problems, the administration was noncooperative and displayed an incompatible management style, many teachers were inexperienced, and all were overwhelmed with competing demands. Teaching resources were in short supply as well.

2. Here is a *partial* list from a 4-year project involving 11 schools in a new curriculum opportunity: drug intervention, teen pregnancy, standardized testing, accreditation self-studies and site-review visits, child abuse awareness, on-campus violence, Chapter I programs, self-esteem curricula, critical thinking units, School Improvement programs, suicide prevention, clinical teaching and supervision, at-risk programs, mainstreaming, integrating the LEP student, career counseling, work-study programs, computer literacy, curriculum revision and text adoption cycles, writing across the curriculum, global education, special education meetings, science fairs (B. B. Tye & K. A. Tye, 1992, pp. 112–113).

3. The Study of Schooling data revealed that "Teachers tend to be isolated in their own classrooms, in control of what goes on there, and satisfied with the situation as it is. They feel impotent to affect school-wide decisions, they do not wish to call upon resource people, they individually select their own inservice or post-credential college coursework, and they are basically traditional in their educational beliefs" (K. A. Tye, 1981, p. 52).

7

The Unique Personality Level—
Where Change Is More Likely to Succeed

Any . . . critique rests, ultimately, on a vision of an alternative possibility.
It is futile to struggle against that which cannot be different than it is.
                                        Kathy E. Ferguson (1984, p. x)

Having come this far in our analysis, readers may well be feeling discouraged—is everything we try doomed to fail? Certainly not. It *is* possible to make change in schools—and to make it permanent. But we must clearly separate what can be done from what probably cannot.

HOPE LIES IN THE UNIQUE PERSONALITY OF EVERY SCHOOL

Although the deep structure of schooling that exists in our society shapes much of what goes on and thus creates a pervasive similarity of schools, it is also true that *every school in the nation is different from every other.* "Schools differ," note Lieberman and Miller (1984), "even as schooling appears similar" (p. 84). This is one of the persistent paradoxes of our system of public education, and it is only partly attributable to our history of local and state, as opposed to federal, control. The unique personality of each school is a function of—among other things—its history, the community of which it is a part, and internal factors such as the quality of its adult relationships, the number and intensity of its problems, and the climate of most of its classrooms (Page, 1999). The key to changing a school lies in the particular configuration of characteristics that give *that* school its distinctive identity.

   In Chapter 1, I cited Michael Katz's (1975) image of school reform as basically a matter of "moving things around inside the box." It seemed discouraging to think of being constrained in that way. But being aware of the limits inherent in the deep structure may free us to focus on projects that can be more satisfying. Perhaps, in the process, we can also break free of the endless cycle of fads and symbolic rituals of "educational change" undertaken primarily for the satisfaction of external constituencies. In short, "moving things around inside the box" can improve individual schools tremendously. Many successful reforms have been achieved at the unique personality level of schooling. Some have been well documented in the literature; others simply exist without fanfare. All, however, testify to the power of change that is focused within a single school.

I am not alone in calling for constructive efforts at the single school level. On the contrary, many thoughtful people have made the same argument through the years. Juxtaposing the dynamics of the deep structure with the possibilities of successful work at the unique personality level can, however, give a new appreciation of the complexity of the institution of schooling.

Granted, change efforts at the unique personality level are by definition going to seem comparatively modest. They are unlikely to include projects that try to dramatically alter deeply-rooted practices such as the subject-matter structure of the curriculum, the basic architecture of the school building, and the custodial role of the school.

Larry Cuban (1984) made this point in his historical analysis of the teaching profession. Using a farming metaphor to talk about the limits of what is possible in teaching, he points out that farmers can only do the best they can within the limits of soil capability, weather, insects, plant characteristics, and so forth. Similarly, "The variety of what teachers do in classrooms is finite. It is limited by a number of circumstances over which teachers have little influence . . . concentrating upon what teachers can do well in classrooms, on what schools can achieve successfully within certain boundaries is a sensible response to the potent processes at work in schools" (pp. 267–268).

More recently, after documenting the change processes in the life of one school, Laraine Hong (1996) observed that "Schools . . . need to be realistic about the kinds of change they can institute and how far they can proceed at any given time" (p. 181).

EVIDENCE OF THE UNIQUE PERSONALITY

Notwithstanding the presence of a deep structure of schooling that creates profound similarities across all schools in the nation, no one is going to dispute the fact that differences between schools are real. Furthermore, most practitioners can see how it would make sense to focus change efforts at the individual school site rather than trying to implement sweeping mandates formulated by people far removed from the daily life of American schools. But what evidence is there of a "unique personality" that can actually play a role in helping or hindering a site-based innovation? Is this a real phenomenon or just a hypothetical construct? Evidence of the existence of a unique personality dynamic can be found at three levels: in theory, in research, and in practice.

. . . In Theory

"We start from the assumption that good schools are unique," said Ted Sizer in a 1995 interview. "We offer no model. There's nothing you can just 'put into place'" (O'Neil, 1995, p. 4). Sizer's *assumption* is a theory about uniqueness that informs the ways in which his Coalition of Essential Schools functions. This assumption isn't new; for example, in the early 1930s the staff of the Eight-Year Study, recognizing that each participating school would have to find its own best way, deliberately chose *not* to impose a single model of curriculum change. After the study ended, Wilford Aikin (1942), the study's director, observed that "A school faculty might choose an easy solution by copying what some other school had done. . . . Such a procedure would be a serious mistake and the results would certainly be unsatisfactory. All teachers, all faculties must go through the hard experience of thinking their own problems through" (pp. 131–132).

In the early 1970s, a number of works called attention to the premise that the culture of individual schools could impede or facilitate the adoption of new ideas. Rogers (1973) proposed that the norms, social status, and hierarchy of a social system influence the behavior of members of that system. To the extent that these norms, status and hierarchy structures, and so on, differ from school to school, it followed that the adoption and implementation of new ideas and practices would vary from school to school.

In 1974, House noted the sometimes huge gap between what administrators assume to be innovation and what actually goes on in the classrooms of their district. Two years later, Weick's (1976) seminal essay on education as a loosely coupled system appeared, providing a theoretical explanation for the gap noted by House. As we found in Chapter 3, the notion of the institution of schooling as being loosely coupled at the instructional level is heuristically helpful for understanding why things happen— or fail to happen—at the classroom or building level.

In pondering the reasons that a truly interactive, postbureaucratic organization probably cannot be created in a large-scale operation, Krackhardt (1994) suggests that it is simply a matter of size: The number of possible links in the network gets too cumbersome. In the final analysis, he concludes, "communication patterns will localize geographically" (p. 214). Here we have yet another theory that supports the concept of a unique personality: If action for change is based on communication and the needed communication is more likely at the local level, then it is school-based dialogue and decision-making—and not mandates from the superordinate system—that will be most conducive to the implementation of lasting improvements.

. . . In Research

A good deal of research evidence exists to indicate that schools really do have unique "personalities" as well as many characteristics in common. In revisiting the findings of the RAND Change Agent Study of the 1970s, McLaughlin (1990) commented that "Local variability is the rule; uniformity is the exception" (p. 13).[1] Gold and Miles (1981) attributed this local variability not to school characteristics alone but to the community context in which a school is located. "The schools we studied were not freestanding," they noted, "but embedded in a local public school district. . . . The local district also includes a surrounding community populated by parents and other citizens, with characteristic sets of values and ideologies about education, which set the stage" (pp. 22–23).

Louis (1990), too, found evidence that community values shape the work lives of teachers. Indeed, the contextual embeddedness of the school has been understood by both scholars and practitioners for many years. Raywid's (1997–1998) review of recent research on school size is careful to remind us that—even in small schools where the advantages of a human-scale enterprise seem to make reform success more likely—still there is no magic bullet or fail-safe recipe, because successful education is both complex and context-specific. What works in one place may well not work in another.

The work of Mary Haywood Metz (1990) reveals the existence of a unique personality related to the internal culture that develops among teachers. "Within individual schools," she points out, "teachers develop common perspectives . . . that are distinctive to that school. They then tend to socialize newcomers into those perspectives. . . . Schools in communities of fairly homogeneous social class at high, middle, and low levels become very different places. Students and teachers have markedly different social and academic experiences in these schools, despite their common schedule, curriculum, and textbooks" (pp. 44, 102).

Another perspective on the power of the unique personality to sustain localized change can be found in Fullan and Pomfret's (1977) meta-analysis of 15 different studies of innovation, including the RAND study already mentioned. One of the many interesting points made by Fullan and Pomfret was that innovations that had been adopted opportunistically—because money was available for them—were far less likely to become permanent than were innovations adopted because they truly met locally identified needs.

Many educators over the years have found how difficult it is to disseminate a change across schools. House, Kerins, and Steele (1972) critiqued the once-popular RD&D paradigm (research, development, and dissemination) by noting that the assumption that dissemination would lead to implementation was flawed to begin with: "The facts," they said, "belie this assumption. Of far greater importance are the variables controlling the would-be adopter's everyday world in his home district. The individual is caught in a powerful social web that determines his behavior more than do his individual impressions gleaned at a demonstration visit. The variables that influence whether he will adopt are those that shape his home environment" (p. 12).

Wasley (1991) came to the same conclusion after studying teacher leadership projects at three sites: "Each site had its own distinct culture. It is unlikely that Gwen's model of teacher leadership could be exported to Mary's school. Nor is it likely that Ted's model could be transplanted to Gwen's school. . . . In each case, the conception of teacher leadership and the development and implementation of each role was contextually bound" (p. 151).

A provocative suggestion made by Meyer in 1983 began with the observation that because instructional matters are highly decentralized in American schools, replication is virtually impossible. He went on to propose an *inverse* relationship between the amount of national attention that a reform receives and the likelihood of successful grass-roots implementation. (If Meyer is correct, one might predict that *none* of the popular, highly visible reforms of the present are likely to find their way into daily practice but that some of the more modest ones might.)

Meyer's (1983) thesis offers hope for useful, locally appropriate and lasting reform in individual schools. And in fact it does appear that reform efforts at the unique personality level are alive and well. Shields and Knapp (1997) did a relevant study for the U.S. Department of Education in the early 1990s. Designed to provide a national snapshot of school-based reform activity, the findings showed that such localized activity "has been both widespread and extremely varied in recent years" (p. 294).

. . . In Practice

Much of the evidence for the existence of a "unique personality" that I find most persuasive comes from the experiences of practitioners and the stories they tell. For example, in her description of the change process at one school, Hong (1996) describes how the faculty managed to survive the third-year crisis phase that so often accompanies the implementation of an innovation. What it boiled down to was that the school had managed to assemble all the ingredients for success: a group identity, a decision-making process, time for dialogue, an actively supportive principal, and a community that understood what the school was trying to accomplish. "No single factor in itself, however, could make the difference. Everything had to work together, all the gears grinding at the same time; stop one, and the rest would cease turning" (p. 149). It sounds a bit precarious—(what would have happened if, for example, that principal had been transferred?)—and it is pretty obvious that *this* particular idiosyncratic combination of school and community characteristics would be impossible to replicate anywhere else (or, even if it could be, that it would produce the same results).

When I interviewed the school and community pioneers in Columbia, Irvine, and Reston, I kept hearing the same basic message—that right from the start each of the schools had its own unique personality. Two pioneer teachers at one Irvine school, for example, told me that the culture of their school was almost isolationist but that, in their opinion, this was surprisingly constructive. They credited the original principal—still in place in 1998—with serving as a buffer, resisting fads and bandwagons and thus creating space within which the faculty could focus on doing even better what they already did well. In terms of the goal-orientation typology discussed in Chapter 3, this principal was "goal-focused" (B. B. Tye & K. A. Tye, 1992). Despite a district ethos that valued and encouraged openness to change, this particular school had earned a reputation in its community for being cautious—and everyone was happy about it. The faculty was not resistant to change per se—just very selective about which changes to adopt.

To my surprise, I also learned that an element of the unique personality of one Reston school was connected to its distinctive *architecture*, coupled with an early decision to structure the school by grade-level subschools. According to Diana Schmeltzer, the principal of South Lakes High when I visited Reston for the first time in 1994, the culture that developed included a tradition whereby each subschool "physically moves, when they get promoted, from one part of the school building to another. The subschool principal, the two counselors and the secretary move with them—they all move every year. It makes us clean out our offices! The culture is so strong that when the seniors graduate and we have two or three more days of class for the underclassmen, literally the juniors move into that space. It's a physical taking-over that became a tradition almost immediately."

A pioneer Columbia teacher felt that her school had changed somewhat in the years since it opened, but—significantly—that most of the changes had happened in-house and *not* as a response to external pressures. On the whole, she acknowledged, some of the changes had been for the better—and some had not. "If I had a magic wand," she admitted, "I would bring back some things that we did ten or fifteen years ago, that in my opinion we no longer do as well." Her statement brings to mind the useful caution by Shields and Knapp (1997) that the assumption that change will *always be for the better* is "logically shaky" (p. 291).

No Recipes. There was also widespread skepticism among educators in the three communities that what worked at one school could be effectively exported to other schools. "One of the biggest mistakes that policymakers make, over and over again, is to insist that if something is 'good,' it must work at every school," one pioneer superintendent told me. This viewpoint implicitly accepts the notion that each school is a unique unit, and echoes Sarason's (1995) conclusion, formed after years of studying school change, that what is demonstrated in a single classroom or school never spreads.

During the 1980s and 1990s, however, top-down mandates continued despite a growing consensus among educators that this is *not* the way to promote school improvement. The effective schools research of the 1980s, for example, was seized upon and its findings twisted into a prescription: If these are the things one finds at schools that are identified as being "effective and successful," then all one has to do is to replicate these characteristics at one's own school and—hey, presto!—your school, too, will be an effective and possibly even an "excellent" school. It just doesn't work that way, as Lieberman and Miller (1984) point out: "While some schools may do well to model their structure for school improvement on the Effective Schools research, others may find this approach totally inappropriate" (p. 90).

One of our problems as a nation, Lightfoot (1983) suggests, is that we too often think dichotomously. We tend to see schools as being either "good" or "bad," and this limited viewpoint lends itself to simplistic prescriptions: "Only do these things, and your 'bad' school, too, can become a 'good' one." Instead, she argues that we try to recognize, applaud, and nurture *emergent* goodness in schools and to "see them whole, changing and imperfect" (p. 311).

McAdams (1997), citing lessons learned (by both practitioners and researchers) from Kentucky's state-mandated school reforms of the 1990s, concluded that "A convincing argument can be made that substantive school reform is easiest to achieve at the individual school level. While school reform at the district level is possible, it is difficult to achieve, and lasting school reform initiated at the state level is highly unlikely to occur under existing political conditions" (p. 142).

Local Adaptation. The strength of *adaptation* as a process is another strong argument for the existence and power of the unique personality of each school; it also underlines the fact that the system is far more loosely coupled than many people realize. By "adaptation," I mean the process whereby an innovation adjusts to fit local circumstances. The process has been shown to be unavoidable (Gold & Miles, 1981; Lukas, 1975; McLaughlin, 1990; Pauly, 1991; Poole, 1991): Rarely, if ever, will a reform be implemented with absolute fidelity to its original conception. "Nothing of any importance or potential significance," observed Goodlad in 1975, "enters a school to become a permanent part of it and remains there in its original form" (p. 59). A quarter-century later, adaptive implementation is considered not only inevitable but quite acceptable. Many influential educators now believe that teachers not only can but *should* "hybridize" reforms to fit their local circumstances.

Another characteristic of the adaptation process seems to be its non-linearity (Fullan, 1996). This is something that bureaucratic minds are likely to find distressing but that practitioners recognize and some researchers have documented. For example, Bryk et al. (1994), who studied the Chicago school reforms of the early 1990s, concluded that change isn't smooth and predictable, and that transitions from old practices to new are often confusing and conflicted. The 1997 Shields and Knapp study of site-based reforms mentioned earlier found that "no particular sequence was inherently more sensible than any other"—some schools started here, others there—and that the schools that seemed to be making the clearest progress were ones that didn't try to tackle everything at once but "aimed for more modest goals and allowed for changes to take place on a longer time line than other schools" (pp. 292–293). This absence of a clear recipe for how to proceed suggests not only that idiosyncratic adaptation will take place at individual school sites but that it does so *because each school has a unique personality*. And *that* means that each school must find its own way of achieving its improvement goals.

That is not easy to do. It takes a fair amount of collective nerve to venture into what may be—for one's own school or district—uncharted territory. It's tempting to look around for other schools that are already "doing it." One of two things might happen then: An attempt might be made to imitate what one sees working well elsewhere, whether or not it suits one's own school; or the visiting team might truly discover that what they have in mind for their school really *isn't* happening anywhere else and that they truly *are* on their own. That's what the planning team from Howard County, Maryland, found when they were given a federal grant to develop the schools for the new town of Columbia:

> We got this Title III money and for the very first time we were able
> to do so many things. Some of us traveled all over the country
> visiting other schools which were said to be innovative. What we

found was that there were interesting things going on, good things that were really successful but which were not transferrable. We never found a school where the whole school was involved; and we couldn't find what we had in mind for Columbia.

The School–Community Connection

Each school's distinctly unique personality is in large measure a function of the type of community of which it is a part. The schools that were built in Columbia and Reston were part of the preexisting county school systems and bound by many policies already in place. Columbia was established in what had been a quiet rural area populated by settled farming families and disturbed the long-standing equilibrium of that part of Howard County. In the early years, the unique personalities of the first schools to be built included, in varying degrees, some tension between the established county residents and the "new town pioneers." At the same time, however, there was a certain excitement in the air. As one key player recalls, in Howard County all the pieces came together to create a magic moment:

> Even a James Rouse (the developer), a new city, a new citizenry and a willing school board couldn't bring about the changes by themselves. There had to be a superintendent in the leadership role and a staff willing to work hard with imagination and deep commitment. Howard County at that point in time had them all . . .

Today, Columbia feels more suburban than rural. Newcomers are drawn to its attractive wooded neighborhoods, its proximity to Washington, D.C., and its good schools. They are likely to be fairly affluent, well-educated, and cosmopolitan families. There are tangible differences, however, in the personalities of the schools in the various neighborhoods. A greater range of affordable housing in the original sections of Columbia has given Wilde Lake High School a more diverse student body than is apparent at the high schools built later, for example. This is regarded as an advantage by Wilde Lake parents, who are vocal in their support of the school.

A former member of the Howard County Board of Education made an interesting connection between the first open-space elementary school built for Columbia and its parent community:

> There was a great deal of parent involvement, because the open structure lent itself to—you know, in the four-walls system, if the door opens and your mother comes in, everybody wonders what

you did! Whereas in open space it was a natural flow, a mother could come in and work two hours, helping in various ways; they would move in and out of the classroom without too much distraction.

The unique personality of that school, at that point in time, included this comparatively easy movement of parents and other community volunteers or visitors through the building. As visual barriers, and eventually walls, went up between the formerly open learning spaces, this aspect of the life of the school also changed, though subtly. No one was made to feel unwelcome, but as this board member recognized, the structural changes simply created a different kind of environment.

Unlike Columbia and Reston, the new school district established in Irvine in the early 1970s was not bound by a preexisting county system. In addition, Irvine had a pioneer superintendent who very deliberately established a district ethos built on a philosophy of decentralized decision-making: Site-based management was a reality in Irvine long before it became a national movement in the 1990s. It would not have occurred to the board of education in Irvine to insist upon policies that would standardize practices district-wide. The individual schools and the neighborhoods they served were free to solve their own problems and develop the structures that would serve their needs. As one of the pioneer principals, who later became the assistant superintendent, recalls, "Given the participation of the parents and staff in decision-making, there were—and still are—things that they design in response to the issues at their school that *they own*. And if you told them that they could no longer do that, they wouldn't give it up easily."

Site-based educators interested in identifying their own school's unique personality need to take a clear look at its relationship to the surrounding community. This includes analysis of the local power structure as it relates to the school. McCarty and Ramsey (1971) identified a typology of communities based on the politics of their school boards. In the first type, a small community *elite* dominates school matters, with little opposition. In the second, two approximately equal *factions* vie for power. The *pluralistic* type includes several community interest groups, with no one of them dominant. Finally, in an *inert* community there is little interest in the schools and no competition for seats on the school board.

Many of us can see our own local school district in one or another of these categories, perhaps with some variations on these themes. Being aware of our own local reality is important when we decide to embark upon changes in the school where we work. Assuming that we are going to avoid deep structure changes that are likely to fade in a few years and concentrate our energies instead on projects at the unique personality level of our school, the power structure can work for us or against us.

For example, an *inert* community would probably not get involved with the project one way or another. The school people could tackle whatever site-based changes they chose and work on them with little or no interference—but also with little or no support. In a community characterized by *pluralism*, on the other hand, there might be a good deal of support. There might also be differences of opinion between the various community interest groups. There might be room for coalition politics to develop around certain school policies or practices, with a danger of bitter factionalism if the disagreements became really contentious. In a community where a small *elite* dominates the school board, the values of those few people can make or break a proposed change. The men and women working in a school in such a district may have a clear sense of what is or is not possible, and that may be comforting if the power brokers are supportive of the school people. But it can be stifling if the policymakers are wary of change, authoritarian in their exercise of power, and patronizing in their dealings with teachers and staff.

The extent to which the type of community surrounding a school can have an impact upon attempted change is profound, and communities can be very different in this respect. Even communities that may seem similar can have markedly different capacities for change, as Lewis (1995) noted in documenting the results of a well-financed 5-year math project in 12 urban middle schools:

> During the five years of the project, about one-half of the schools made progress. The other half had little to show for the time and investment. That the outcomes were so different is not so much a reflection of what the schools did as the result of an uneven capacity of urban systems to change. . . . Schools that floundered from the very beginning were still doing so at the end, not because anyone intentionally wanted to fail, but because the desired reforms could not overcome the unwillingness of systems to change, or leadership unable to move the systems. (p. 19)

The Adult Work Environment of the School

The environment of a school for the adults who work there has already been discussed but can be mentioned again here insofar as it connects to the unique personality of the school. In this respect, I'd almost be tempted to say that no two schools in the nation are likely to have exactly the same configuration of adult interpersonal dynamics. A great many studies have explored teacher/teacher and teacher/administrator relationships, and a number of helpful typologies can be found in the literature by any who wish to probe this topic further. A study of interaction among teachers by Blase and Anderson (1995), for example, identified both positive and negative teacher behaviors that affect the sociocultural context of the school (pp. 69–73). Positive behaviors included being tactful and diplomatic and being friendly and supportive of colleagues. Being self-centered, aloof, overly critical, and not doing one's share of the work load were some of the many negative teacher behaviors identified in that study.

Rosenholz (1989) focused on the extent to which a norm of self-reliance (related to teacher autonomy) existed in the schools she studied. Schools in which self-reliance was highly valued tended to be places in which there was little sense of community or mutual support among the teachers and little sense of a collective ability to solve school problems. Low morale, a good deal of complaining, and a certain amount of fatalism about the possibility of real change or improvement would be more likely in such schools (pp. 206–208).

Identifying the Positives. Instruments that permit teachers to examine their own school's adult work environment have been developed. An example of such an instrument is the SWEPT inventory, which when properly used yields a profile of adult interaction that can be quite useful to teachers in setting some internal school-improvement goals at the unique personality level.[2] The extent to which the faculty regards itself as being task-oriented, mutually supportive, and self-renewing can be identified, as can the amount of job satisfaction, enjoyment of each other as colleagues, and the quality of problem solving and decision-making by the staff. Faculty perception of school leadership is included, as well. If the teachers view the principal as being open to their ideas, that will show up. The amount of respect and affection that the staff members feel for the principal will also emerge.

If a school faculty and administration were to self-assess using such an instrument and discover significant agreement that communication is a problem in the school, for instance ("Information is not shared between teachers from different teams, departments, or grade levels," "Staff members don't listen to each other," etc.), that area could become the focus for some coordinated improvement efforts. One is more likely to look forward to going to work each morning if one works in a school where the adults enjoy each other and work well together.

"Organization development specialists have demonstrated that school personnel can learn to study their social condition and improve it," Bruce Joyce said in 1982 (p. 45). And if one believes, as I do, that high faculty morale and a positive adult work climate in a school can have an effect on student productivity, such site-specific reforms are well worth the effort.

Changing the culture of *our own schools* for the better is something that is within our reach, and—in the words of one pioneer principal in Irvine—"Human interaction is more important than structural change."

POSSIBLE PROJECTS AT THE UNIQUE PERSONALITY LEVEL

As Fullan (1991) has observed, each one of us must act—however modestly—to improve our own work environment: "Individuals, regardless of their institutions, will have to take affirmative action to make positive changes in their own situations, affecting as many as possible around them" (p. 354). We must also act collectively, including not only teachers and the administrative team but students, parents, and community supporters as well. The education literature is full of accounts of worthwhile site-based school improvement projects that failed when everyone wouldn't "buy in."

Finally, we come to this key question: If we are unlikely to be successful in changing characteristics of our school that are grounded in the deep structure, what kinds of undertakings *are* likely to succeed? It has already been pointed out that staff interpersonal work relationships can be made the focus of improvement efforts, using a data-feedback strategy and a reliable survey instrument. I would like to conclude this book with a brief discussion of some other possible efforts that could improve a school. Before I do, however, some cautions.

First, experience as well as research shows that we are more likely to succeed in our efforts at site-specific reform if we pick a few goals and really *focus* on them, emphasizing depth over breadth, allowing ourselves a long time line for achievement, and resisting the inclination to jump on every new idea that comes along (Hargreaves, 1995; Shields & Knapp, 1997; Tyack & Cuban, 1995; B. B. Tye & K. A. Tye, 1992; Weil, 1997). Michael Fullan's (1991) words are apt here: "Meaning cannot be masterminded at a global level. It is found through small-scale pursuits of significant personal and organizational goals" (p. 348). Organization development guru Peter Senge (1990) concurs: "small, well-focused actions can produce significant, enduring improvements, if they are in the right place" (p. 15).

Second, before we choose our improvement goals, we can—and should—take a really fresh look at both our school and our community. Let's step outside the hurtling, incessant pressure for "change" and take a look at our school as if we have never seen it before (Greene, 1973; Sarason, 1982): to "arrive where we started," as T.S. Eliot said, "and know it for the first time." *Then* we can think about how each of us can best devote our energies and choose, together, two or three things to do—and do well, determined to make them stick—no matter how long it takes.

Third, let's not lose sight of the things we already do well as a school. We should start from and make use of our strengths to work on our weaknesses, advises Meier (1996). Too, it might be wise to acknowledge up front that we cannot necessarily know what the outcome will be but that we can put faith in the process and in ourselves. The process may be complex and nonlinear; but we can handle it (Heckscher et al., 1994).

Finally, we are going to need both process goals and substantive goals. By "process goals," I mean those tools that we use collectively to get things done. By "substantive goals," I mean specific work in curriculum and pedagogy, designed to improve student learning. In the remainder of this chapter, examples of both kinds are discussed.

Skill Building as Site-based Reform

Projects that emerge from analysis of the school's work environment, formed by consensus, using a data-feedback process and with the participation of the entire faculty and staff, have already been mentioned. We can also turn to the classic literature on organization development for process assistance that we can actually put to real, practical use in addressing our substantive goals. Goal setting, decision-making, problem solving, open communication, shared leadership, and conflict resolution are the process-skill areas generally understood to be important to improving organizational health. Obviously, there would be a close connection between these process skills and the substantive work a school staff choose in order to improve its adult work environment. Using the following process skills, groups of teachers can build on their strengths and shore up their weaknesses. As they do, their school may become a happier place.

Problem Solving. If a principal, an assistant principal, the teachers, and other nonteaching professionals in a school were to decide to work on their problem-solving skills, their eventual improvement in this area would be likely to show up in increased feelings of efficacy. Results would be tangible as specific problems actually got solved. There would be less to deal with, less to complain about, and energy formerly expended in coping with a problem could be released for other tasks. Over time, the school culture might shift from one in which problems simply seem overwhelming to one characterized by confidence, resilience, and greater staff cohesiveness. So important is problem solving to the life of any school, in fact, that it may be the single most critical determinant of whether that school can or cannot be considered a healthy, self-renewing place for adults to work (Bentzen & Tye, 1973).

It may be helpful to know that there are established problem-solving models that can be systematically learned and applied by groups that have problems to solve. The value in using such process models lies in the way they are structured to guide the group *away* from what is a common mistake of inexperienced problem-solving groups: a premature focus on solutions before all aspects of the problem have been analyzed. Simply learning to use such a model (and then *using* it, of course) might be an excellent goal for a school faculty, staff, and community; and it would be a good example of a unique personality-level project that could improve the adult work environment of a school.

Open Communication. Another process area that is vital to the life of a healthy organization is open communication. Shortly, we consider some reform projects that involve improved communication between the school and its community; for now, however, let's focus on communication *within* the school—which is just as important (Kernan-Schloss & Plattner, 1998; Soholt, 1998). An agreement to work on open communication could well be the focus of school improvement efforts at the unique personality level. Wasley, Hampel, & Clark (1997) studied five schools, all active members of the Coalition of Essential Schools but each very different from the others, and found—among other things—that the successful ones had vital, open communication. An "ongoing conversation," civil discourse, and receptivity to external feedback were all present in those schools.

Conflict Resolution. Interestingly, those schools were also able to deal openly with controversial issues. Evidently conflict resolution (another component of organization development) was either a healthy by-product of open communication or had become an identified process-skill goal in those schools. Either way, in the schools in which faculty members "had developed processes for airing controversy, the faculty made changes that endured and grew stronger over time. Where faculty members had no capacity to grapple with controversy, they were unable to move beyond existing practices. In addition, the tone of such a school was less hopeful because the unresolved issues rankled" (Wasley et al., 1997, p. 694).

Schools participating in a reform effort in Tucson have developed an internal communication structure, the dialogue group, which provides a forum for sharing ideas, formulating goals, and making decisions (Heckman, 1995; Oakes & Lipton, 1999). It didn't happen overnight and there may have been some rough times, but after more than 6 years of good-faith effort, the dialogue groups seemed to be firmly in place. Such a strategy is well within the range of possibility for any school staff.

Shared Decision-making. Decision-making is, of course, intrinsic to the processes already described—problem solving, open communication, and conflict resolution. Within each of these process contexts, decisions must be made by the group. As those decisions lead to successful outcomes, a faculty will presumably become more and more confident about its decision-making as well. However, it is also true that shared decision-making could be the primary improvement goal instead of a secondary one. If that were the case, what kinds of issues, policies, and projects could be the *substantive* focus of the decision-making effort? One possibility might be the choice to do some work on improving the levels of cooperation between the adults in the school. Structural elements, however, can make this difficult, so some problem solving and creative rethinking might be needed first.

It has already been suggested elsewhere in this book that radical changes in the use of time and space are unlikely to be successful because time and space allocation are deep structure areas. Without dramatically altering the school day, week, or year, or the basic structure of the school building, however, it *is* possible for a school faculty and administration to make it easier for teachers to work together if they choose to do so:

> Routinely coordinated planning times can bring together teachers who teach the same grade or subject. Placing 1st and 6th grade teachers in adjacent classrooms can begin to break down stereotypes and the boundaries between the upper and lower ends of the elementary school. (Hargreaves, 1995, p. 17)

In Chapter 6 it was established that collaboration cannot and should not be forced. But it is also clear that a smoothly functioning school with a happy adult work environment does require a certain amount of willing teamwork. Shields and Knapp (1997), in their national study of school-based reforms under way in the mid-1990s, discovered that "a substantial portion of school-based professional development activity was devoted to inculcating the skills and commitments necessary for collaborative teamwork" (p. 292). When it comes to teachers' ability to learn to work together, Ron Edmonds is emphatic: "If I can show you *one* school that can do it, it can be done" (Barth, 1990, p. 32).

Obviously, choosing to work on building a collaborative culture is a decision that can be made only on a school-by-school basis; and so are the decisons as to how to go about doing it. There can be no formula applicable across schools, *precisely* because each school's unique personality must be taken into account. Only those who work in each separate school can negotiate the division of tasks that will be acceptable to all, drawing on each person's strengths and interests and carefully avoiding a situation in which anyone feels either left out or—at the other extreme—forced to participate beyond his or her ability or comfort level at that point in time.

As an aside, I've noticed that educators today are *very* conscientious about honoring and working with differences among students but less so when it comes to differences within their own ranks. Not all teachers are skillful lecturers—but some are terrific. Not all can plan and teach inductively or use constructivist methodologies. Some are better working with students one-on-one and don't do as well with large classes, and others are just the opposite. Some are gregarious; others are not. Unless a principal has hired with a certain philosophy in mind, every school faculty is likely to contain a wide range of belief systems and teaching styles. These affect what we choose to do and how we do it in our classrooms, as well as how we relate to our colleagues outside of class.

Another substantive arena for group decision-making is the realm of curriculum. A good many decisions about what will or will not be taught in a school are made by people or groups outside the school and handed to teachers as givens, and up to a point this seems to be a deep structure reality. Parents, as we saw in Chapter 5, have some pretty set ideas about what their children should be learning. So do most policymakers, who support state or even national standardized tests that, in turn, drive the curriculum. The Carnegie unit, long the established way of dividing the secondary-school curriculum into semester- or year-long segments, is so deeply embedded in our thinking that even creative people can have difficulty imagining alternative ways of organizing a high school course of study.

And yet . . . I believe that there are cracks in this monolith, where teachers in a school can do some exciting curriculum work together. I also believe, just as firmly, that these opportunities are site-specific and that they can be neither mandated across schools in advance nor replicated after the fact. Each faculty must assess its own situation, identify what it can do, and decide how to proceed. Perhaps some cross-disciplinary curriculum integration is possible. Maybe a core curriculum model would work. Perhaps a faculty might decide to use a writing-across-the-curriculum model school-wide. A new charter or magnet school might select global education as its unifying curricular concept. There are ways in which educators can still be proactive in curriculum decision-making if they choose.

Goal Setting. Goal setting, like decision-making, is inseparable from the processes of problem solving, open communication, and conflict resolution: It can't be avoided. The trick for the adults who work in a school is to learn to set goals that are not only worth doing but also achievable: a stretch—but not out of reach. And, I would add, if goals are to be achievable, they should be explicitly aimed at unique personality changes. It would be frustrating over the long haul for a faculty to set deep-structure change goals and find their efforts thwarted. Like Sisyphus, they would be able to see their goal; but the rock would keep rolling back down before they could get it up there.

Shared Leadership. Shared leadership is the final element of organizational health that I propose as a possible focus for school-improvement process work at the unique personality level. Shared leadership is an essential feature of a collaborative school culture but could conceivably exist in a school even where autonomy, rather than collaboration, is the dominant ethos. As committees and task groups form, do their work, and disband, a norm of shared decision-making would mean simply that no one acts as an official chairperson or group leader but that all members accept responsibility for helping the group to work efficiently and harmoniously. As in the case of problem solving, there are models that can be used to help groups learn and use small-group dynamics skills, including shared decision-making.

Unless a school is very small, shared leadership may be difficult at the whole-school level because of the deep structure reality that, above the instructional level, school systems are bureaucratic and hierarchical. School administrators are expected (by everyone, including teachers more often than not) to assume a leadership role within their building. Some principals are able to transcend this expectation and genuinely work collaboratively with their teachers, yielding the leadership role to others for various purposes; but many are not. Even in this latter case, however, teachers could agree to use a shared-leadership process among themselves in their work as subject departments, grade-level teams, or when special projects bring them together to work across the conventional groupings. It is a choice that teachers *could* make and a goal they could set among themselves: "Communities of practice" are possible (Marsh, 1999, p. 195).

Substantive Projects

All of the suggestions I have sketched thus far would be modest, achievable efforts that I believe could lead directly to increasing faculty morale and from there to improved school experiences for children and young people. Other site-specific projects, less focused on faculty skill building but equally worthwhile, might include the following:

1. *Projects designed to connect the school more closely with the community it serves.* These can range from home phone calls (Gustafson, 1998), to es-

tablishing benchmarks to use in keeping the community informed about the progress of a reform effort in the school (Rallis & Zajano, 1997), to setting up focus groups of parents when a change is being considered (Hargreaves & Fullan, 1998). Town meetings on education, despite challenging obstacles, have worked well in some places, particularly when they involve all constituencies, including teachers *and* students (Wagner, 1997). A Reston principal commented during an interview that "That's the best way to make decisions—to have parents, students, and administrators doing it jointly." Karen Seashore Louis (1990), reviewing how community values can shape and affect the quality of teachers' work lives, noted that although "it is not impossible to find schools and teachers who have begun to create solidarity communities . . . it is to a large extent the teacher's effort that pulls parents into schools rather than the parents' initiative" (pp. 31–32). Evidently, the ball is in our court. But more than a ball is needed: James Comer (1995), who has devoted many years to creating a successful community schools model, believes that parent involvement can become a permanent and constructive part of the life of a school. But various kinds of support—both for parents and for teachers—are needed if this is to happen.

2. *Becoming a full-service school.* Teachers working in schools that serve needy inner-city or rural communities could make a project of collaborating with local social service agencies and providers to create a school that is truly the hub of its community, 7 days a week and 12 months a year. Children could receive the extra help they need (glasses, breakfast, group counseling) in order to improve their academic performance. Before-school programs and after-school supervised play and guided homework or extracurricular programs would provide enrichment as well as safety and friendship. Adults, too, could receive services ranging from dental care to night-school classes and group activities such as book or movie discussion groups, parenting programs, and guest speakers on topics of interest. Parents, senior citizens, and other adult volunteers would be welcome to help with what would necessarily become a permanent project involving the entire neighborhood.

3. *Developing a teacher-advisor system within a school.* Where these exist, they have proven enormously popular, although frequently teachers feel out of their depth at first. As one Columbia principal told me, "My teachers would not give up the advisory group. Many of them would tell you, 'This is the highlight of my day; many days when everything else is going down the tubes, it's neat to meet with my advisees.'" Several teachers at a school in Irvine told me basically the same thing, and I have seen the teacher-advisor system work well in secondary schools from coast to coast. It takes work—that's where the goal setting, problem solving, decision-making,

and open communication (and yes, no doubt, conflict resolution too) come in. Teachers need some help in learning to perform this role well, and the entire school needs to get used to it. But it can be done.

4. *Coordinated efforts to speak out on behalf of public schools.* As we enter the 21st century, teachers can no longer afford to be as passive as we have been through most of the 20th. In 1932, George Counts issued a clarion call for teachers to speak out; since the mid-1980s many others have reminded us of our responsibility to take the initiative and reclaim our voices, establishing ourselves as thoughtful practitioners who know whereof we speak.[3] Why shouldn't America's teachers organize locally to provide speakers for neighborhood groups, civic organizations, church groups, and other audiences who are interested in the state of our public schools? After all, who else can speak with such authority on this topic? Why shouldn't we step forward to make ourselves heard at PTA meetings, local and state board of education meetings, hearings of our state legislatures when schooling matters are on the table, and professional meetings—not just of teachers' organizations but at state and national meetings of administrators and policymakers as well—at the Associations of School Administrators, for instance, and at the National Governors' Conference. The much more active participation of teachers in the ongoing civic conversation about public schooling could be—why not?—another component of school reform at the unique personality level. The specifics of such activism would remain, by definition, home-grown: initiated, decided upon, designed, and carried out by each school's own faculty members as they see fit.

5. *Playing together: activities to build staff cohesion.* Gathering for happy hour on Fridays or for occasional potluck lunches may seem trivial but can in fact be important to the health of any organization (Deal, 1990). Though conviviality cannot be mandated, teachers could—if they chose—socialize occasionally. There is some evidence that in schools where teachers express high levels of job satisfaction, symbolic activities are often found to bond the group with ties of friendship and support that go well beyond saying hello in the hallways. The unique personality of a school will shape the social activities that its staff might choose, but why not consider family picnics to mark the beginning and the end of a school year? An intramural softball tournament? A miniature golf showdown? A monthly book or movie discussion group? A really ambitious faculty might even organize a group summer travel tour to somewhere exciting in the United States, Canada, or Mexico— or even further afield; why not?

OUTSIDE SUPPORT FOR UNIQUE PERSONALITY CHANGE

When I propose that lasting reforms are more likely to succeed if they are changes that target aspects of the unique personality of a specific school, I do not mean to suggest that a faculty, staff, and parents should go it alone, with no outside support. In fact, external support is not only helpful but necessary, as Fullan and Miles made clear in 1992: "Successful change efforts are most likely when the local district office is closely engaged with the changing school in a collaborative, supportive way and places few bureaucratic restrictions in the path of reform" (p. 751).

Shields and Knapp (1997) found that the superordinate system can influence change efforts under way in individual schools, either positively or negatively, in as many as nine significant ways; and even this is probably not an exhaustive list. For example, the school district, county, or state education authorities can be a catalyst for specific reforms; can influence—through hiring and transfer policies—the makeup of a school faculty and staff; can give or withhold decision-making authority; and can set boundaries upon reform activity. They can set—or waive—requirements; provide (or fail to provide) needed technical help, resources, and staff development opportunities; serve (or fail to serve) as a buffer to give the school people that important "psychic space" within which to work; and determine the accountability mechanisms that the teachers will have to deal with (p. 293).

Part of the necessary activism of teachers who want to make some unique-personality-level changes at their school involves finding ways to gain the support of those external agencies that might otherwise erect barriers to their efforts. In this, enthusiastic parents can play a pivotal role. The more closely bound they feel to the life of the school their children attend, the more likely they are to be advocates for the school when the need arises.

For example, one of the innovations that endured for over 20 years at Wilde Lake High School in Columbia was a "no-fail" grading system. Essentially, a student could not pass out of a course until he or she earned at least a grade of C. No D's or F's were given; an Incomplete would remain on the record until an acceptable grade had been earned. This is a system that would make most parents—and many teachers—uncomfortable. But in the Wilde Lake community, one of the original teachers told me, the parents became enthusiastic supporters: "There are a lot of parents who would tell you, this grading system is hell but it's the best thing that ever happened to my kid, to finally be held accountable for what he has to do, and not get any credit until he does it right."

We would do well to bear in mind that neglecting to inform and include parents and to actively solicit their support for our projects can cause real problems with implementation. Another lesson that was learned from the Eight-Year Study, for example, was that failure to include parents doesn't mean simply an absence of parent voice; it can mean active opposition that might have been avoided: "The schools which did not draw patrons into the planning . . . encountered parental misunderstanding. Unwarranted criticism and opposition were the results" (Aikin, 1942, p. 128).

SUCCESS IS POSSIBLE: IF . . . (A REMINDER)

In the final analysis, I believe that there is cause for optimism when it comes to effective local action. Many opportunities for improvement exist—taking steps to establish a healthier, happier adult work environment at one's own school is a big one. Success in that area could lead to the identification of other worthwhile in-school and school/community projects. It is important to remember, however, that just because a reform project is "site-based" doesn't automatically mean it is a unique personality effort. A school might tackle a deep structure element but not recognize it as such because both the initiative and the change effort are site-based.

Deep structure reforms try to change components of the educational system that Americans assume are what a "real school" should look like, and, as I have tried to show in this book, they run into all kinds of interference that pull and pick at them until they collapse. *Unique personality reforms* focus on other aspects of school life that do not pose a confrontational challenge to the deep structure regularities.

CLOSING THOUGHTS

Deep structure theory posits that a system of schooling will remain stable indefinitely, until sea-changes in the surrounding culture lead to changes in what citizens throughout the society expect from their schools, *whether or not they are aware of it*. Further, identifiable forces can be seen to assist in this preservation of the status quo. There is enormous pressure on schools to remain as they are, as I have tried to demonstrate in this book.

I do not know the answer to the question, Is our culture changing again? Is America's sense of itself as a public entity, with common values, yielding to a new self-image based on market-driven competitive individualism? If so, are this society's expectations for its schools also changing? In what ways? Readers will have to answer these questions for themselves, trying (and it isn't easy) to avoid getting tangled in wishful thinking. We must remember, as well, that we are all culture-bound: It is difficult to accurately recognize large-scale cultural shifts when one is actually living through them. On the other hand, we sometimes mistake smaller and more transitory changes for the Real Thing.

Unfortunately, what I think might happen and what I hope will happen are two very different things. Much as I hate to admit it, I do think the United States may be on the brink of a shift in what it asks of its public schools. This shift is grounded in what seems to be an increasingly fragmented society, in which individuals are no longer committed to a vision of the common good. I fear that such a society will move away from the Great Experiment of universal public education, in the direction of a scattering of public and private alternatives that would, in turn, contribute to even further fragmentation and an ever-widening socioeconomic gap. That is what I fear. What do I hope for?

Actually, I believe the public schools are basically on the right track and have been doing a far better job—with fewer resources and against the persistent negativity of the opinion-shapers—than is acknowledged. There is plenty of room for improvement, and reform efforts developed and carried out at the site level have a good chance of success as long as they don't tackle deep structure elements that are impervious to change. If we make that mistake, we are likely to see our efforts begin to slide back in 3 to 5 years. In the final analysis, every school faculty must set its own course; there are no sure-fire recipes.

Some states are starting to play a helpful supporting role by finding ways to reduce class size, equalize funding, or increase teacher salaries and to encourage the use of schools as community centers offering a range of needed health and social services. Two questions come to mind, however. First, can state policymakers and state-level education agencies resist the temptation to micromanage these efforts? Second, will *all* of the states take such steps? If not, those that do may also slip back as other priorities come to the fore. I hope the answer is *yes* to both of these questions.

The federal government could help in a number of ways, and some attempts to do so were made during the Clinton years but none were as vigorous as needed; I hope this will change, too. First, Congress could increase the funding for Head Start, to reach 100% of eligible children for the very first time—it has never reached even half of them. Second, funds for new school construction and deferred maintenance are badly needed. Third, some block grants for schools to acquire and use new technological tools have been provided, but these need to be expanded, so that our schools will not fall behind our workplaces and so that *all* schools will be equally well-equipped.

Fourth, while some support for school-to-work and work-study programs has been forthcoming, it is not yet clear either whether it is enough or whether it is being optimally utilized. Washington should take the lead in generating policy based on the assumption that the nation can't afford to lose even *one* youngster to the chaos and despair of poverty, chronic unemployment, or incarceration. This is a moral position, but it can become empty rhetoric if it isn't backed with the necessary appropriations. We can't, for example, continue to pay lip service to the importance of K–12 education and child support services, and then continue to spend more money for new prisons than for new school buildings.

That is what I hope will happen. In the best of all possible worlds, it would. In the world we have, we must be aware of the power of the deep structure and the pull of the inhibiting forces that protect it.

> *The Model Schools Project staff person who visited the school at the end of the project found that for all practical purposes the program had disappeared, although some students and some staff members remembered it.*
> Trump and Georgiades (1977, p. 124)

Deep structure analysis requires a big step back, to see the *macro* view. Closeups always reveal variations within the larger pattern, like the individual dots of color in a Seurat painting; only from a distance can one see the whole picture. I think again of Sarason's (1982) space visitor, who looks without preconceptions and so can ask fresh questions about why schools are as they are. My question isn't new and—as I said in Chapter 1—others have asked (and answered) it before. My hope is that I have contributed to a better understanding of pitfalls that can be avoided, so that our efforts to build happy, productive schools are more likely to be successful. Let's have done with tilting at windmills. Noble as the effort might be, the vitality of our educational system is too important for us to dissipate our energy on battles that cannot be won.

NOTES

1. McLaughlin (1990) went on to add, "Although classrooms, schools, and school districts share common features—curriculum structures, grade structures, and student placement policies—they also differ in fundamental and consequential ways. A high school English course in a wealthy suburban classroom differs substantially from a course offered under the same title in an inner-city school. The problems faced by California school administrators differ markedly from those faced by colleagues in Kansas. Dade County's site-based decision-making project will bear only a scant resemblance to a restructuring activity in Santa Fe" (p. 13).

2. The SWEPT was developed for use in the study of schooling and is not, as far as I know, still in use. It was similar to the OCDQ (Organization Climate Description Questionnaire), the classic instrument of this type. Other climate surveys have been developed since and may be useful to school faculties interested in assessment of their word environment.

3. A classic call for teacher activism was George S. Counts's (1932) *Dare the School Build a New Social Order?* Readers interested in more recent calls for teacher voice and action might begin with Henry Giroux's 1985 plea that teachers act as "transformative intellectuals"; Gail McCutcheon's 1988 essay, "Curriculum and the Work of Teachers"; Michael Apple's 1990 *Phi Delta Kappan* essay, "Is There a Curriculum Voice to Reclaim?" and the 1998 book by Hargreaves and Fullan, *What's Worth Fighting for Out There?*

References

Adelman, N., & Pringle, B. (1995). Education reform and the uses of time. *Phi Delta Kappan, 77*(1), 27–29.

Agger, R. E. (1969). The politics of local education. In A. Rosenthal (Ed.), *Governing education: A reader on politics, power, and public school policy* (pp. 44–85). Garden City, NY: Doubleday Anchor.

Aikin, W. M. (1942). *The story of the Eight-Year Study.* New York: Harper & Bros.

Aikin, W. M. (1953). The Eight-Year Study: If we were to do it again. *Progressive Education, 31*, 11–14.

Airasian, P. W. (1988). Symbolic validation: The case of state-mandated, high-stakes testing. *Educational Evaluation and Policy Analysis, 10*(4), 301–313.

Anderson, J. G. (1968). *Bureaucracy in education.* Baltimore: The Johns Hopkins Press.

Anyon, J. (1995). Race, social class, and educational reform in an inner-city school. *Teachers College Record, 97*(1), 69–94.

Apple, M. W. (1985). Making knowledge legitimate: Power, profit, and the textbook. In A. Molnar (Ed.), *Current thought on curriculum, the 1985 ASCD Yearbook* (pp. 73–90). Alexandria, VA: Association for Supervision & Curriculum Development.

Apple, M. W. (1988). *Teachers and texts: A political economy of class and gender relations in education.* New York: Routledge.

Apple, M. W. (1990). Is there a curriculum voice to reclaim? *Phi Delta Kappan, 71*(7), 526–530.

Apple, M. W. (1993). *Official knowledge: Democratic education in a conservative age.* New York: Routledge.

Apple, M .W. (1995). *Education and power* (2nd ed.). New York: Routledge.

Associated Press (1997, December 18). Use of property tax for schools illegal in N.H. *Los Angeles Times*, p. A46.

Bailey, S. K., & Mosher, E. K. (1968). *ESEA; The Office of Education administers a law.* Syracuse, NY: Syracuse University Press.

Barker, B. O. (1986). The advantages of small schools. ERIC Digest. (ERIC Document Reproduction Service No. ED 265 988)

Barker, R. G., & Gump, P. V. (1964). *Big school, small school: High school size and student behavior.* Stanford, CA: Stanford University Press.

Barnes, J. E. (1997, September 22). Segregation, now. *U.S. News & World Report*, 22–28.

Barth, R. S. (1990). *Improving schools from within.* San Francisco: Jossey-Bass.

Bellah, R. N., Madsen, R., Sullivan, W. M., Swidler, A., & Tipton, S. M. (1985). *Habits of the heart*. Berkeley: University of California Press.

Benham, B. J. (1978a). *A comparison of instructional materials used by teachers in 39 schools nationwide*. Unpublished study, I/D/E/A & the C. F. Kettering Foundation, Los Angeles, CA.

Benham, B. J. (1978b). None so holy as the recently converted: Malefic generosity and multicultural education. *Educational Studies, 9*(2), 125–131.

Benham, B. J. (1979a). *The lives of students: A substudy of the data from A Study of Schooling*. Unpublished study, I/D/E/A & the C. F. Kettering Foundation, Los Angeles, CA.

Benham, B. J. (1979b). More is less. *The Review of Education, 5*(4), 301–310.

Bennis, W. (1993). *Beyond bureaucracy: Essays in the development and evolution of human organizations*. San Francisco: Jossey-Bass.

Bentzen, M. (1974). *Changing schools: The magic feather principle*. New York: McGraw-Hill.

Bentzen, M. M., & Tye, K. A. (1973). Effecting change in elementary schools. *NSSE Yearbook 1973*, 350–379. Chicago: University of Chicago Press.

Berliner, D. C. (1993). Mythology and the American system of education. *Phi Delta Kappan, 74*(8), 633–640.

Berliner, D. C., & Biddle, B. (1995). *The manufactured crisis: Myths, fraud, and the attack on America's public schools*. Reading, MA: Addison-Wesley.

Berman, P., & McLaughlin, M. W. (1974). *Federal programs supporting educational change*. Santa Monica, CA: The RAND Corporation.

Blase, J., & Anderson, G. L. (1995). *The micropolitics of educational leadership: From control to empowerment*. New York: Teachers College Press.

Bliss, T., & Mazur, J. (1998). *Secondary and middle school teachers in the midst of reform: From control to empowerment*. New York: Teachers College Press.

Boutwell, C. E. (1997a). Profits without people. *Phi Delta Kappan, 79*(2), 104–111.

Boutwell, C. E. (1997b). *Shell game: Corporate America's agenda for schools*. Bloomington, IN: PDK Foundation.

Bowles, S., & Gintis, H. (1976). *Schooling in capitalist America: Educational reform and the contradictions of economic life*. New York: Basic Books.

Bracey, G. W. (1994). The media's myth of school failure. *Educational Leadership, 52*(1), 80–83.

Bracey, G. W. (1996). The sixth Bracey report on the condition of public education. *Phi Delta Kappan, 78*(2), 127–138.

Brantlinger, E., Majd-Jabbari, M., & Guskin, S. L. (1996). Self-interest and liberal educational discourse: How ideology works for middle-class mothers. *American Educational Research Journal, 33*(3), 571–597.

Bridge, G. R. (1978). Parent participation in school innovations. In D. Mann (Ed.), *Making change happen?* (pp. 101–119). New York: Teachers College Press.

Bruckerhoff, C. E. (1994). School routines and the failure of curriculum reform. In R. A. Martuzewicz & W. M. Reynolds (Eds.), *Inside out: Contemporary critical perspectives in education* (pp. 80–98). New York: St. Martin's Press.

Bryk, A. S., Easton, J. Q., Kerbow, D., Rollow, S. G., & Sebring, P. A. (1994). The state of Chicago school reform. *Phi Delta Kappan, 76*(1), 74–78.

Bullough, R. V. (1988). *The forgotten dream of American public education.* Ames: The Iowa State University Press.

Burby, R. J. (1977). *Schools in new communities.* Cambridge, MA: Ballinger.

Butts, R. F., & Cremin, L. A. (1953). *A history of education in American culture.* New York: Henry Holt.

Callahan, R. F. (1962). *Education and the cult of efficiency.* Chicago: University of Chicago Press.

Carlson, R. O. (1972). *School superintendents: Careers and performance.* Columbus, OH: Charles Merrill.

Charters, W. W., & Pellegrin, R. (1972). Barriers to the innovation process. *Educational Administration Quarterly, 9*(1), 3–14.

Chomsky, N. (1987). The manufacture of consent. In J. Peck (Ed.), *The Chomsky reader* (pp. 121–136). New York: Pantheon.

Cohn, M., Kottcamp, R. B., McCloskey, G. N., & Provenzo, E. F. (1987). *Teachers' perspectives on the problems in their profession: Implications for policymakers and practitioners.* Washington, DC: Office of Educational Research and Improvement/U.S. Department of Education.

Comer, J. P. (1980). *School power: Implications of an intervention project.* New York: Free Press.

Comer, J. P. (1995). Parent participation: Fad or function? In K. Ryan & J. M. Cooper, *Kaleidoscope* (7th ed., pp. 450–456). Boston: Houghton Mifflin.

Corcoran, T. B. (1990). Schoolwork: Perspectives on workplace reform in public schools. In M. W. McLaughlin, J. E. Talbert, & N. Bascia (Eds.), *The contexts of teaching in secondary schools: Teachers' realities* (pp. 142–166). New York: Teachers College Press.

Counts, G. S. (1927). *The social composition of boards of education.* Chicago: University of Chicago Press.

Counts, G. S. (1932). *Dare the school build a new social order?* New York: John Day.

Craig, C. J. (1998). Issues to address, assets to engage: Parents in classrooms and schools. *Journal of Curriculum & Supervision, 13*(3), 279–286.

Crain, R. L., & Street, D. (1969). School desegregation and school decision-making. In A. Rosenthal (Ed.), *Governing education: A reader on politics, power, and public school policy* (pp. 342–362). Garden City, NY: Doubleday Anchor.

Crandall, D. P., Bauchner, J. E., Loucks, S. F., & Schmidt, W. H. (1982). Models of the school improvement process: Factors contributing to success. Paper presented at the annual conference of the American Educational Research Association, New York. (ERIC Document Reproduction Service No. ED 251 918)

Cremin, L. A. (1951). *The American common school: An historic conception.* New York: Teachers College Press.

Cremin, L. A. (1961). *The transformation of the school.* New York: Knopf.

Crews, A. C., & Weakley, S. (1995). *Hungry for leadership.* Atlanta, GA: The Southern Regional Education Board.

Cuban, L. (1984). *How teachers taught: Constancy and change in American classrooms, 1890–1980.* New York: Longman.

Cuban, L. (1994, June). The great school scam. *Education Week,* 44.

Cuban, L., & Shipps, D. (1997, December 14). The limits of turning schools into businesses. *Los Angeles Times*, p. M1.

Cusick, P. A. (1992). *The educational system: Its nature and logic.* New York: McGraw-Hill.

Danzberger, J. P., & Friedman, W. (1997). Public conversations about the public's schools. *Phi Delta Kappan, 78*(10), 744–748.

Darling-Hammond, L. (1997). *The right to learn: A blueprint for creating schools that work.* San Francisco: Jossey-Bass.

Darling-Hammond, L., & McLaughlin, M. W. (1995). Policies that support professional development in an era of reform. *Phi Delta Kappan, 76*(8), 597–604.

Davies, L. (1990). Limits of bureaucratic control. In L. Davies & E. Schragge (Eds.), *Bureaucracy and community: Essays on the politics of social work practice* (pp. 81–101). Montreal, Canada: Black Rose Books.

Deal, T. (1990). Reframing reform. *Educational Leadership, 47*(9), 6–12.

Doyle, W. J. (1978). A solution in search of a problem: Comprehensive change and the Jefferson Experimental Schools. In D. Mann (Ed.), *Making change happen?* (pp. 78–100). New York: Teachers College Press.

Eicholz, G. C. (1963, December). Why do teachers reject change? *Theory Into Practice, 2*, 264–268.

Eisner, E. W. (1987). Why the textbook influences curriculum. *Curriculum Review, 26*, 11–13.

Eisner, E. W. (1992). Educational reform and the ecology of schooling. *Teachers College Record, 93*, 610–627.

Eisner, E. W. (1994). *The educational imagination: On the design and evaluation of school programs* (3rd ed.). New York: Macmillan.

Elam, S. (1996). Phi Delta Kappa's young leaders of 1980 tackle today's issues. *Phi Delta Kappan, 77*(9), 610–614.

Eliot, T. H. (1969). Toward an understanding of public school politics. In A. Rosenthal (Ed.), *Governing education: A reader on politics, power, and public school policy* (pp. 3–35). Garden City, NY: Doubleday Anchor.

Elkind, D. (1995). School and family in the postmodern world. *Phi Delta Kappan, 77*(1), 8–14.

Elliott, D. L., & Woodward, A. (Eds.) (1990). *Textbooks and schooling in the United States, the 89th yearbook of the National Society for the Study of Education.* Chicago: University of Chicago Press.

Elliott, M. (1998). Learning not to panic. *Newsweek, 131*(13), 2.

Fallon, B. (1967). *Fifty states innovate to improve their schools.* Bloomington, IN: Phi Delta Kappa.

Ferguson, K. E. (1984). *The feminist case against bureaucracy.* Philadelphia: Temple University Press.

Ferguson, B. T., Forte, P., Regan, J., Alter, J., & Treacy, S. (1995). Maximizing cooperative learning success. *Journal of Instructional Psychology, 22*(3), 214–224.

Fishkin, J. S. (1995). *The voice of the people.* New Haven, CT: Yale University Press.

Fitzgerald, F. (1979). *America revised.* Boston: Atlantic/Little, Brown.

Frahm, R. A. (1994). The failure of Connecticut's reform plan: Lessons for the nation. *Phi Delta Kappan, 76*(2), 156–159.

Fraley, A. E. (1981). *Schooling and innovation: The rhetoric and the reality*. New York: Tyler Gibson.

Freire, P. (1970). *Pedagogy of the oppressed*. New York: Seabury Press.

Fullan, M. G. (1991). *The new meaning of educational change*. New York: Teachers College Press.

Fullan, M. G. (1996). Turning systemic thinking on its head. *Phi Delta Kappan, 77*(6), 420–423.

Fullan, M. G. (1998). Breaking the bonds of dependency. *Educational Leadership, 55*(7), 6–10.

Fullan, M. G., & Miles, M. B. (1992). Getting reform right: What works and what doesn't. *Phi Delta Kappan, 73*(10), 745–752.

Fullan, M., & Pomfret, A. (1977). Research on curriculum and instruction implementation. *Review of Educational Research, 47*(1), 335–397.

Galbraith, J. K. (1958). *The affluent society*. Boston: Houghton Mifflin.

Gardner, J. (1963). *Self-renewal: The individual and the innovative society*. New York: Harper & Row.

Giroux, H. A. (1985). Teachers as transformative intellectuals. *Social Education, 376–379.*

Gold, B., & Miles, M. B. (1981). *Whose school is this anyway? Parent-teacher conflict over an innovative school*. New York: Praeger.

Goldberg, M. F. (1995). Portraits of educators: Reflections on 18 high achievers. *Educational Leadership, 52*(8), 72–76.

Goodlad, J. I. (1975). *The dynamics of educational change*. New York: McGraw-Hill.

Goodlad, J. I. (1984). *A place called school*. New York: McGraw-Hill.

Goodlad, J. I. (1990). *Teachers for our nation's schools*. San Francisco: Jossey-Bass.

Goodlad, J. I., & Klein, M. F. (1974). *Looking behind the classroom door*. Worthington, OH: Jones.

Gould, S. J. (1981). *The mismeasure of man*. New York: W.W. Norton.

Grant, C. A., & Sleeter, C. E. (1996). *After the school bell rings* (2nd ed.). London: Falmer Press.

Greene, M. (1973). *Teacher as stranger*. Belmont, CA: Wadsworth.

Greene, M. (1976). *Pedagogy and praxis: The problem of malefic generosity*. Paper presented at the Institute for Critical Studies, Buffalo, NY.

Gronn, P. (1986). Politics, power, and the management of schools. In E. Hoyle (Ed.), *The world yearbook of education 1986: The management of schools* (pp. 45–54). London: Kogan.

Gross, N. (1958). Who applies what kind of pressures? In A. Rosenthal (Ed.), *Governing education: A reader on politics, power, and public school policy* (pp. 86–104). Garden City, NY: Doubleday Anchor.

Guba, E. G., Jackson, P. W., & Bidwell, C. E. (1959). Occupational choice and the teaching career. *Educational Research Bulletin, 38*, 1–12.

Gustafson, C. (1998). Phone home. *Educational Leadership, 56*(2), 31–32.

Gutek, G. L. (1972). *A history of the western educational experience*. Prospect Heights, IL: Waveland Press.

Gutek, G. L. (1991). *An historical introduction to American education* (2nd ed.). Prospect Heights, IL: Waveland Press.

Hall, G. E. (1987). *Strategic sense: The key to reflective leadership in school principals.* Paper presented at the Reflection in Teacher Education Conference, Houston, TX. (ERIC Document Reproduction Service No. ED 334 690)

Hall, G. E., & Loucks, S. F. (1977). A developmental model for determining whether the treatment is actually implemented. *American Educational Research Journal, 14*(3), 263–276.

Hall, S. (1986). The toad in the garden: Thatcherism among the theorists. In C. Nelson & L. Grossberg (Eds.), *Marxism and the interpretation of culture* (pp. 35–73). Urbana: University of Illinois Press.

Hargreaves, A. (1984). Contrastive rhetoric and extremist talk. In A. Hargreaves & P. Woods (Eds.), *Classrooms and staffrooms: The sociology of teachers and teaching* (pp. 215–231). Milton Kynes, England: The Open University Press.

Hargreaves, A. (1991). Contrived collegiality: The micropolitics of teacher collaboration. In J. Blase (Ed.), *The politics of life in schools: Power, conflict, and cooperation* (pp. 46–72). Newbury Park, CA: Sage.

Hargreaves, A. (1992). Cultures of teaching: A focus for change. In A. Hargreaves & M. G. Fullan (Eds.), *Understanding teacher development* (pp. 216–240). New York: Teachers College Press.

Hargreaves, A. (1994). *Changing teachers, changing times.* New York: Teachers College Press.

Hargreaves, A. (1995). Renewal in the age of paradox. *Educational Leadership, 52*(7), 14–19.

Hargreaves, A., & Fullan, M. G. (1998). *What's worth fighting for out there?* New York: Teachers College Press.

Havelock, R. G. (1971). *Planning for innovation through dissemination and utilization of knowledge.* Ann Arbor, MI: Institute for Social Research.

Hawley, W. D. (1978). Horses before carts: Developing adaptive schools and the limits of innovation. In D. Mann (Ed.), *Making change happen?* (pp. 224–253). New York: Teachers College Press.

Heckman, P. (1995). *The courage to change.* Thousand Oaks, CA: Crown Press.

Heckscher, C. (1994). Defining the post-bureaucratic type. In C. Heckscher & A. Donellon (Eds.), *The post-bureaucratic organization: New perspectives on organizational change* (pp. 14–62). Thousand Oaks, CA: Sage.

Heckscher, C., & Donellon, A. (Eds.). (1994). *The post-bureaucratic organization: New perspectives on organizational change.* Thousand Oaks, CA: Sage.

Heckscher, C., Eisenstadt, R. A., & Rice, T. J. (1994). Transformational process. In C. Heckscher & A. Donellon (Eds.), *The post-bureaucratic organization: New perspectives on organizational change* (pp. 129–271). Thousand Oaks, CA: Sage.

Hedges, L. V., Laine, R. D., & Greenwald, R. (1994). Does money matter? A meta-analysis of studies of the effects of differential school inputs on student outcomes. *Educational Researcher, 23*(3), 5–14.

Henke, R. R., Choy, S. P., Chen, X., Geis, S., & Alt, M. N. (1997). *America's teachers: Profile of a profession 1993–94, NCES 97–460.* Washington, DC: U.S. Department of Education. (Available: www.ed.gov/NCES/pubs97/97460.html)

Hill, P. T. (1978). Comments on an essay by Willis Hawley. In D. Mann (Ed.), *Making change happen?* (pp. 253–260). New York: Teachers College Press.

Holland, H. (1997). KERA: A tale of one teacher. *Phi Delta Kappan, 79*(4), 265–271.

Hong, L. K. (1996). *Surviving school reform: A year in the life of one school.* New York: Teachers College Press.

Hord, S. M., & Hall, G. E. (1986). Institutionalization of innovations: Knowing when you have it and when you don't. Paper presented at the 67th annual conference of the American Educational Research Association, San Francisco, April 16–20, 1986. (ERIC Document Reproduction Service No. ED 276 103)

House, E. R. (1974). *The politics of educational innovation.* Berkeley, CA: McCutchan.

House, E. R., Kerins, T., & Steele, J. M. (1972). A test of the research and development model of change. *Educational Administration Quarterly, 8*(1), 1–15.

Hovet, M. (1971). *A study to identify and describe productive school-community relationships in Howard County, Maryland.* Unpublished dissertation, George Washington University, Baltimore, MD.

Hummel, R. P. (1977). *The bureaucratic experience.* New York: St. Martin's Press.

Jackson, P. W., & Guba, E. G. (1957, Summer). The need structure of in-service teachers: An occupational analysis. *The School Review, 65*(2), 176–192.

Jenkins, J. M. (1977). Wilde Lake High School. In J. L. Trump (Ed.), *NASSP Bulletin, 61*(412), 108–116.

Johnson, S. M. (1990). Redesigning teachers' work. In R. Elmore et al., *Restructuring schools: The next generation of educational reform* (pp. 125–151). San Francisco: Jossey-Bass.

Johnson, J., & Immerwahr, J. (1994). *First things first: What Americans expect from the public schools.* New York: Public Agenda.

Joyce, B. (1975). Conceptions of man and their implications for teacher education. In *Teacher Education, the seventy-fourth yearbook of the National Society for the Study of Education* (pp. 117–157). Chicago: University of Chicago Press.

Joyce, B. (1982). Organizational homeostasis and innovation: Tightening the loose couplings. *Education and Urban Society, 15*(1), 42–69.

Judis, J. B. (1997, October 20). Honor code. *The New Republic, 4,* 45.

Kaestle, C. F. (1973). *The evolution of an urban school system.* Cambridge, MA: Harvard University Press.

Kaestle, C. F. (1983). *Pillars of the republic: Common schools and American society.* New York: Hill and Wang.

Kahne, J. (1994). Democratic communities, equity, and excellence: A Deweyan reframing of educational policy analysis. *Educational Evaluation and Policy Analysis, 16*(3), 233–248.

Katz, M. B. (1975). *Class, bureaucracy, and schools: The illusion of educational change in America* (2nd ed.). New York: Praeger.

Katz, M. B., Fine, M., & Simon, E. (1997). Poking around: Outsiders view Chicago school reform. *Teachers College Record, 99*(1), 117–157.

Kernan-Schloss, A., & Plattner, A. (1998). Talking to the public about public schools. *Educational Leadership, 56*(2), 18–22.

Kerr, N. D. (1964). The school board as an agency of legitimation. *Sociology of Education, 38,* 34–59.

Kimbrough, R. B. (1969). An informal arrangement for influence over basic policy.

In A. Rosenthal (Ed.), *Governing education: A reader on politics, power, and public school policy* (pp. 105–136). Garden City, NY: Doubleday Anchor.

Kirst, M. (1974). The growth of federal influence in education. In C. W. Gordon (Ed.), *Uses of the sociology of education, 73rd yearbook of the National Society for the Study of Education, part II* (pp. 448–477). Chicago: University of Chicago Press.

Kleine-Kracht, P., & Wong, K. K. (1991). When district authority intrudes upon the local school. In J. Blase (Ed.), *The politics of life in schools* (pp. 96–119). Newbury Park, CA: Sage.

Kohn, A. (1998). Only for my kid: How privileged parents undermine school reform. *Phi Delta Kappan, 79*(8), 569–577.

Kozol, J. (1991). *Savage inequalities.* New York: Harper Collins.

Krackhardt, D. (1994). Constraints on the interactive organization as an ideal type. In D. Heckscher & A. Donellon (Eds.), *The post-bureaucratic organization* (pp. 211–222). Thousand Oaks, CA: Sage.

Kuttner, R. (1993, March 18). Training programs alone can't produce $20-an-hour workers. *Business Week,* 16.

Labaree, D. F. (1987). Politics, markets, and the compromised curriculum. *Harvard Educational Review, 57*(4), 483–494.

Labaree, D. F. (1999). Too easy a target. *Academe, 85*(1), 35–39.

Lasch, C. (1978). *The culture of narcissism: American life in an age of diminishing expectations.* New York: W.W. Norton.

Lee, V. E., Smith, J. B., & Croninger, R. B. (1995). Another look at high school restructuring. *Issues in Restructuring Schools* (Issue Report No. 9). Madison, WI: Center on Organization and Restructuring of Schools.

Leonard, P. (1990). Fatalism and the discourse on power. In L. Davies & E. Schragge (Eds.), *Bureaucracy and community: Essays on the politics of social work practice.* Montreal: Black Rose Books.

Levin, R. A. (1991, Winter). The debate over schooling: Influences of Dewey and Thorndike. *Childhood Education, 68*(2), 71–75.

Lewis, A. C. (1995). *Believing in ourselves: Progress and struggle in urban middle school reform.* New York: Clark Foundation.

Lieberman, A. (1995). Practices that support teacher development. *Phi Delta Kappan, 76*(8), 591–596.

Lieberman, A., & Miller, L. (1984). *Teachers: Their world and their work.* Alexandria, VA: Association for Supervision and Curriculum Development.

Lightfoot, S. L. (1983). *The good high school: Portraits of character and culture.* New York: Basic Books.

Lindblom, C. E. (1994). Success through inattention in school administration and elsewhere. *Educational Administration Quarterly 30*(2), 199–213.

Little, J. W. (1981). *School success and staff development in urban desegregated schools: A summary of recently completed research.* Boulder, CO: Center for Action Research.

Little, J. W. (1990). The persistence of privacy: Autonomy and initiative in teachers' professional relations. *Teachers College Record, 91*(4), 509–536.

Lortie, D. C. (1975). *Schoolteacher.* Chicago: University of Chicago Press.

Louis, K. S. (1990). Social and community values and the quality of teachers' work life. In M. W. McLaughlin, J. E. Talbert, & N. Bascia (Eds.), *The contexts of teaching in secondary schools: Teachers' realities* (pp. 17–39). New York: Teachers College Press.

Lukas, C. V. (1975). Problems in implementing Head Start planned variation models. In A. M. Rivlin & P. M. Timpane (Eds.), *Planned variation in education: Should we give up or try harder?* (pp. 113–125). Washington, DC: The Brookings Institute.

Maeroff, G. (1998). *Imaging education: The media and schools in America.* New York: Teachers College Press.

Marsh, M. S. (1999). Life inside a school: Implications for reform in the 21st century. In D. D. Marsh, *Preparing our schools for the 21st century* (pp. 185–202). Alexandria, VA: Association for Supervision & Curriculum Development.

Martin, D. T. (1991). The political economy of school reform in the United States. In M. B. Ginsburg, *Understanding educational reform in global context: Economy, ideology, and the state* (pp. 341–361). New York: Garland.

Martin, R. C. (1962). *Government and the suburban school.* Syracuse, NY: Syracuse University Press.

Martin, R. C. (1969). School government. In A. Rosenthal (Ed.), *Governing education: A primer on politics, power, and public school policy* (pp. 260–290). Garden City, NY: Doubleday Anchor.

Mason, W. S. (1961). *The beginning teacher* (Circular No. 644). Washington, DC: The U.S. Department of Health, Education, and Welfare, Office of Education.

Mathews, D. (1997). The lack of a public for public schools. *Phi Delta Kappan, 78*(10), 741–743.

Maurer, R. (1996). *Beyond the wall of resistance: Unconventional strategies that build support for change.* Austin, TX: Bard Books.

McAdams, R. P. (1997). A systems approach to school reform. *Phi Delta Kappan, 79*(2), 138–142.

McCarty, D., & Ramsey, C. (1971). *The school managers: Power and conflict in American public education.* Westport, CT: Greenwood.

McCloskey, G., Provenzo, E. F., Cohen, M., & Kottkamp, R. B. (1987). *A profession at risk: Legislated learning as a disincentive to teaching.* Washington, DC: Office of Educational Research and Improvement, U.S. Department of Education.

McCutcheon, G. (1988). Curriculum and the work of teachers. In L. E. Bayer & M. W. Apple (Eds.), *The curriculum* (pp. 191–203). Albany: State University of New York Press.

McLaren, P. (1998). *Life in schools: An introduction to critical pedagogy in the foundations of education* (3rd ed.). New York: Addison Wesley Longman.

McLaughlin, M. W. (1978a). Implementation as mutual adaptation: Change in classroom organization. In D. Mann (Ed.), *Making change happen?* (pp. 19–31). New York: Teachers College Press.

McLaughlin, M. W. (1978b). Implementation of ESEA Title I: A problem of compliance. In D. Mann (Ed.), *Making change happen?* (pp. 162–180). New York: Teachers College Press.

McLaughlin, M. W. (1990). The RAND Change Agent Study revisited: Macro perspectives and micro realities. *Educational Researcher, 19*(9), 11–16.

McLuhan, M., & Fiore, Q. (1967). *The medium is the message.* New York: Bantam Books.

Meek, A. (1998). America's teachers: Much to celebrate. *Educational Leadership, 55*(5), 12–16.

Meier, D. W. (1996). Afterword. In L. K. Hong, *Surviving school reform: A year in the life of one school* (pp. 187–190). New York: Teachers College Press.

Meier, D. W. (1998). Can the odds be changed? *Phi Delta Kappan, 79*(5), 358–362.

Metz, M. H. (1986). *Different by design: The context and character of three magnet schools.* New York: Routledge & Kegan Paul.

Metz, M. H. (1989). Real school: A universal drama amid disparate experience. In D. E. Mitchell & M. E. Goertz (Eds.), *Education politics for the new century. The twentieth anniversary yearbook of the Politics of Education Association* (pp. 75–91). New York: The Falmer Press.

Metz, M. H. (1990). How social class differences shape the context of teachers' work. In M. W. McLaughlin, J. Talbert, & N. Bascia (Eds.), *The contexts of teaching in secondary schools: Teachers realities* (pp. 40–107). New York: Teachers College Press.

Meyer, J. W. (1983). Innovation and knowledge use in American public education. In J. W. Meyer & W. R. Scott (Eds.), *Organizational environments: Ritual and rationality* (pp. 233–260). Beverly Hills, CA: Sage.

Meyer, J. W., & Rowan, B. (1977). Institutionalized organizations: Formal structure as myth and ceremony. *American Journal of Sociology, 83*(2), 340–363.

Meyer, J. W., & Rowan, B. (1983). The structure of educational organizations. In J. W. Meyer & W. R. Scott (Eds.), *Organizational environments: Ritual and rationality* (pp. 71–97). Beverly Hills, CA: Sage.

Michels, R. (1949). *Political parties: A sociological study of the oligarchical tendencies of modern democracy* (pp. 389–390). Glencoe, IL: Free Press.

Miles, M. B. (1965). Planned change and organizational health: Figure and ground. In R. O. Carlson, *Change processes in the public schools* (pp. 11–34). Eugene, OR: Center for the Advanced Study of Education Administration.

Molnar, A. (1997). Why school reform is not enough to mend our civil society. *Educational Leadership, 54*(5), 37–39.

Mort, P. R. (1957). *Principles of school administration.* New York: McGraw-Hill.

Nachtigal, P. (1972). *A foundation goes to school: The Ford Foundation Comprehensive School Improvement Program, 1960–1970.* New York: Ford Foundation.

Nohria, N., & Berkley, J. D. (1994). The virtual organization: Bureaucracy, technology, and the implosion of control. In C. Heckscher & A. Donellon (Eds.), *The post-bureaucratic organization: New perspectives on organizational change* (pp. 108–128). Thousand Oaks, CA: Sage.

Oakes, J. (1981). A question of access: Tracking & curriculum differentiation in a national sample of English and math. *Study of Schooling* (Technical Report No. 24). Los Angeles, CA: I/D/E/A and C. F. Kettering Foundation.

Oakes, J. (1985). *Keeping track: How schools structure inequality.* New Haven, CT: Yale University Press.

Oakes, J. (1995). Great news—greater challenges. *Issues in Restructuring Schools* (Issue Report No. 9). Madison, WI: Center on Organizing and Restructuring of Schools.

Oakes, J., & Lipton, M. (1999). *Teaching to change the world.* New York: McGraw-Hill.

Ohanian, S. (1996). Is that penguin stuffed or real? *Phi Delta Kappan, 78*(4), 277–284.

O'Neil, J. (1995). On lasting school reform: A conversation with Ted Sizer. *Educational Leadership, 52*(5), 4–9.

O'Neil, J. (1994). Taking stock of school-based management. *ASCD Update, 36*(7), 4–8.

Osipow, S. H. (1973). Holland's career typology theory of vocational behavior. In *Theories of career development* (pp. 41–81). New York: Appleton-Century-Crofts.

Overman, B. C. (1980). *Variety and intensity of school-related problems as perceived by teachers, parents, and students.* (I/D/E/A Study of Schooling Report No. 17). (ERIC Document Reproduction Services No. ED 214-887)

Packard, V. (1981). *The hidden persuaders.* New York: Penguin.

Page, R. N. (1999). The uncertain value of school knowledge: Biology at Westridge High. *Teachers College Record, 100*(3), 554–601.

Parish, R., & Aquila, F. (1996). Cultural ways of working and believing in school: Preserving the way things are. *Phi Delta Kappan, 78*(4), 298–305.

Pauly, E. W. (1978). The decision to innovate: Career pursuit as an incentive for educational change. In D. Mann (Ed.), *Making change happen?* (pp. 261–284). New York: Teachers College Press.

Pauly, E. W. (1991). *The classroom crucible: What really works, what doesn't, and why?* New York: Basic Books.

Pinchot, G., & Pinchot, E. (1994). *The intelligent organization.* San Francisco: Berrett-Koehler.

Pincus, J. (1974). Incentives for innovation in public schools. *Review of Educational Research, 44*, 113–144.

Pipho, C. (1995). Urban School problems and solutions. *Phi Delta Kappan, 77*(2), 102–103.

Poole, W. (1991). *Resistance to change in education: Themes in the literature.* Unpublished paper, Syracuse University, Syracuse, NY. (ERIC Document Reproduction Service No. ED 330 307)

Postman, N. (1985). *Amusing ourselves to death: Public discourse in the age of show business.* New York: Penguin Books.

Purpel, D. E. (1989). *The moral and spiritual crisis in education.* New York: Bergin and Garvey.

Purpel, D. E., & Shapiro, S. (1995). *Beyond liberation and excellence: Reconstructing the public discourse on education.* Westport, CT: Bergin and Garvey.

Rallis, S. F., & Zajano, N. C. (1997). Keeping the faith until the outcomes are obvious. *Phi Delta Kappan, 78*(9), 706–709.

Raven, B. H., & French, J. R. P. (1957). An experimental investigation of legitimate and coercive power. *American Psychologist, 12*, 393.

Raven, B. H., & French, J. R. P. (1958a). Group support, legitimate power, and social influence. *Journal of Personality, 26*, 400–409.

Raven, B. H., & French, J. R. P. (1958b). Legitimate power, coercive power, and observability in social influence. *Sociometry, 21*, 83–97.

Raywid, M. A. (1994). Alternative schools: The state of the art. *Educational Leadership, 52*(1), 26–31.

Raywid, M. A. (1997–1998). Small schools: A reform that works. *Educational Leadership, 55*(4), 34–39.

Redefer, F. L. (1950). The Eight Year Study . . . eight years after. *Progressive Education, 28*(2), 33–36.

Reich, R. (1991). *The work of nations: Preparing ourselves for 21st century capitalism.* New York: Alfred A. Knopf.

Rogers, E. M. (1962). *Diffusion of innovations.* Glencoe, IL: Free Press.

Rogers, E. M. (1965). What are innovators like? In R. O. Carlson, A. Gallaher, M. B. Miles, R. J. Pellegrin, & E. M. Rogers (Eds.), *Change processes in the public schools* (pp. 55–61). Eugene, OR: Center for the Advanced Study of Educational Administration.

Rogers, E. M. (1973). Social structure and social change. In G. Zaltman (Ed.), *Processes and phenomena of social change* (pp. 75–92). New York: John Wiley.

Rose, L. C., & Rapp, D. (1997). The future of public schools—a public discussion. *Phi Delta Kappan, 78*(10), 767.

Rosenblatt, R. A. (1993, March 7). Digging ever deeper: A short account of taxman's long arm. *Los Angeles Times*, D1, D10.

Rosenholz, S. (1989). *Teachers' workplace.* New York: Longmans.

Rosenthal, A. (Ed.). (1969). *Governing education: A reader on politics, power, and public school policy.* Garden City, NY: Doubleday Anchor.

Rowan, B. (1982). Organizational structure and the institutional environment: The case of the public schools. *Administrative Science Quarterly, 27*, 259–279.

San Antonio School District v. Rodriguez, 411 U.S.1 (1973).

Sarason, S. B. (1982). *The culture of the school and the problem of change* (2nd ed.). Boston: Allyn and Bacon.

Sarason, S. B. (1983). *Schooling in America: Scapegoat and salvation.* New York: Free Press.

Sarason, S. B. (1991). *The predictable failure of school reform.* San Francisco: Jossey-Bass.

Sarason, S. B. (1993). *The case for change: Rethinking the preparation of educators.* San Francisco: Jossey-Bass.

Sarason, S. B. (1995). Some reactions to what I have learned. *Phi Delta Kappan, 77*(1), 84–85.

Schultz, T. W. (1968). Investment in human capital. In M. Blaug (Ed.), *Economics of education* (pp. 22–24). Middlesex, England: Penguin.

Schumacher, E. F. (1973). The greatest resource—education. In *Small is beautiful: Economics as if people mattered* (pp. 79–101). New York: Harper & Row.

Scott, W. R. (1995). *Institutions and organizations.* Thousand Oaks, CA: Sage.

Sedlak, M. W. (1989). "Let us go and buy a school master": Historical perspectives on the hiring of teachers in the United States, 1750–1980. In D. Warren

(Ed.), *American teachers: Histories of a profession at work* (pp. 257–290). New York: Macmillan.

Senge, P. M. (1990). The leader's new work: Building learning organizations. *The Sloan Management Review, 32*(1), 7–24.

Shen, J. (1998). Do teachers feel empowered? *Educational Leadership, 55*(7), 35–36.

Shields, P. M., & Knapp, M. S. (1997). The promise and limits of school-based reform. *Phi Delta Kappan, 79*(4), 288–294.

Shor, I. (1986). *Culture wars: School and society in the conservative restoration, 1969–1984.* Boston: Routledge & Kegan Paul.

Sizer, T. (Ed.) (1964). *The age of the academies.* New York: Teachers College Press.

Soholt, S. (1998). Public engagement: Lessons from the front. *Educational Leadership, 56*(2), 22–23.

Sokoloff, H. (1996, November). A deliberative model for engaging the community: Use of community forums can undercut special-interest politics. *School Administrator,* 12–18.

SooHoo, S. (1990). School renewal: Taking responsibility for providing an education of value. In J. I. Goodlad & P. Keating (Eds.), *Access to knowledge* (pp. 205–222). New York: College Entrance Examination Board.

Spring, J. (1986). *The American school 1642–1985.* New York: Longmans.

Spring, J. (1998). *Conflict of interests* (3rd ed.). New York: McGraw-Hill.

Stern, G. C., Stein, M. K., & Bloom, B. S. (1956). *Methods in personality assessment.* Glencoe, IL: Free Press.

Stiles, L. J., & Robinson, B. (1973). Change in education. In G. Zaltman (Ed.), *Process and phenomena of social change* (pp. 257–280). New York: John Wiley & Sons.

Stuart, J. (1949). *The thread that runs so true.* New York: Simon & Schuster.

Tanner, D. (1998). The social consequences of bad research. *Phi Delta Kappan, 79*(5), 345–349.

Tanner, D., & Tanner, L. (1980). *Curriculum development: Theory into practice* (2nd ed.). New York: Macmillan.

Theobald, P., & Mills, E. (1995). Accountability and the struggle over what counts. *Phi Delta Kappan, 76*(6), 462–466.

Thompson, J. B. (1990). *Ideology and modern culture: Critical social theory in the era of mass communication.* Stanford, CA: Stanford University Press.

Trump, J. L., & Georgiades, W. (Eds.). (1977). NASSP's Model Schools Project. *The NASSP Bulletin, 61*(412), 1–138.

Tyack, D., & Cuban, L. (1995). *Tinkering toward utopia: A century of public school reform.* Cambridge, MA: Harvard University Press.

Tyack, D., & Tobin, W. (1994). The "grammar" of schooling: Why has it been so hard to change? *American Education Research Journal, 31*(3), 453–479.

Tye, B. B. (1985). *Multiple realities: A study of 13 American high schools.* Lanham, MD: University Press of America.

Tye, B. B., & Tye, K. A. (1984). Teacher isolation and school reform. *Phi Delta Kappan, 65*(5), 319–322.

Tye, B. B., & Tye, K. A. (1992). *Global education: A study of school change.* Albany: State University of New York Press.

Tye, K. A. (1978). The politics of decline—Catastrophe or opportunity. *The Review of Education, 4*(1), 23–30.

Tye, K. A. (1981). *Changing our schools: The realities* (I/D/E/A Study of Schooling Technical Report No. 30). Los Angeles: The C.F. Kettering Foundation and I/D/E/A.

Tye, K. A. (1992). Restructuring our schools: Beyond the rhetoric. *Phi Delta Kappan, 74*(1), 8–14.

Tye, K. A., & Novotney, J. M. (1975). *Schools in transition: The practitioner as change agent.* New York: McGraw-Hill.

Tye, K. A., & Tye, B. B. (1998). *Global education: A study of school change* (2nd ed.). Orange, CA: Interdependence Press.

Tyson, H. (1994). *Who will teach the children? Progress and resistance in teacher education.* San Francisco: Jossey-Bass.

Wagner, T. (1997). The new village commons. *Educational Leadership, 54*(5), 25–28.

Waller, W. (1932). *The sociology of teaching.* New York: Wiley & Sons.

Warren, C. (1978). The nonimplementation of EEP: All that money for business as usual. In D. Mann (Ed.), *Making change happen?* (pp. 150–161). New York: Teachers College Press.

Wasley, P. A. (1991). *Teachers who lead: The rhetoric of reform and the realities of practice.* New York: Teachers College Press.

Wasley, P., Hampel, R., & Clark, R. (1997). The puzzle of whole-school change. *Phi Delta Kappan, 78*(9), 690–697.

Watson, A. (1998). The newpaper's responsibility. *Phi Delta Kappan, 79*(10), 729–734.

Weick, K. E. (1976). Educational organizations as loosely-coupled systems. *Administrative Science Quarterly, 21*, 1–19.

Weil, R. (1997). The view from between a rock and a hard place. *Phi Delta Kappan, 78*(10), 760–764.

Weingartner, C. (1977). "Mind-forg'd manacles . . .". *Educational Studies, 8*(1), 21–27.

Weisman, J. (1991, March 13). Business's words, actions to improve education at odds, economist argues. *Education Week*, 1, 26.

Wells, A. S., & Serna, I. (1996). The politics of culture: Understanding local political resistance to detracking in racially mixed schools. *Harvard Educational Review, 66*(1), 93–118.

Wise, A. E. (1979). *Legislated learning.* Berkeley: University of California Press.

Wise, A. E., & Gendler, T. (1995). Rich schools, poor schools. In K. Ryan & J. M. Cooper (Eds.), *Kaleidoscope: Readings in education* (pp. 498–504). New York: Houghton Mifflin.

Woodward, A., Elliott, D. L., & Nagel, K. C. (1988). *Textbooks in school and society: An annotated bibliography and guide to research.* New York: Garland Press.

Yeo, F. L. (1997). *Inner-city schools, multiculturalism, and teacher education: A professional journey.* New York: Garland Press.

Yeo, F. (1998). Thoughts on rural education: Reconstructing the invisible and the myths of country schooling. *Educational Foundations, 12*(2), 31–44.

Zacker, J. (1973). Authoritarian avoidance of ambiguity. *Psychology Reports, 33*, 901–902.

Index

Ability grouping, 108, 113–114, 116, 119–120
Academic goal of schooling, 27
Academies, 14
Accountability
quest for, ix
role differentiation and, 48
of students, 129, 175
of teachers, 129
Adelman, N., 137
Age-grading, 40–41
Agger, R. E., 88
Aging population, 32, 88
Aikin, Wilford M., 122, 140, 157, 176
Airasian, Peter, 23, 33
Alt, M. N., 130
Alter, J., 153–154 n. 1
American Federation of Teachers (AFT), ix
American School Boards Association, 50
American Superintendent Association, 53
America Revised (Fitzgerald), 102–103
Anderson, G. L., 110, 139, 141, 148, 166
Anderson, J. G., 126, 129, 134
Anderson, Robert H., 53, 98, 149
Anyon, Jean, 45, 134
Apple, Michael W., 37, 102, 103, 106 n. 2, 128, 134, 179 n. 3
Aquila, F., 142
Association of School Administrators, 174
At-risk students, 87
Autonomy of teachers, 133, 142–144

Bailey, S. K., 4, 80, 102
Banking model of schooling, 38
Barker, Bruce O., 134
Barker, R. G., 134
Barnes, J. E., 108, 114
Barth, R. S., 170
Bauchner, J. E., 55
Benham, B. J., 16, 90, 102, 114
Bennis, Warren, 64
Bentzen, M. M., 46, 168

Berkley, J. D., 42
Berliner, David C., 35
Berman, P., 5, 97
Biddle, Bruce, 35
Bidwell, C. E., 132
Bilingual programs, 70
Bill for the More General Diffusion of Knowledge (Jefferson), 31
Blaming the victim, 32
Blase, J., 110, 139, 141, 148, 166
Bliss, T., 149
Bloom, B. S., 132
Boston, Massachusetts, 135
Boutwell, C. E., 87, 88
Bowles, S., 132
Bracey, Gerald W., 34–35
Brandt, Ron, ix–x
Brantlinger, E., 108, 124 n. 1
Bridge, G. L., 108, 115
Bruckerhoff, C. E., 64
Bryk, Anthony S., 58, 85, 122–123, 162
Bullough, Robert V., 32, 37–38, 124 n. 1
Burby, R. J., 10, 117
Bureaucracy in schooling, 11, 40–77
culture of, 42–43
documentation requirements in, 42, 44, 68–70, 75
hierarchy in, 40, 42, 43, 45–48
historical perspective on, 40–42
impersonal environment in, 42, 44, 62–66
informal structure versus, 61–62
loosely coupled instructional system within, 44–45, 70–76
nature of, 42–45
personnel evaluation in, 42, 66–67
resistance to innovation and, 45–70
role differentiation in, 42, 43, 48–62
teachers and, 126–127, 129, 131
technical competence in, 42, 43–44, 66–67
textbook industry and, 103

195

About the Author

Barbara Tye's career as an educator began in 1967 in a Title III fine arts project for the Dayton, Ohio public schools. During the 1970's she helped write the Kettering Foundation's Individually Guided Education program for high schools, and then became involved in implementing it at a high school in Greer, South Carolina while also teaching at Furman University. She was a member of John Goodlad's Study of Schooling team from 1977 until the project ended in 1980. Following two years overseas, Dr. Tye and her husband returned to the United States and she joined the Chapman faculty in 1983. She is the author of *Multiple realities: A study of 13 American high schools* (1985) and co-author of *Global education: A study of school change* (1992, 1999). Dr. Tye has been a Fulbright Scholar and holds the Hassinger Chair in Education at Chapman University in Orange, California.